# GRANDS PRIX

## 75 YEARS OF FORMULA ONE RACING

ACC ART BOOKS

24

# GRANDS PRIX

## 75 YEARS OF FORMULA ONE RACING

*Introduction by Sir Jackie Stewart*

# CONTENTS

## FOREWORD



## CHAPTER 1
## PHOTOGRAPHERS



## CHAPTER 2
## CHAMPIONS AND HEROES

UBS
ETRONAS
2016
GBR0236
PHOTO

# CONTENTS

## CHAPTER 3
## CIRCUITS



## CHAPTER 4
## ICONS



## CHAPTER 5
## RIVALRIES

## CHAPTER 6
## THE GREAT CARS



## CHAPTER 7
## MOMENTS

# FOREWORD

## by Sir Jackie Stewart

**Formula One World Champion**
**1969, 1971, 1973**

**SPEED IS THE ESSENCE OF FORMULA ONE.** Capturing speed is the essence of Formula One photography.

And it is through the images caught on camera since the 1950 British Grand Prix that we can best appreciate the grace, artistry and drama of this most compelling and dangerous sport.

We might linger on the view of the great Juan Manuel Fangio holding his Maserati 250F in perfect power slide. Or of my friend and hero Jim Clark guiding his rapier-like Lotus 25 with such precision none could touch him.

Maybe we would pause to reflect on the skill and daring of a young Jackie Stewart at the Nürburgring in 1968; or the courage of Niki Lauda returning to the sport with his wounds not healed after his terrible, fiery crash in 1976. What of Alain Prost, jumping for joy alongside his McLaren after securing the 1986 world title against the odds? All of these moments and so many more are contained in this wonderful record of 75 years of Formula One.

Many of these images stir deep memories – happy ones, of course, as they take me back to my youth, trying to forge a career in motorsport and ultimately winning my three World Championships. There is great sadness, too. Formula One was a deadly sport when I was racing and to see the faces of Jim, Jochen Rindt and François Cevert, among many others, is a bitter reminder of the price demanded in pursuit of Grand Prix glory.

It is a great comfort that Formula One is a far less dangerous sport than it once was and that the likes of Sir Lewis Hamilton and Max Verstappen have been able to race ferociously in recent years without the peril once attached to Grand Prix motor racing.

Their achievements, like those of their predecessors, are celebrated in these pages and we can doff our caps to the craft and passion of the many immensely talented photographers who have preserved the sport forever through their work.

It is with heartfelt encouragement that I invite you to enjoy this feast of Formula One and Formula One photography.

*Six of the most evocative images from eight F1 decades – as explained by the men who took them.*

# PHOTOGRAPHERS

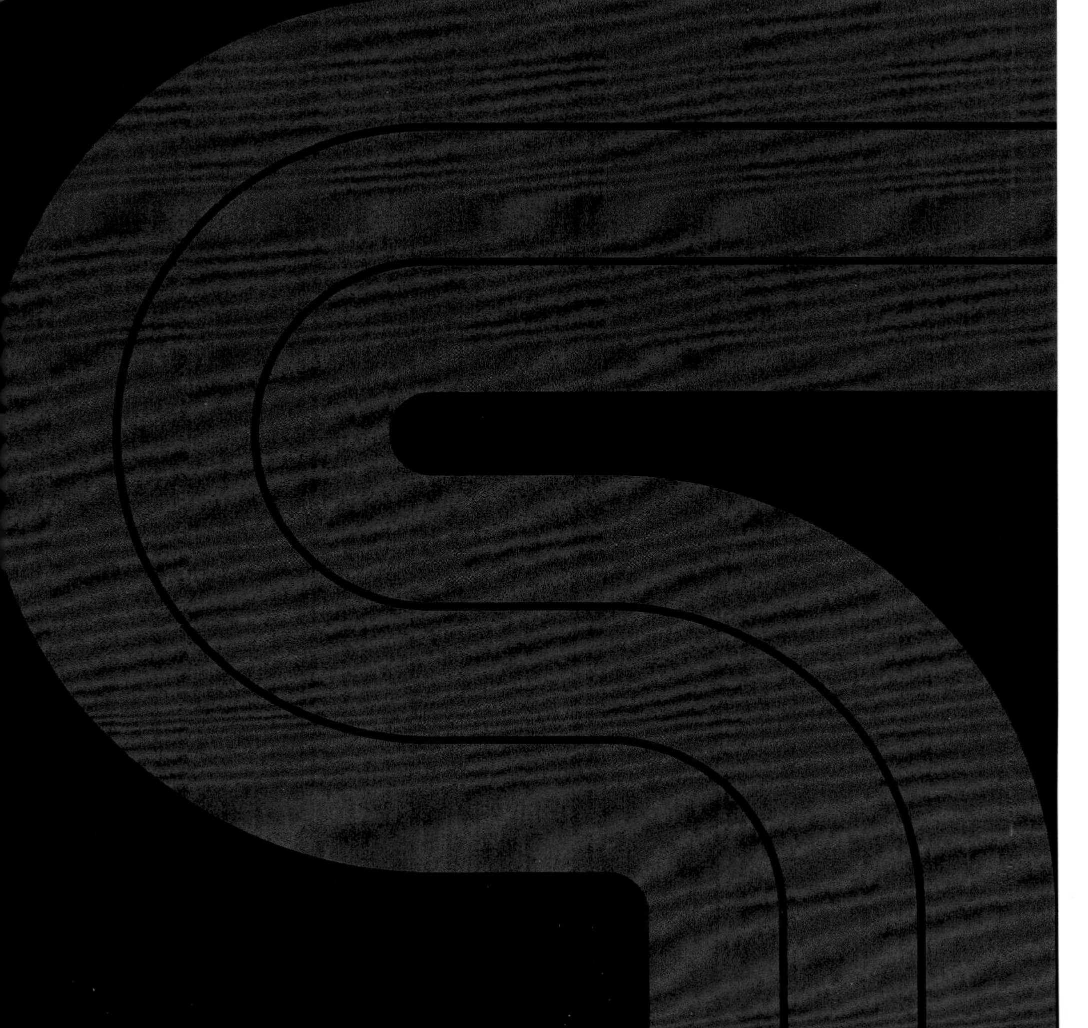

Steven Tee on Ayrton Senna

Michael Tee on Juan Manuel Fangio

Rainer Schlegelmilch on Stefan Johansson

Keith Sutton on Ayrton Senna

Mark Sutton on Mika Häkkinen

Ercole Colombo on Gilles Villeneuve

# STEVEN TEE ON
# AYRTON SENNA
# Winning his first Grand Prix

**1985 Portuguese Grand Prix**
**Estoril race circuit, 21 April 1985**
**Lotus-Renault 97T**

**THIS WAS MY FIRST FULL SEASON IN THE** sport, and I was still young – only 23. Portugal was the second race of the year, and the abiding memory is that it was the most atrocious day on Earth, weather-wise. The rain wouldn't stop, and it was really, really dark. We all went down to the first corner early to get a good, clean shot of the start – there were no photographers' towers or anything like that – and we just stood there in the pouring rain, getting soaked. The most important thing when it's like that is to keep your equipment clean. You spend a lot of time worrying about that.

I had come up through the sport with Senna, shooting him in Formula Ford and Formula Three and then in Monaco the year before, in similar conditions, where he should have won his first race. So, I knew how good he was in the wet. But, in 1985, I had the added pressure of being the team photographer for Lotus. Their team boss, Peter Warr, wasn't completely convinced – sort of, 'You've only been here two minutes and you're our team photographer?' Anyway, as the day unfolded, knowing how good Senna was in the rain and how good he was in general, it became obvious that he was probably going to win. So, then it's all about being at the podium to get the pictures that I knew all our magazines and sponsors would want.

We used to shoot on colour and black-and-white film – no digital photography, of course – and I'd made the pragmatic decision to start shooting the podium in black and white. I found a little spot right at the end of the pit wall – a sort of raised concrete bollard – which I thought would be a good spot. I also knew that the cars would have to come past me to get to Parc Fermé. So, I stood there with my Canon F1, a 50mm lens and black-and-white film – all very basic. Just before I took the shot, Peter Warr wandered up to Parc Fermé and it became one of those things when there's no real time to think. Senna came down the pitlane, taking his belts off, and he saw Peter to his right, who has his arms outstretched. Manual focus, obviously, motor drive – and you're just making sure your lens is clean. It was all a bit higgledy-piggledy. You don't know what you've shot.

After the race, there's the usual rush to the airport, then back to the office to drop off the films for processing. Then, on Monday morning, there's the nervous look along the lightbox...and this frame is the one that stands out – literally this one frame where it all comes together. Peter Warr's got the perfect expression on his face and Senna is half out of the car. Then, on the left, you can see the two Goodyear-tyre guys, Kenny and Clive – that's Kenny in mid-air – which adds to the picture. It probably works better in black and white than it would have in colour. There's more depth of field. Also, the car is black with gold lettering and Senna's helmet is yellow, of course, which all adds to the classic, monochrome feel. I think the picture has really stood the test of time.

When I first saw the shot, I remember thinking, 'Peter can't really argue about this'. He'd said to me on the plane home, 'I hope you got some good pictures from today'. It was a big deal for Lotus because they hadn't won a race since 1982 and they put all their eggs in the Senna basket. Obviously, it was a coming-of-age moment for Senna because he'd won his first Grand Prix, proving to everyone how talented he was. But it was a coming-of-age moment for me as well – a monkey off my back, in a way. I had shown that I could deliver to a team and their sponsors, and I was pleased on a personal level that the shot was completely exclusive. I'd found this one little place to stand, which could have been the worst, but turned out to be the best. Peter Warr had the picture framed soon afterwards and hung it on the wall of his office at Lotus HQ.

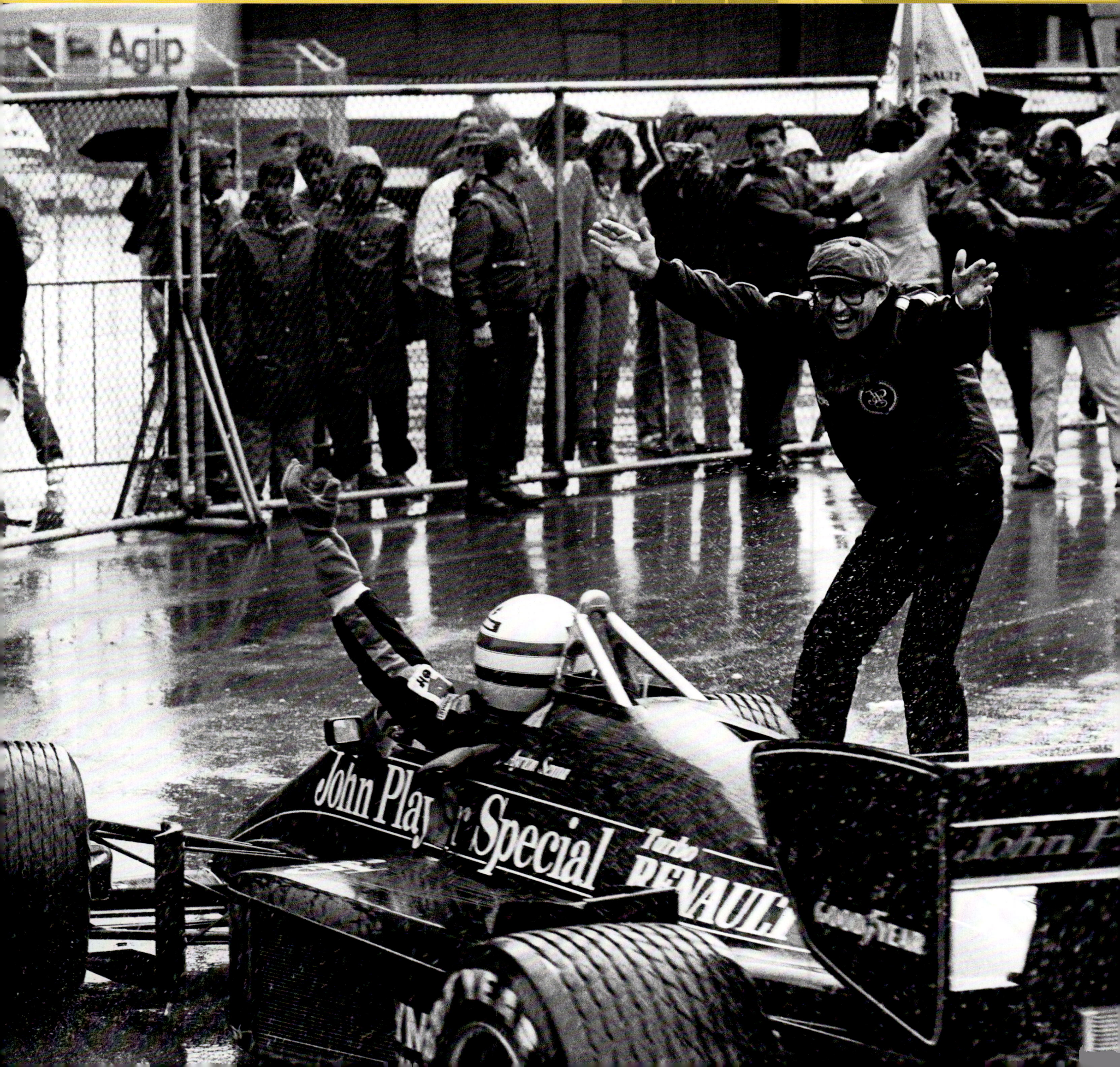
Agip
John Play r Special
Turbo
RENAULT
GOODYEAR

2

# MICHAEL TEE ON
# JUAN MANUEL FANGIO
# Holding a perfect four-wheel drift

**1957 French Grand Prix**
**Rouen-Les Essarts circuit, 7 July 1957**
**Maserati 250F**

**I THINK THE POINT TO MAKE ABOUT** Fangio in this picture is that he was absolutely on the limit. But this isn't a driver fighting a car that he is struggling to control – he has the Maserati perfectly balanced in a four-wheel drift at a very fast, downhill section of the circuit. What you can see is the greatest driver of his era showing what it took to drive a Grand Prix car as fast as it would go. This is 100 per cent Fangio holding the car with absolute precision, exactly where he wants it to be. The drivers who weren't able to do this would be too slow and those who went beyond 100 per cent would crash. But Fangio could hold a car like this at will, every lap, with absolutely perfect balance.

If you look closely, you can see a puff of smoke coming up from the left rear tyre. That gives you an indication of how much of the car's speed and position is being controlled with the throttle. You can also see the damage to the car's nosecone – another sign that Fangio was pushing hard.

The 1957 race was Fangio's first (and only) Grand Prix at the circuit, but I knew that once he found his feet and settled down, he would be exciting. This is actually a very fast and incredibly dangerous section of the track after the start/finish line. It runs down in sweeping right and left curves and, at this point, Fangio has just passed a section of rock face that lined the track. It's unthinkable now, of course, that races would be held on such obviously dangerous circuits – no Armco, no crash barriers – but that's just how it was then. This aspect is part of what made Fangio such a great driver; beyond his skill was his sheer bravery and control of his mind. Going into a corner like that, which would have been at maybe 120mph, he had to know exactly what he was going to do on the way in. There were an awful lot of drivers who just drove on tramlines, and others who would be all over the grass, which you had to be careful of as a photographer. But standing at the trackside, which we were able to do then, you could see very clearly which drivers were in control and which weren't.

I shot from this point for three laps and, every time, Fangio came past using exactly the same bit of track and with the car in the same perfectly balanced drift. Before the race, I had in mind that I wanted to try to get this picture, but it wasn't straightforward. It was quite a hike out to the corner, and it was a long lap, so you had to wait a bit for the car to come round. Also, you had to set your focus to a spot on the track before the car arrived in your frame. I was using a Contax without auto-focus and it could be a little bit hit-and-miss unless you had a point on the track you could aim at, like a white stone or something. I ended up with six or seven pictures and this one was sharpest.

At the time, my sole job was to shoot pictures for *Motorsport* magazine – just racing pictures, no atmosphere or portraits – so I always knew I had to come back with strong track shots. This one must have been ok because they used it on the cover (August 1957 edition).

# RAINER SCHLEGELMILCH ON STEFAN JOHANSSON
## 'Frozen Speed'

**I STARTED TO SHOOT FORMULA ONE IN** the 1960s and I began using the zoom technique you see here in 1969. The idea is that you have the centre of the car sharp – ideally the driver's helmet – but the rest of the image has a speed-blur effect created by a very fast zoom on the image as the shutter closes. I took it during Saturday morning practice, and I'd been shooting other cars head-on at La Rascasse corner as they approached me. But when Stefan came past, I turned at the same time and my movements were totally synchronised with the car as it passed. And you can see this because the centre of the car is completely sharp, even as the background is blurred. Like a painting. I was deliberately trying to achieve this effect, but I was also lucky because, just as I pressed the shutter button, Stefan got back on the throttle as he exited the corner. That created two bursts of flame from the exhausts into the diffuser. This is what makes the photo so exciting, I think. You can try a thousand times to capture flames in a photograph, but it's almost impossible, so there was definitely some good luck involved.

By 1985, I had already been shooting F1 for more than 20 years, so I was quite experienced in terms of what I was trying to shoot, and also in terms of knowing how to work a circuit. Finding the right location for a shot is very important and if you stay in the sport for a while, you learn that track staff are often the same from year to year. So, if you get to know the marshals working on a particular corner, maybe they will let you stand in a place that's not strictly permitted. That's what happened with this shot: I was actually leaning against the barrier at La Rascasse, which you wouldn't be able to do now. The barrier wasn't high – maybe just a metre or so – and my camera was touching it. It was incredibly close to the cars; they were just the other side of the barrier, almost touching the metal.

People have asked if the '80s were the best time to shoot Formula One but I don't think it's as simple as that. It's not the cars themselves that make pictures spectacular, it's the opportunities that you have as a photographer. With this picture, you know, there was just a little barrier between me and the car – in the decades before, there was nothing at all. Now there are many more restrictions on where you can shoot, which limits the possibilities. It's all for safety of course.

When I first saw this picture on the Monday after the race, once the film had been developed, I was really happy with it. It had Monaco, a Ferrari, flames... all the elements, really, to make it work. But, still, you can never know if you'll capture an image like this. A good picture can work without words. The picture itself is the language and I think that's the case here. When Stefan saw it, he loved it, and you can still see it on the homepage of his website. It's funny... it was entered into a photography competition that year. It didn't win.

**1985 Monaco Grand Prix**
**Monte Carlo circuit, 18 May 1985**
**Ferrari 156/85**

FIAT

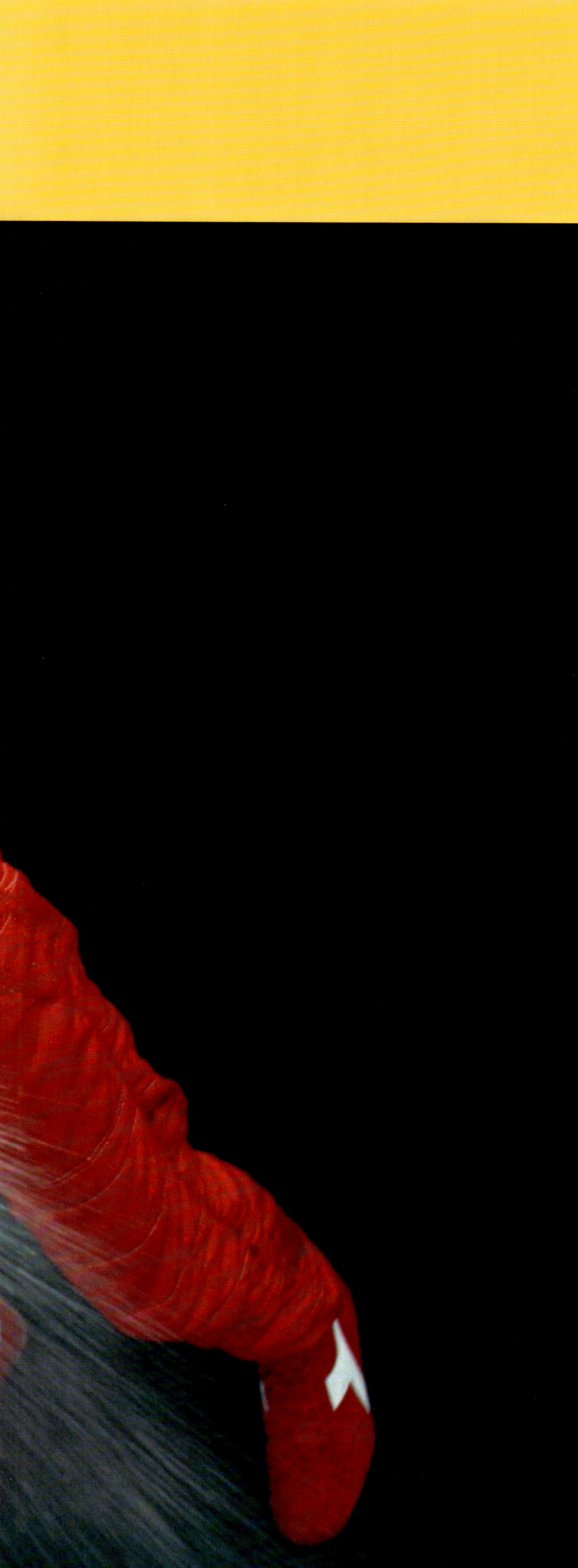

# KEITH SUTTON ON AYRTON SENNA Celebrating victory

**Belgian Grand Prix**
**Spa-Francorchamps circuit,**
**25 August 1991**

**MY ASSOCIATION WITH AYRTON WENT** back to 1981, when he first came over from Brazil to race in the UK. I worked as his photographer in the junior British racing categories, and we were both at the same stage in our lives – young, ambitious, trying to prove ourselves and determined to get to Formula One. Ayrton made it with the Toleman team in 1984, after winning the British Formula Three title the year before. Over the next decade, I took thousands of shots of him.

This one is of his podium champagne celebration after winning the 1991 Belgian Grand Prix. What makes it unique is that it's shot from overhead, and Ayrton is looking right into my camera as he sprays the champagne. Most podium shots are effectively head-on and from beneath the drivers, but the special angle for this one is thanks to a little office I'd found in the circuit buildings on the morning of the race. I'd been walking out of the press room and saw a room with a door ajar and I went in for a look. I could see straight away that the window had a view straight down onto the podium. Even better, the window wasn't locked, so I was able to hold my camera out and over the podium. I remember thinking, 'This could be amazing,' then shut the window and shut the door and kept very quiet about it for the rest of the day. I knew I couldn't tell anyone and would just have to sneak up there.

After the race, which Ayrton won, I headed back to the room, hoping I'd still be able to get in – and thankfully when I got there it hadn't been locked. So, there I am, all on my own, looking down onto the podium, waiting for the drivers to come out. Then I saw them. I shouted to Ayrton when he got hold of the champagne and he looked up and sprayed at me. I was shooting film, as we all were then, and I had five or ten frames left on my roll of 36. It was over in a few seconds, but I remember thinking, 'I'm sure I've got something amazing'. I sort of knew straight away.

Then it was a matter of rushing back to wherever we'd parked the hire car, to escape the crowds and head to the airport. I went straight to the office from the plane to process the film and soon I was on the lightbox with the magnifying glass to check the sharpness and everything. There were probably three or four frames that were good, but this one was exceptional.

You always keep quiet if you think you have something special. In those days, you didn't say anything until it was on the lightbox... and then you see the picture, your colleagues gather round, they see the frame and go, 'Oh, wow!'

One of the things that's so nice about it is that there's no advertising in the background, just artificial grass and that lovely row of flowers. I shot on Fuji Velvia film so the colours are really bright. But what makes this so special is that Ayrton is so happy, so joyful, and that makes me remember him that way, and smile. Those 10 incredible years he was in Formula One and the three world titles... Whenever I look at this picture, the sadness of Imola 1994 sort of goes away. You can just remember the good times.

# MARK SUTTON ON MIKA HÄKKINEN The Flying Finn

**Australian Grand Prix**
**Adelaide circuit, 7 November 1993**
**McLaren MP4-8**

**THIS WAS ONE OF THOSE PICTURES THAT** you can't possibly anticipate. It's a moment that happens; maybe you'll be in the perfect spot to capture it; maybe not. It was my second full year of covering the Grands Prix and it was a warm, sunny Saturday when I headed down to Brewery Bend, the right-hander onto the main straight.

I'd been doing pan shots there against the kerb and the fencing, shooting with a fixed 300mm lens at 1/25 of a second on Fuji Velvia film. I was in a group of about 10 photographers in quite a confined space behind a concrete wall and up against an advertising board. I heard a screech of brakes – really locked up – and in a blink of an eye, this car jumped high over the kerb, crashed down, and headed back to the pits.

My shots were all reaction – there was no time to think or frame anything, so I just aimed and kept on shooting. I only got three frames, but they capture the sequence, from launch to landing. I have him hitting the kerb and taking off, flying in mid-air, then crashing back down and heading to the pits. There were other photographers with me, and they were asking, 'Did you get it?' I wasn't sure, but no one else thought they had it. The whole thing was over in a split second.

We had the film processed locally in Adelaide and when my brother Keith was going through them the next day, he gave a bit of a scream. He was looking at the lightbox and shouted, 'Oh my fucking god! What an amazing picture!' and everyone came over. The shot of Mika in mid-air was taken with a very slow shutter speed but it's still pin-sharp, so it was very lucky in a way. What makes it so unusual is that you just don't see F1 cars that high in the air and it's so level that it really does look like it's flying.

Obviously, we wanted some prints, so we went back to the lab and asked if they could do a rush job for us if we let them keep one print, which I promised I would get Mika to sign. I went to find him back at the track, with a print in hand. Initially, he wanted to keep it away from the team because it looked like he had made a mistake. He could hardly believe it was him when he saw it, but then he showed the shot to his engineer, who said, 'That's why there was a blip on the telemetry...'

It's become quite an iconic photo, but really it shows that sometimes you just have to be in the right place at the right time, and then maybe you make your own luck. I'd been doing regular panning shots and I come back with this! I couldn't possibly have planned it – there was no time to refocus and I had a slow shutter speed and a fixed lens – but sometimes everything just comes together. I remember it so clearly; it still feels like yesterday that I was standing there.

The picture put me on the map in F1. I was still new in the sport, and everyone knew Keith as 'the Senna photographer'. This one helped me establish my own name and was a big commercial success for us. It still sells to this day. There's one other aspect to this picture that isn't apparent unless you know Häkkinen's story. It was at this very corner, two years later, that he had the accident that nearly killed him. Happily, of course, he survived and went on to win his world titles. He's still signing that picture as 'The Flying Finn' to this day.

BOSS
Marlboro
COURTAULDS
Shell

MICHELIN MIC
Labatt
LONGINES

# ERCOLE COLOMBO ON GILLES VILLENEUVE
## On the ragged edge

**IF I HAD TO CHOOSE ONE SHOT FROM THE** millions I have taken in more than 50 years of F1 photography, that really defines the sport and really defines Gilles Villeneuve, it would be this one. Why? Because, for me, it's the symbol of Formula One: skill, bravery, and going above and beyond the limit. I remember it so clearly. It was taken on Saturday morning, 11 April, at the 1981 Argentinian Grand Prix – the third race of the season that year. I had wanted to take some frontal shots because those were quite hard to find at the Buenos Aires circuit, which mostly consisted of long corners where you couldn't really get in front of the car. There was one place I knew, though, just behind the pits. So, I thought I would go there. It was on the exit of Ombu corner, before Cajon – a relatively slow and technical section. I could see Gilles coming off the long straight and right away I knew he was flat-out and that this was going to be entertaining. So, I got ready to take the photo, but then I could see he was sliding through the corner at the very limit. He went hugely wide and, to be honest, I thought he was going off.

As all this was happening, I took the shots and hoped for the best. Back then, of course, you developed your film only on the Tuesday after a long-haul race, so you had absolutely no idea what you'd got until then. I was hoping that the shot was in focus because, of course, I had focused on the apex and Gilles was nowhere near there. It was also a pretty grey and cloudy day, so my hopes weren't too high. Unbelievably, he came round the next time; I was lined up for another shot and did the same again! Then once more the following lap. It was incredible, but that was Gilles for you. Always going over the line. I took as many photos as I could because, back in those film days, you didn't get many chances.

The photo you see here is actually from the first time he came round, which turned out to be the best one. I took it using an Olympus OM2 camera with a 500mm telephoto lens – I was an Olympus ambassador at the time. When it came out, I was really excited because I could see straight away that it had captured everything I wanted it to. It went on to become quite a famous image and, as I said, my personal favourite. Gilles saw it too, of course, and he really liked it. 'Did I give you a good shot?' he asked. 'But I should have been more sideways...'

He was crazy, but he was also very curious about photography. Every so often he would rifle through my camera bag to see what was in there, and he was fascinated by the zoom lenses that were state-of-the-art at the time. He would ask me what I could see through there, and often take a good look himself. Gilles was a real gift for photographers and could always spot a camera as he was going round the lap.

**Argentinian Grand Prix**
**Buenos Aires circuit, 11 April 1981**
**Ferrari 126C**

2

# CHAMPIONS AND HEROES

*The stories of every world champion since 1950, plus those of a dazzling supporting cast.*

Giuseppe Farina
Juan Manuel Fangio
Alberto Ascari
Jean Behra
Stirling Moss
Mike Hawthorn
Peter Collins
Tony Brooks
Jack Brabham
Phil Hill
Wolfgang Berghe von Trips
Graham Hill
Jim Clark
Dan Gurney
John Surtees
Denny Hulme
Bruce McLaren
Jackie Stewart
Jochen Rindt
François Cevert
Emerson Fittipaldi
Jacky Ickx
Niki Lauda
James Hunt
Carlos Reutemann
Mario Andretti
Ronnie Peterson
Jody Scheckter
Gilles Villeneuve
Alan Jones
Nelson Piquet
Didier Pironi
Keke Rosberg
René Arnoux
Alain Prost
Ayrton Senna
Gerhard Berger
Nigel Mansell
Jean Alesi
Michael Schumacher
Damon Hill
David Coulthard
Jacques Villeneuve
Mika Häkkinen
Fernando Alonso
Juan Pablo Montoya
Kimi Räikkönen
Felipe Massa
Robert Kubica
Lewis Hamilton
Jenson Button
Sebastian Vettel
Nico Rosberg
Max Verstappen

FARINA

# GIUSEPPE FARINA
# 1950 WORLD CHAMPION

**CAREER STATS**

**World title: 1950**
**Wins: 5**
**Pole positions: 5**
**Fastest laps: 5**

**IT SEEMS ALMOST UNIMAGINABLE FROM** a 21st-century perspective that a driver might win the F1 world title with 30 points and a haul of three victories from the season's six Grands Prix. Yet that's how it was in 1950 for Formula One's first World Champion, Dr Giuseppe 'Nino' Farina, enshrined forever by his pioneering achievements.

The scale of the first World Championship was diminutive in comparison with the globe-straddling contest of more than 20 races that has become familiar. Farina and his rivals battled six European Grands Prix that year, with the anomalous inclusion of the Indianapolis 500 justifying the 'World' tag. Nonetheless, the fundamentals were the same: the best drivers of the day competing in the fastest machinery available on closed-road courses, to an agreed set of rules and regulations.

Farina, driving for the pace-setting Alfa Romeo factory team, was every inch the grandee of his day. He was an established ace of pre-war motor racing and in the late 1940s raced for Ferrari, Maserati and Alfa. He looked forward to the 1950 racing season with expectation, if not quite a sense of entitlement. Aged 44 in his title year, racing had been Farina's life for a quarter of a century. He had been introduced to the automotive world as a boy via his father's automobile bodywork business located in Turin, the heart of Italy's auto industry. Farina's uncle Pinin would go on to found the legendary Pininfarina coachbuilding and design house.

Almost by osmosis, Nino was absorbed by the world of motoring and motorsport, though not before proving himself in other sporting disciplines, including skiing and football. Academic ambitions, pursued in tandem, led to his completion of a doctorate before taking up full-time competition. The assured background and cool intellect rendered him aloof, earning him the nickname 'The Gentleman of Turin'. He regarded motor racing as a pursuit for those of a certain social standing. It was not, in Dr Farina's view, a sport for every man.

The imperious manner, epitomised by his upright, arms-at-full-stretch stance at the wheel, translated into his on-track etiquette – or lack thereof. Regarded as brave beyond his talent and overly aggressive during racing manoeuvres, Farina's early racing exploits were not without incident. He survived numerous spills in his learning years from which he was fortunate to escape career-ending injury. This was not always the case, however, for those who crossed his path during a race.

Farina displayed enough speed and grit racing through the perilous pre-war Grand Prix scene to attract the attention of Enzo Ferrari, who in the late 1930s was building his future empire by running Alfa Romeos. In 1937, driving for Ferrari, Farina became Italian National Champion, a success he repeated in '38 and '39 as an Alfa works driver.

World War II put international motorsport on hold for almost a decade, but once hostilities had ceased, Farina was straight back to competition. He notably won the 1948 Monaco Grand Prix driving for Maserati but by 1950 he was back with Alfa Romeo, the most distinguished of the 'three Fs' racing for the team that year: Juan Manuel Fangio, Luigi Fagioli and Giuseppe himself.

For the inaugural race in the FIA World Championship of Drivers, held on 13 May at Silverstone, a crowd of between 150,000 and 200,000 (estimates vary) assembled to watch an event attended by King George VI. Farina duly delivered a commanding victory from pole position, and he might have considered the world title his by right. He had reckoned without the abilities of Fangio, five years younger and soon to become the standard-setter of his, and future, generations. Both men won three Grands Prix in the Alfa 158 that year, but only at the Swiss Grand Prix, on the Bremgarten road circuit, did they stage a true head-to-head. Their Alfas were dominant and lapped the entire field, Farina and Fangio exchanging the lead as they progressed. Farina was determined to hold back his younger, faster rival and profited from a late-race mechanical failure for Fangio.

By the season's final round at Monza, Fangio held a points advantage and qualified on pole position. A win or second place would guarantee him the title. Farina, though, made the better start and led all 80 laps, as Fangio retired with a broken gearbox on lap 23. Farina's victory secured him the title on home soil and he raced on with Alfa through 1951, winning the Belgian GP but slipping to fourth in the drivers' table behind champion Fangio.

Alfa's withdrawal at the end of the season brought a switch to Ferrari for the remainder of Farina's F1 career, where he was outpaced by the dashing young Alberto Ascari. Never comfortable with defeat, 'The Man of Steel', as Enzo Ferrari once referred to him, retired at the end of the '55 season to begin post-racing life as an Alfa Romeo dealer. His death in a road accident in 1966 came as little surprise to those who knew him well. 'I never understood how he survived so long,' noted Fangio. 'On the track he was not too bad, but on the road, he was a madman.'

**IN HIS FINAL SEASON AS A GRAND PRIX** driver in 1957, Juan Manuel Fangio drove a race still regarded as one of the greatest-ever in Formula One. Aged 46, he won the German Grand Prix at the fearsome Nürburgring Nordschleife, displaying mastery of his car, the circuit, and – though barely – of himself.

Notorious as The Green Hell, the Nürburgring circuit, built in 1927, is a 14-mile carousel through the Eifel mountains, encompassing more than 150 corners and constant elevation change. Every contour reeks of jeopardy; it demands the utmost skill and concentration to conquer. Fangio was already a four-time World Champion by the time of the '57 race and a figure of towering eminence. He raced that year for Maserati, piloting their 250F with a mesmeric combination of finesse and relentless speed.

He had qualified the 'beautifully balanced' car on pole position, ahead of rivals Mike Hawthorn and Peter Collins of Ferrari, his teammate Jean Behra and the Vanwall pair, Tony Brooks and Stirling Moss. Still very much The Man, Fangio was favourite to win on the most demanding circuit of all: the perfect stage for his skills and stamina. Maserati were confident in their advantage, too. They had planned a pit stop for Fangio, allowing him to run the race in two sprints, each with a lighter fuel load that would allow him to maximise the handling advantage of the 250F. All went well until lap 11, when Fangio entered the pits with a 30-second advantage over the non-stopping Collins and Hawthorn. A mechanic's fumble during the stop delayed re-fitting of the left-rear wheel and Fangio rejoined 48 seconds down on Collins. To win, he would have to be almost five seconds per lap faster than the Ferraris over the final 10 laps.

A man already so successful and at an advanced stage of his career, moreover one who had survived a near-fatal racing accident five years earlier, could be forgiven for letting younger, hungrier rivals let rip. Not Juan Manuel Fangio. Not on this day. He set about the task with such commitment that he was lapping around 15 seconds per lap quicker than his own fastest time from the previous year. He drove lap 20 in 9'17.4s – more than eight seconds faster than his own pole position time. Passing Collins, then Hawthorn on the penultimate lap to win by 3.6 seconds, he had driven, he said, at a level he believed he 'would never be able to again'. The exhilaration of the performance prevented him from sleeping for two days.

Fangio went on to win that year's title comprehensively, his fourth in succession, having set standards that would take decades to match. He had won almost half the Grands Prix he entered (24 out of 51) and no driver won five titles until Michael Schumacher in 2002. Fangio's raw statistics, compelling though they are, say nothing of the stature he achieved while racing, and of the aura that continues to surround his legend. He came late to European racing, making the 7,000-mile odyssey from Argentina in 1949, aged 38, with backing from the country's automobile club. Already a feted veteran of epic Latin road races such as the two-week, 6,000-mile Gran Premio Del Norte, there would be little to intimidate him in the Formula One arena, for all the perils of Grand Prix racing in the Fifties.

Driving for Alfa Romeo in the first year of the Formula One World Championship in 1950, Fangio was immediately successful. He started the final round – the Italian GP at Monza – as favourite to win the inaugural title before mechanical failure allowed teammate Giuseppe Farina through to victory. Fangio swept Farina aside in '51, however, to win his first championship ahead of a strongly challenging Alberto Ascari, but he had no chance of mounting a defence. Alfa withdrew ahead of the season, a rule change having made their 159 ineligible and – far more seriously – because Fangio broke his neck in a non-championship race at Monza. He spent months recovering in Argentina before returning with Maserati for 1953, a season dominated by Alberto Ascari and Ferrari.

Thereafter, Fangio locked out '50s Formula One through to his retirement. In consecutive years from 1954 to '57 he won the title for Mercedes, Ferrari and Maserati. He left the sport after two races in 1958, with nothing left to achieve or prove, returning to Argentina, where he died in 1995 aged 84. The domination he achieved would not be seen again in Formula One until the Schumacher–Ferrari 'redwash' of the early noughties.

Unlike Schumacher, however, and latterly Sebastian Vettel and Lewis Hamilton, Fangio won titles with four different teams. With each switch, he displayed his ability to transfer not only his sublime – and devastatingly fast – four-wheel-drifting technique, honed on the endless gravel roads of his homeland, but also his ability to work with new teams and win the confidence of new mechanics. Once dismissed by Enzo Ferrari as a driver without loyalty, Fangio was held in rather different esteem by his Mercedes teammate Stirling Moss, one of the few capable of breathing Fangio's rarified air. In Moss' view, Fangio switched teams frequently because 'he was the best bloody driver. The cheapest method of becoming a successful Grand Prix team was to sign up Fangio!'

Together at Mercedes in 1955, Moss running dutifully in line behind the man he called 'Maestro', they created some of the hallmark images of the era. Yet none could surpass the sight of Fangio in full flight at the wheel of a 250F – man and machine never more perfectly attuned, Fangio manipulating time and space with hands and feet. The definitive driver of his age, Juan Manuel Fangio remains a racing icon for all times.

**CAREER STATS**

**World title: 1951, 1954, 1955, 1956, 1957**
**Wins: 24**
**Pole positions: 29**
**Fastest laps: 23**

# JUAN MANUEL FANGIO
# WORLD CHAMPION 1951, 1954–57

0404
3B 8957
76·9875
66-842
A248
0-34-75
NEW MEXICO
368-55
129

ASCARI
Maserati

CAREER STATS

World title: 1952, 1953
Wins: 13
Pole positions: 14
Fastest laps: 12

# ALBERTO ASCARI WORLD CHAMPION 1952–53

**TIMES MAY CHANGE IN FORMULA ONE,** speeds increase, budgets spiral, calendars fatten, but the fundamentals remain unchanged. Just as the very modern Max Verstappen has spent the early 2020s crushing the competitive spirit of his rivals, so did Alberto Ascari perform a similar number on his opponents across 1952–53.

Driving for Ferrari in both those seasons, Ascari won the world title and, in doing so, became the sport's first multiple champion, as well as the first to win back-to-back titles. His superiority showed itself not simply in the fact of championship victory, but in the manner of it. For a whole calendar year, from June 1952 to June '53, Ascari was the only man to win a Formula One Grand Prix. That equated to nine consecutive victories, a streak not broken until Verstappen won 10 on the trot in 2023. While motor racing from the 1950s seems from the dark ages, when viewed from the perspective of the early 2020s, the opportunity for a great driver, equipped with the best car, to close out his rivals, was as viable then as it is now.

The mechanical excellence of the Ferrari Tipo 500, raced by Ascari in both his title-winning seasons, underpinned his success. It was the only car designed to meet new technical regulations (which had been based on Formula Two engine specifications) and Ascari's cause was further aided in '52 by the absence of reigning champion Juan Manuel Fangio, who had been sidelined with a serious neck injury. Ascari excelled with what he had. Having missed the Swiss GP, the opening race of the season, and then retired from the Indianapolis 500 (then part of the World Championship), Ascari won all six remaining Grands Prix, from five pole positions and with six fastest laps.

His preferred style of controlling from the front ('catch me if you can' – they rarely did) set the template for later double champions similarly capable of paralysing notional opposition from the head of the field: Jim Clark and Mika Häkkinen. Ascari revelled in being the pace setter, because only when running cleanly in first place could he drive with the unfettered urgency and accuracy that were his hallmark. Mike Hawthorn, the 1958 World Champion who was a junior teammate of Ascari in 1953, explained: 'He is spot-on all the time and on every lap. There is never any variation. Bloody Ascari.' Alberto himself reflected later that he wished Fangio had been fit and offering competition during the season, a sentiment later reciprocated by Fangio, who reckoned Ascari and Stirling Moss to be the two drivers he most respected and feared.

Ascari's hot streak continued into '53 and he secured his second title with a race to spare. The season-closing Italian GP would be a coronation, surely, for a national hero in front of his adoring fans. But they were to be disappointed, for against the script, their man became embroiled in a race-long dogfight. Approaching the final corner (Verano – now Parabolica) on the last lap, his teammate Giuseppe Farina, and Fangio in a Maserati, were in his slipstream hoping to tow past for the win. Then – sensation! – Ascari spun as he attempted to lap back markers, allowing Fangio through for his only victory of the season. Had Ascari become so used to leading that he'd lost an edge of race craft in wheel-to-wheel scrapping? At least the crestfallen *tifosi* took consolation from the knowledge that their *Ciccio* (chubby) was unhurt and fit to lead Ferrari again the following season.

They were to be shocked once more, however, for during the winter Ascari switched allegiance to the Lancia team, tempted by a bigger salary and the prospect of taking the innovative D50 car from prototype to race-readiness. He guest-drove for Ferrari at the Italian GP, leading until retirement, but almost the entire 1954 season passed before the debut of the D50 at the Spanish GP, where Ascari took pole position and fastest lap before a clutch failure.

The auguries for 1955 were promising, as the D50, though still unruly, seemed to have the raw pace needed to take on the all-conquering Mercedes W196. Ascari qualified second for the season-opening Argentinian GP and led for 21 laps before retiring after a spin (the corner where he lost control was later named in his honour). And then to Monaco, where he survived a plunge into the harbour waters having run wide at the chicane with fading brakes. Ascari was submerged for several seconds but soon resurfaced, distinctive blue helmet still strapped on, and was helped to a rescue boat by divers. There was soreness and a broken nose, but he had escaped lightly. The Lancia had been quick, too, Ascari qualifying in second place and briefly leading before the accident.

Four days later he was dead, killed at Monza testing a Ferrari sportscar, preparing for an endurance race in which Lancia would not compete. Ascari had not been scheduled to drive but told his co-driver for the race, Eugenio Castellotti, that he wanted to get back in the cockpit, check he hadn't lost his nerve. The accident has never been properly explained, though a driver of Ascari's talents was unlikely to have made a mistake and Ferrari later insisted their investigations showed that no mechanical failure would have been the cause. Mystery gave rise to speculation. The ultra-superstitious Ascari had driven without wearing his lucky blue helmet. Had his tie blown into his face, distracting him? Had the Monaco dive left him concussed? The date of the accident was 26 May 1955. Ascari's father, the great pre-war champion Antonio, had been killed in a racing accident on 26 July 1925. Both were 36.

It mattered little. Italy had lost a favourite son and the streets of Milan, Ascari's hometown, filled with maybe a million mourners on the day of his funeral. He was laid to rest next to his father's grave in the Cimitero Monumentale in Milan.

**IF THE INFANT JEAN BEHRA'S LUNGS HAD** allowed, he might have come into the world singing 'La Marseillaise'. Born in Nice and a musketeer in style – all bravura, dash and mercurial temperament – Behra broke into Formula One, aged 30, with the French Gordini team in 1952, pitched against the might of all-conquering Ferrari.

There was little chance that the blue cars might beat the majestic Alberto Ascari during his world title glory years, despite the ragged speed of their courageous lead driver, who had enjoyed much success racing motorbikes before his switch to cars. But there would be highlights to ignite the passions of his countrymen, such as the 1952 non-championship Formula One Marne Grand Prix.

At the Reims circuit, which would host the French Grand Prix one week later, Behra's Gordini Type 16 was in the lead by the end of lap one and held on to take the chequered flag three hours later, ahead of Ferrari's Giuseppe Farina and a car shared between Ascari and Luigi Villoresi. Had a blind eye been turned to the Gordini's legality? A week later in the Grand Prix proper, blue was no match for red, but no matter: Behra had beaten the Ferraris, and a cult hero was born.

He remained loyal to the national squad through to the end of 1954, despite meagre success. That season, however, did allow Behra another glory day. At the non-championship Pau Grand Prix, held around the streets of the Pyrenean French town, Gordini blue once again prevailed over the red of Ferrari and Maserati, as Behra brought the house down with a passing move for the lead only minutes before the end of the three-hour race. These results were mere crumbs for a man of Behra's competitive bent and the lure of a faster car proved too strong when Maserati offered him a drive for 1955.

His three years racing the 250F brought his greatest Formula One success and during 1956, Behra took five podium finishes from seven races as he succeeded in allying consistency with the trademark tigerish aggression that resulted in multiple heavy accidents and frequent injury. Never, though, did he take the chequered flag in a championship Grand Prix, despite many top-line successes elsewhere.

Maserati's persistent financial troubles led Behra to an abortive year with BRM in 1958, before a combustible part-season with Ferrari in 1959. At the French Grand Prix, scene of Behra's Gordini glory day in '52, he charged from the back of the field after a start-line hold-up, to place third by lap 24, only for his engine to blow seven laps later. Team manager Romolo Tavoni pinned blame for the retirement firmly on Behra, who he accused of over-revving his engine. Jeannot made his contrary view clear with a fist to Tavoni's jaw. He never raced for Ferrari again.

Without team backing, Behra arrived at the German GP meeting one month later, at the Avus circuit, and drove his privately entered Porsche in a sportscar race held the day before the Grand Prix. Chasing the leaders in wet conditions, Behra lost control on lap four. His car spun up and over Avus' banking, hitting a concrete block and throwing Behra into the sky, to his death. His funeral service in Nice was attended by 3,000 mourners.

**CAREER STATS**

**Wins: 0**
**Pole positions: 0**
**Fastest laps: 1**

# JEAN BEHRA

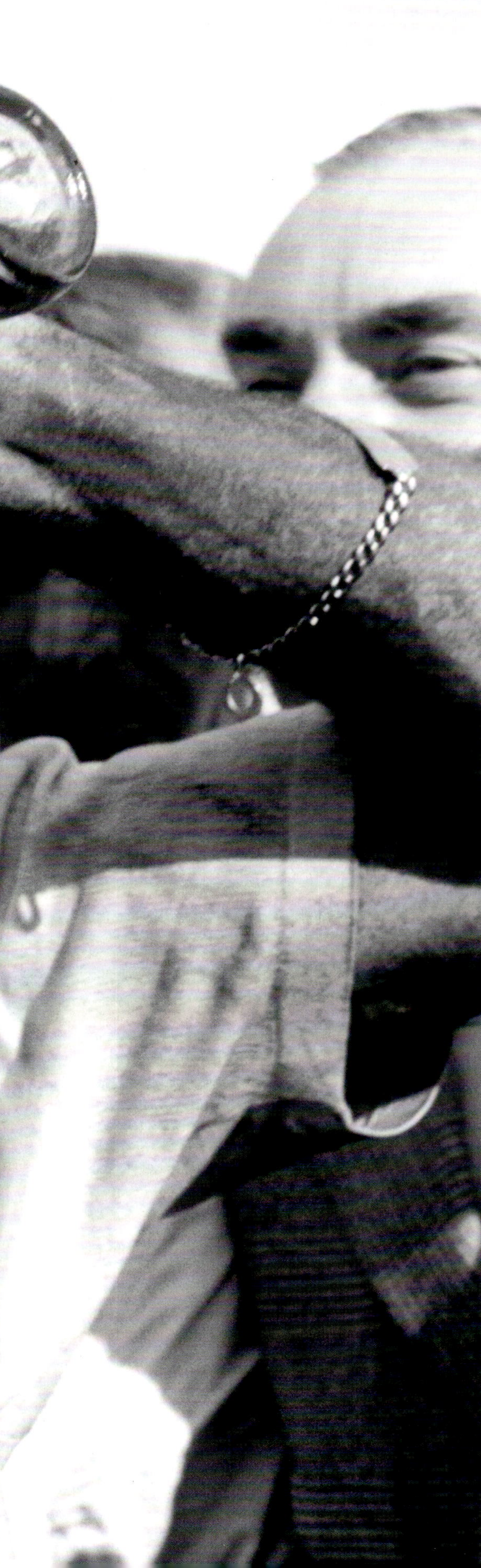

# STIRLING MOSS

**CAREER STATS**

**Wins: 16**
**Pole positions: 16**
**Fastest laps: 19**

**A HANDFUL OF DRIVERS IN THE 75-YEAR** history of Formula One have transcended their status as greats to become timeless icons of the sport itself. Their stature assured, no further explanation is needed of their place in the pantheon. On any such list, hotly debated of course, names such as Ayrton Senna, Niki Lauda and Lewis Hamilton might well be pencilled in early. Before them all, written in ink, would be the name 'Stirling Moss', the very essence of a racing driver in his own time and in the decades that passed after his retirement.

At odds with his status is the fact that he never won the World Championship, despite being a recognised ace, yet that simple truth does more to devalue the world title than it does to diminish Moss's standing. He won 16 Grands Prix in a Formula One career that spanned 1951–61 and broke into the winners' circle at the 1955 British GP, ahead of his Mercedes lead driver Juan Manuel Fangio. Their single-season partnership at Mercedes remains one of the sport's most fabled, the pair often running 1–2, with Moss happy to take the understudy role – a position he was only willing to accept for a driver he regarded as the greatest of all.

The true nature of their relative speed is open to debate and Moss was the faster of the two in sportscar racing outside Formula One. It was in that arena, driving the Mercedes 300 SLR, that he won the 1955 Mille Miglia race – a 1,000-mile sprint around open roads in northern Italy, with co-driver Denis Jenkinson as his navigational aide. Moss's achievement in a race so dangerous that it was banned two years later after an accident that killed driver Alfonso De Portago, co-driver Edmund Nelson and 10 spectators, five of them children, was his greatest, in his own view. In a 2012 interview with distinguished motorsport journalist Maurice Hamilton, he said, 'If you're talking about the skill of driving, not one of [my Grand Prix wins] equals winning the Mille Miglia in 1955. Averaging 97.7mph over 1,000 miles of public roads... The pleasure was remarkable'.

As British drivers and manufacturers began to challenge the supremacy of rivals from continental Europe, Moss's eminence in the late 1950s was huge. He finished runner-up in the World Championship in the four consecutive years from 1955 to '58 and only lost out in that last season because of an act of high sportsmanship towards his countryman Mike Hawthorn At the Portuguese GP, Hawthorn had been penalised for driving against the direction of traffic while returning to the track after a spin. Post-race, with Hawthorn due to be disqualified from second place, Moss offered testimony that, while Hawthorn had indeed driven against the track direction, he had done so off the circuit and therefore should not be penalised. Hawthorn's result stood and he won that year's title by a point, despite having won only a single Grand Prix to Moss's four.

Moss raced for the next three seasons with the independent Rob Walker team, revelling in his underdog status driving customer Cooper and Lotus cars against better-funded factory entries. During this post-Fangio and pre-Jim Clark period, Moss was regarded as without peer by his rivals. His two 1961 victories at Monaco and Germany's Nürburgring, ahead of more powerful Ferrari opposition, showcased his virtuosity, while cementing his legend.

A Ferrari future beckoned for 1962, Moss having agreed terms to race a customer car entered by Walker, but a near-fatal accident at the Goodwood circuit on Easter Monday 1962 guillotined Moss's career. He was unconscious for a month after the crash, partially paralysed for six, and when he did venture back into the cockpit less than a year later, he found instinctive feel, touch and reaction no longer present. In time, his faculties might have returned, but aged 32 and at the peak of his powers, Moss called it quits. While Stirling's racing days were over, the happy outcome was recovery to full health and long life. He died in 2020, aged 90, iconic to the last.

**IDIOSYNCRATICALLY DAPPER IN FLAT CAP,** polka-dot bow tie and collar, Mike Hawthorn appeared almost a parody Englishman in pursuit of motor-racing glory. Yet the first British World Champion won the 1958 drivers' title for an Italian manufacturer, Ferrari, having failed to achieve success with nascent home teams.

Hawthorn, strikingly tall, boisterous and blond, also achieved that singular honour during a period when more obviously gifted compatriots Stirling Moss, Peter Collins and Tony Brooks fell short in their quest to win motorsport's most coveted prize. He was an unlikely champion, and one who retired with only three Grands Prix victories on the scoresheet and a title taken by a single point ahead of Moss, who won four Grands Prix in Hawthorn's title year.

A racer in a monochrome age, the colour of Hawthorn's character shines from contemporary accounts of his generosity, joie de vivre and sheer determination to have a bloody good time with fast cars, fast friends and whatever quantity of liquor was required to fuel the adventure. Being a Grand Prix driver, even winning the world title, seemed subservient to the greater goal of hedonistic fulfilment. Motor racing might have been fun for Mike Hawthorn, but it was never a game. The guts and commitment of his on-track style were evidence of his seriousness about racing and there was no shortage of talent on which to build.

The son of garage owner Leslie Hawthorn, whose premises in Farnham, near London, were licensed to service Ferraris and Jaguars, Mike was an early automobile addict and by the age of nine had decided he wanted to race. The proximity of Brooklands Speedbowl was a further influence and by 1950 Mike was campaigning a Riley sportscar bought for him by his father. Within two years, Hawthorn had begun racing single-seaters and a starring performance during an Easter meeting at the Goodwood circuit encouraged Hawthorn father and son to try their hand at Formula One. Impossibly naïve though such a notion might seem, that's exactly what transpired. In his third Formula One start, Hawthorn placed third in the 1952 British Grand Prix, driving a Cooper-Bristol. Only the Ferraris of Alberto Ascari and Piero Taruffi finished ahead.

The pluck of this dashing Englishman had caught the eye of Enzo Ferrari, leading to the offer of a works drive with the Scuderia for 1953. Now racing in red, Hawthorn's charmed career elevation continued with a famous victory over Juan Manuel Fangio at the French GP, Hawthorn's ninth Formula One start. He was one of four works Ferrari drivers entered that hot July day at the Reims circuit, in the heart of Champagne country. Alongside him were Alberto Ascari, largely dominant throughout 1952–53, Luigi Villoresi and 1950 champion Nino Farina. Chief opposition came in the form of Maserati's factory team, led by Juan Manuel Fangio, the 1951 champion, and fellow Argentinian José Froilán Gonzáles.

Early in the race Gonzales sped away in the lead, benefitting from a light fuel load which would necessitate a mid-distance pit-stop. As the race progressed, Fangio took the lead, Hawthorn tailing him closely. Despite being the junior member of the Ferrari squad, Hawthorn was mounting the team's strongest challenge. With 20 laps remaining, he and Fangio remained locked together, frequently passing and re-passing as they progressed around the wide-open Reims track, which was little more than three straights connected by a couple of fast corners and a hairpin bend. The Ferrari and Maserati were closely matched: Hawthorn's car with an edge in grip and braking; Fangio's Maserati compensating with a slight power advantage. Into the last lap Hawthorn had the lead, but Fangio passed, only to be re-passed by Hawthorn on the approach to Thillois corner. By now, Hawthorn had worked out that Fangio had been trying to disguise the loss of first gear and he was able to out-accelerate his rival on exit. Hawthorn held on for the win by only a second, with Gonzales a mere 0.4s behind, after two-and-three-quarter hours of racing. It was declared 'The Race of the Century' in ecstatic media reports.

Hawthorn won again in 1954 – victory at the Spanish GP during a year of Mercedes domination – before two fallow years spent chasing success with the British Vanwall and BRM teams. His victory with Jaguar in the 1955 Le Mans 24-hour race was marred by an accident that he was involved in, which killed 83 spectators and driver Pierre Levegh. An enquiry found Hawthorn had not been responsible for causing the accident, but the carnage fed his growing concerns about the sport's dangers.

For 1957 he was back with Ferrari, forging an intensely close friendship with teammate Peter Collins – one that was to end in tragedy with Collins' death during the 1958 German GP, only two weeks after he had won his home race at Silverstone. Witnessing Collins' accident hardened Hawthorn's resolve to quit at the end of a year during which fellow Ferrari teammate Luigi Musso was also killed. Musso's death came during the French GP, Hawthorn's only win of the season. He had driven consistently throughout the year, taking seven podium finishes alongside the win to head into the final race, the Moroccan GP, for a title decider with Moss. Driving a Vanwall, Moss was the season's pace setter but finished the season a point behind Hawthorn, despite winning four Grands Prix.

Hawthorn's cause was helped by an act of extreme sportsmanship from Moss earlier in the year at the Portuguese GP. Hawthorn had been disqualified post-race for re-starting his Ferrari against the direction of the circuit after a spin. Moss, who had seen Hawthorn's re-start, intervened, stating that Hawthorn had done nothing wrong. This noble act allowed Hawthorn to keep points which would ultimately secure his title. By season's end, and having seen another driver, Stewart Lewis-Evans, die after an accident at the Moroccan GP, Hawthorn quit racing to return to running the family garage and look forward to married life with fashion model Jean Howarth. Three months later, he was killed in a road accident a few miles from his home, aged 29.

**CAREER STATS**

**World title: 1958**
**Wins: 3**
**Pole positions: 4**
**Fastest laps: 6**

# PETER COLLINS

**AT THE TAIL END OF THE 1950S, A QUARTET** of British drivers raced with unprecedented distinction in motor racing's top flight. Mike Hawthorn won the world title in 1958 to become the first British champion; Stirling Moss became a legend; Tony Brooks shone as one of the sport's most silken talents. And then there was Peter Collins, a three-time Grand Prix winner for Ferrari and a favourite of Enzo himself, yet a figure sometimes overlooked in this elevated company.

Like many of his era, Collins ventured into the sport racing the skeletal 500cc cars that were cheap, simple, popular and well suited to Britain's austere post-war years. Consistently good results, coupled with a charming off-track manner, led to conversations with Aston Martin and, soon enough, opportunities to race their sportscars. Strong performances for Aston, including second place at Le Mans in 1955 and '56, alongside occasional Formula One outings for the British teams HWM, BRM and Vanwall, kept Collins' name in lights, but it was his victory at the 1955 Targa Florio that placed him in the front rank. For the 600-mile road race around Sicily, Collins shared a Mercedes 300 SLR with Moss, very much the ace of the day, and proved both his talent and team-first ethic.

Ferrari took note, and for 1956 Collins was one of their works drivers, racing both their sportscars and in Formula One. In only his second Grand Prix start for the team, he finished second at Monaco, in a car shared with Juan Manuel Fangio. Collins' next race was the Belgian GP, which he won by almost two minutes from teammate Paul Frère, to stand atop the drivers' table. He won the following Grand Prix in France, and was suddenly being spoken of as champion-elect – Britain's first.

He remained in title contention until the final round in Italy, where an act of remarkable selflessness ensured that the honour would instead go to Fangio, Ferrari's number one. Earlier in the race, Fangio had retired with a broken steering arm and was forced to watch the laps tick down and await the final order to decide the championship. Although Moss was leading the race comfortably, it was mathematically possible for Collins still to take the title, were he to win and set fastest lap. Collins took matters into his own hands by pitting on lap 35 for a tyre change, exiting his D50 and handing it over to his exalted team leader, allowing Fangio to finish in second place with points shared between him and Collins. Fangio later confessed to being moved to tears by Collins' gesture; Collins himself explained that it was simply, 'the right thing to do'.

The year 1957 was a weaker, winless year for Ferrari, though the signing of Hawthorn, Collins' closest friend in racing, was a considerable compensation. Two young fun-loving Brits driving for the world's most famous racing team... what could possibly go wrong? Tales of their antics were legion, and they became largely inseparable, off-track and on.

Things got more serious in 1958, once Ferrari's Dino 246 emerged as a front-running machine. By mid-season, Hawthorn was tied with Moss for the championship lead, though Collins, with only two point-finishes, occupied a lowly tenth spot. Matters changed at the British Grand Prix, where Collins led the full 75 laps, drifting his Ferrari through Silverstone's broad sweeps, revelling in the joy of driving flat-out.

A fortnight later, at Germany's Nürburgring, he and Hawthorn once again set the pace, Collins ahead, before a mid-race challenge from Brooks in the Vanwall, who snuck into the lead on lap 11. Collins immediately gave chase, but lost control of his car after the Pflanzgarten section, was thrown out and hit a tree, suffering head injuries to which he later succumbed. The accident happened immediately ahead of Hawthorn, who withdrew a lap later but went on to win the '58 title, ahead of Moss and Brooks. Collins' absence from the top of the table left an echoing void.

**CAREER STATS**

**Wins: 3**
**Pole positions: 0**
**Fastest laps: 0**

# TONY BROOKS

**CAREER STATS**

**Wins: 6**
**Pole positions: 3**
**Fastest laps: 3**

**THE BEST 'UNKNOWN' FORMULA ONE** driver was a trained dentist who raced for fun, yet almost won the 1959 World Championship. For a handful of glittering seasons in the late '50s, Tony Brooks ran with the elite – Fangio, Moss, Brabham, Hawthorn, Collins, Behra – winning six Grands Prix at some of the sport's most hallowed circuits, but retired before he was 30.

Brooks was the son of a dentist and pursued an academic path that would have led him to follow in his father's footsteps, had it not been for his parents' enthusiasm for fast cars and Brooks' discovery of a rare talent at the wheel. Early forays in club racing were pursued for pleasure, not with any notion of a career as a professional driver and certainly not with designs on the world title.

All that changed when he took a call from the Connaught team, a few days ahead of the 1955 Syracuse Grand Prix, a non-championship Formula One race in Sicily which would be Brooks' first in the category. History records Brooks taking a famous victory ahead of five Maseratis, and a first Formula One win for a British car, before flying home to sit his dentistry finals. Exams duly passed, he accepted F1 drives with another British team, BRM, in '56, the highlight of which was running in a strong second place during the early stages of the British GP at Silverstone, before a major accident, from which he escaped mostly unharmed.

A year later, by now racing as teammate to Moss for the ambitious British Vanwall team, he co-drove the winning car at the British GP, this time at the Aintree circuit, making Vanwall the first British team to win a World Championship Grand Prix. Brooks shared the car with Moss, having entered the race still recovering from injuries sustained in an accident at Le Mans and, fatigued, was glad to vacate his seat for Moss mid-race, as the regulations then permitted.

Moss won twice more for Vanwall that season, but in 1958, victory honours amounted to seven wins for the team (four for Moss and three for Brooks) – though both men were pipped to the title by Ferrari's Mike Hawthorn in a heady season for British motor racing. Brooks' wins came at three high-speed tracks well-suited to the Vanwall's characteristics: Spa-Francorchamps in Belgium, Germany's Nürburgring and Monza, Italy. The victories also drew on the calm authority of Brooks' style: he was a graceful, unhurried driver but also devastatingly fast.

Those elegant skills earned a call from Ferrari for 1959 to race the powerful Dino 246 against the growing threat from the rear-engined Cooper cars. He won twice, as did that year's champion Jack Brabham. Brooks might have taken the title at the final round, held at the US Sebring circuit, had he chosen to ignore a self-imposed rule that he would not race in a car he believed to be mechanically compromised. On the first lap of the race, Brooks' Ferrari was hit from behind, prompting him to pit for the car to be checked over. Nothing was amiss and he was waved out, having lost half a lap, to eventually finish third. Brooks' stop was the result of a belief, formed during recovery from earlier accidents, that to race with a damaged car was inconsistent with his religious views regarding the sanctity of life. 'My decision may have cost me the World Championship,' he later said, 'but I think I did the right thing'.

Brooks left Ferrari at the end of the year, already with an eye on building the garage business that would service his post-racing career. He quit racing altogether after the 1961 season, having finished third in his final Grand Prix. Unlike so many of his peers, he went on to enjoy a long and fulfilled life, reaching 90 as the father of five children.

# JACK BRABHAM
# WORLD CHAMPION 1959–60, 1966

**CAREER STATS**

**World title: 1959, 1960, 1966**
**Wins: 14**
**Pole positions: 13**
**Fastest laps: 12**

**MORE THAN 60 YEARS ON, THE SCALE OF** Sir Jack Brabham's Formula One achievements stand in epic scale: distant peaks that only gain enormity on closer inspection. Aside from the three world titles, which place him alongside fellow legends Sir Jackie Stewart, Niki Lauda, Nelson Piquet and Ayrton Senna, there was the pioneering trek from Australia to Europe to further his career; the founding of his own race team, with which he won his third drivers' title; and survival, just staying alive during Formula One's most perilous era.

A fascination with all things mechanical that drew Brabham inevitably towards motorsport began during his wartime service as a mechanic for the Royal Australian Air Force. Soon enough, he was using those fettling skills to gain a competitive advantage racing on Australian dirt ovals, where he'd begun to learn the rough-and-tumble race-craft that would become his hallmark as he progressed to the elite.

'The most important step I had in my career was seven years on the speedway,' he said in a 2013 interview with *F1 Racing* magazine. 'I learned not just racing, also from the engine point of view. We started with a 1000cc engine which wasn't anywhere near big enough and we stretched it to 1640cc. We made virtually every part of the engine.' Seeking mechanical advantage would become a theme of Brabham's career. Arriving in England in the early 1950s, leaving behind his wife and son, he immediately set about improving the sub-par machinery at his disposal: 'The thing I missed most was my lathe,' he said. 'I struggled to get whatever I could, as I didn't know the right people, and I made mistakes like buying the wrong car. I got talked into buying a new Cooper-Alta in England – which was an absolute disaster.'

Nonetheless, during visits to the Cooper Car Company, seeking better performance from his tardy steed, Sir Jack struck up a friendship with founder John Cooper. By 1959, the two were conquering the world: Brabham hustling the game-changing rear-engined Cooper T51 to a drivers' title, as Cooper vanquished mighty Ferrari in the Constructors' Championship. A back-to-back title double played out in 1960, Ferrari out-smarted by a teak-tough Aussie and some impudent *garagistas* from South-West London.

And Brabham couldn't get enough: 'I loved beating Ferrari. In 1960 they invited me to meet Enzo in Italy, to talk about driving for him, and I never even went. I was only interested in beating them, not joining them.' Given these sentiments, it's little surprise Sir Jack selected his 1960 French GP win as his favourite. At the fast Reims circuit, whose long straights should have given the technically obsolete but still powerful Ferraris of Phil Hill and Wolfgang Berghe von Trips a top speed advantage, Brabham prevailed. 'It was the most thrilling race I ever had. It was so close and then to nail them was great satisfaction.'

As the '60s progressed, Formula One entered its notorious 'killer years': a decade of rapidly escalating speeds that accelerated car performance way ahead of safety provision. Brabham flourished, despite the peril and ferocity of competition. Among his rivals were the likes of Stirling Moss, Jim Clark, Graham Hill, Dan Gurney, John Surtees and Tony Brooks – winners and champions all. Moss's track smarts in particular stood out: 'He was a very hard driver and one to learn from – mainly about race tactics and determination. That sort of rubbed off.'

Brabham soon earned a spiky reputation of his own: a driver who'd think nothing of dropping a rear wheel off the track edge to pepper his pursuers with gravel, or of brushing a straw bale to fill their faces and radiator intakes with grassy scurf. Grit and technical acumen helped earn Brabham his third title in 1966, aged 40, in a car designed by his founding partner in the new Motor Racing Developments company, Ron Tauranac. With engines supplied by Melbourne machinists Repco – highly regarded by Sir Jack from his aero mechanic days – Brabham, team and driver, were F1 pace setters, as Brabham's teammate Denny Hulme became champion in '67. 'Winning our own title was probably the pinnacle,' he said. 'It was a great achievement.' To say nothing of simply not being killed in a race car at a time when Grand Prix racing was deadly.

In his autobiography, *The Jack Brabham Story* (2004), Sir Jack recalled his most serious accident during a test at Silverstone in 1969: 'I'd got as far as Club Corner where we used to blast through at 115mph, and three-quarters of the way through, as I leaned on the left-front tyre, it popped off the rim and deflated. The car understeered into a bank [and] the impact smashed the left-front wheel into the side of the cockpit where it crushed the frame inwards, into my legs. The throttle was jammed wide open and behind me the engine was absolutely shrieking. The pain in my twisted legs and feet was unbelievable. There was a terrible stench of fuel. Looking over the cockpit side I could see a spreading lake of petrol and I knew if it ignited, I'd stand no chance.' Brabham eventually found the engine kill switch, before being rescued by his senior mechanic, a certain Ron Dennis.

'Black Jack' remained a force through the late '60s and was a race winner even in his 1970 retirement year. But it was the counsel of his father, Tom, after the 1970 Dutch GP, during which Piers Courage had crashed fatally, that convinced him to hang up his helmet. Bruce McLaren and Jochen Rindt had also died that year (Rindt becoming posthumous F1 Champion) and, while Brabham later considered he'd quit too soon, he had the priceless consolation of being able to reflect in his comfortable dotage on a unique racing career: that of a giant who bestrode F1's shift from black and white to technicolour.

**CAREER STATS**

**World title: 1961**
**Wins: 3**
**Pole positions: 6**
**Fastest laps: 6**

**AGONY AND ECSTASY DEFINED THE** briefly luminous Formula One career of Phil Hill, the first American to win the World Championship. He loved the experience of racing, thrilled to its speed, but hated what the sport drew from his character in pursuit of success.

A naturally shy character, humble enough in later life to introduce himself with: 'Hi, I'm Phil Hill,' he found a release through motorsport from childhood introversion that followed him for life. While he loved racing like a drug, he was uncomfortable with the 'selfish, irritable' person he became when competing. In Robert Daley's classic account of 1960s motor racing, *The Cruel Sport* (2005), he confessed: 'I don't want to beat anybody. I don't want to be the big hero. I'm a peace-loving man, basically.'

A hero he would become to many, however reluctantly, by winning a world title with Ferrari to cement a place in F1's hall of fame. Hill's '61 triumph was the culmination of an association with Ferrari that stretched back to the mid-1950s, with endurance racing and victory at the Le Mans 24-hour race in 1958. His success in sportscars, which were then regarded with a stature comparable to Formula One, eventually brought a call from Enzo Ferrari to join the F1 team, after both Peter Collins and Luigi Musso had been killed in Grand Prix racing that year.

Drafted in for the final three races of the season, his brief was to help teammate Mike Hawthorn win the title, an understudy role he performed with rather more élan than was strictly required. On his Monza debut, he led, or ran near the front, for much of the race before finishing third. At the season finale in Casablanca he was running second, ahead of Hawthorn, before obeying a pit call to let him past for the points needed to win the title.

Hill was clearly a driver capable of running with the best but in 1959, Ferrari were leapfrogged by the Cooper team's technical innovation: a mid-engined chassis. The forerunner of all subsequent successful F1 designs, the Cooper T51 outperformed front-engined rivals such as the Ferrari 246 in all aspects except power. Jack Brabham used his to win his first drivers' title comfortably. Cooper were also that year's winning constructor, which should have instructed Ferrari that the technical winds had shifted. Ever the traditionalist and a disciple of the 'power first' philosophy, Enzo Ferrari insisted his Formula One cars remain front-engined in 1960. His decision rendered the Scuderia also-rans, although Hill did enjoy one notable day in the sun that season – though not, coincidentally, at the Italian GP.

For the 1960 edition, race organisers had chosen a circuit configuration that included Monza's ultra-fast banked section of track. This high-speed, high-danger curve would automatically favour the more potent Ferraris and, crying 'foul', the British teams stayed away. No matter for Ferrari, whose trio of 246s hurried to a 1–2–3 finish, Hill out front, to the delight of their *tifosi* army. It was the last Grand Prix win for a front-engined car, but the first of only three for Hill, though it was his sweetest. He repeated the feat a year later, though in infinitely darker circumstances.

In 1961, it was a Ferrari year. Their unmistakable, petite-yet-aggressive 156 'Sharknose' was the only bespoke design for a revised set of technical regulations mandating 1.5-litre engines. Ferrari's new V6 offered up to 30bhp more than rival motors and it was finally located behind the driver, Enzo Ferrari having bowed to technical inevitability. Hill would lead the Scuderia's charge, alongside Germany's Count Wolfgang Berghe von Trips and fellow Californian Richie Ginther.

Strong pre-season favourites, Ferrari nevertheless had to suffer the brilliance of Stirling Moss at the season-opening Monaco Grand Prix. In inferior Lotus-Climax machinery, Moss, majestic, held back the Ferrari trio for 100 laps to take what he would come to regard as his greatest win. The red tide could only be resisted for so long and by the penultimate race – the Italian GP at Monza – 'Taffy' von Trips held a four-point advantage over Hill. He placed his 156 on pole, three places ahead of Hill, but started poorly and was passed by five cars, one of which was Jim Clark's Lotus. Approaching the Parabolica Curve at the end of lap two, Clark clipped von Trips, causing the Ferrari to fly from the track into a line of spectators. Fourteen were killed, as was von Trips, who had been thrown from the car.

The race was not stopped, and Hill drove to a forlorn victory and the world title. Having won both titles, Ferrari withdrew from the season-closing US Grand Prix and Hill never won another Grand Prix. He raced on until 1967, winning a third Le Mans with Ferrari in 1962, but never came close to repeating the F1 glories of '61. Returning to the US West Coast, Hill spent his post-racing life building a successful classic car restoration business, shunning the limelight, but secure in the knowledge of his unique place in the annals of American motorsport.

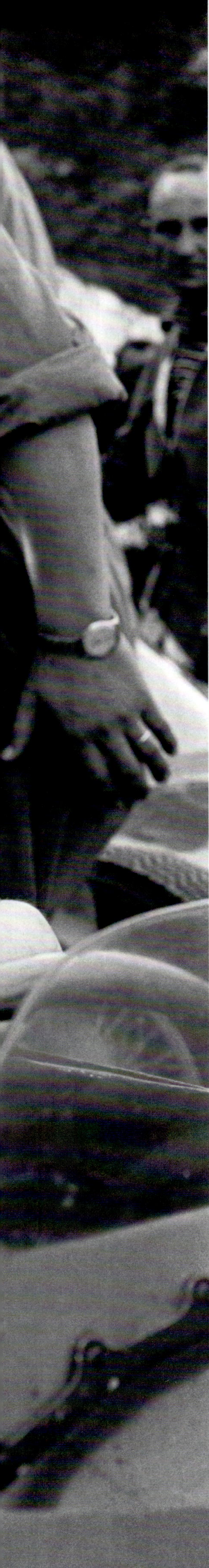

# WOLFGANG BERGHE VON TRIPS

**CAREER STATS**

**Wins: 2**
**Pole positions: 1**
**Fastest laps: 0**

**IN A BRIEF AND PUNCTUATED FORMULA** One career, Wolfgang Berghe von Trips completed only the 1960 season in full. Yet, heading into the penultimate round of the 1961 Championship, the Italian Grand Prix, he topped the drivers' table for Ferrari and started from pole position, before a fatal accident on lap two. At that late stage of the year, von Trips was favourite for the crown. Ferrari had the best car – the 156 'Sharknose'; their first rear-engine design – and only the genius of Stirling Moss, who won for Lotus in Monaco and Germany, kept them from a clean victory sheet. (Ferrari did not enter the final race of the year, the US GP, having already won both titles.)

Events at Monza decided the title in favour of von Trips' teammate, Phil Hill, in the most macabre fashion. 'Taffy' von Trips, as he had become affectionately known, made a poor start from pole, losing five places, as Hill – his only true title rival – surged into the lead. Attempting to fight back on the second lap, von Trips was clipped by the Lotus of Jim Clark, just as the cars began to brake on the high-speed approach to the Parabolica curve. The contact tipped the Ferrari out of control onto the grass to the left of the track. In a split-second, it rode up a grass bank, spinning wildly in mid-air, and hurtled into a line of spectators before crashing to the ground and rolling to destruction. Von Trips, who had been thrown from the car, was killed, along with 14 spectators, though the race was not stopped. Hill ran untroubled to a 30-second victory and the world title. The accident remains the most lethal in Formula One.

By 1961, von Trips had established himself as a Grand Prix front-runner, having earned the respect of Enzo Ferrari through a series of combative drives in sportscar categories outside F1. The dogged nature of his progress to the top flight belied his aristocratic background. Born into an aristocratic family, Count Berghe von Trips might have chosen a life of leisure, but was instead consumed by a desire to be a racing driver.

Without family financial support for his chosen career, von Trips relied mostly on talent to achieve his results, racing through the early 1950s in domestic German championships, before getting a break with the Mercedes sportscar team in 1955. This was a period when top drivers would combine Formula One with sportscar racing (competing at Le Mans and other classic endurance events) and von Trips was soon rubbing shoulders with the stars of the day: Mike Hawthorn, Moss, Peter Collins, Juan Manuel Fangio, and other aces.

A call from Ferrari came in 1956 for a one-off drive at the Italian Grand Prix, which resulted only in a huge practice accident. A year later, von Trips finished third at Monza for the Scuderia in his third Grand Prix start. A six-race programme for 1958 brought another podium in France, but it was not until 1961 that von Trips would enjoy the consistent support from Ferrari that allowed him to set up a title run with two wins and two second places.

He came within touching distance of becoming Germany's first World Champion before his life was cut so brutally short. In an interview with *The New York Times*, published on the day of the tragic Monza race, von Trips commented on the dangers of motorsport: 'It could happen tomorrow. That's the thing about this business. You never know.'

# GRAHAM HILL
# WORLD CHAMPION 1962, 1968

**CAREER STATS**

**World title: 1962, 1968**
**Wins: 14**
**Pole positions: 13**
**Fastest laps: 10**

**ALONGSIDE JIM CLARK, JOHN SURTEES** and Jackie Stewart, Graham Hill was one of a quartet of British F1 Champions who pretty much wrapped up the 1960s. Between them, they won six of that decade's drivers' titles, Hill's coming in 1962 and '68. Ever since those twin peaks, and even while racing, he has routinely been categorised as the least naturally blessed of the illustrious bunch – graft over gift – though somewhat unfairly, for his achievements are most definitely comparable to those of his estimable peers. Two titles, plus five Monaco Grand Prix wins, then victories at the Indy 500 in '66 and the Le Mans 24-hour race in 1972. The haul speaks to Hill's versatility, and he remains the only driver to have completed the unofficial 'Triple Crown of motorsport': victory at the Indy 500, Le Mans and Monaco. It also reveals a grittiness to Hill's ambition, essential for a man not blessed with family wealth, connections, or a benefactor to smooth his career path.

He didn't sit in a racing car until he was 24, when, curious to get a taste of motorsport, he bought what he could afford: five-shilling laps in a Formula Three car at the circuit nearest his London home, Brands Hatch. It was 1953 and he was hooked, but without any immediate means to go racing, he had to tout teams for work as a mechanic, using skills learned as an apprentice engineer and later as a Royal Navy conscript. Hill's hustle took him to Lotus, where he began to take drives in return for spannering.

By 1958 he was part of the Formula One race team, remaining with Lotus throughout 1959, before a switch to BRM for 1960. It was here that Hill began to make an impression, taking his first podium with a third place at the Dutch GP. At the same venue two years later, he won his first Grand Prix to set up a title campaign that brought four wins for BRM, including a flawless drive at a drenched Nürburgring which Hill later described as the most mentally draining of his life. It lasted more than two-and-a-half hours and at flag-fall the top three finishers, Hill, Surtees and Dan Gurney, were covered by 4.4 seconds. Two further wins in Italy and South Africa sealed the title for Hill and also for BRM, who took their sole constructors' title.

The World Champion tag suited Hill immensely. A natural showman with sharp wits and a penchant for hell-raising away from the circuit, he revelled in the celebrity conferred by his title and became a fixture across UK newspapers and television. But the new champion had no answer in 1963 for an immaculate Clark, who won seven out of 10 races. The following year was a different matter and Hill headed to the 1964 season finale in Mexico as favourite to win a second title. With a five-point lead over Surtees and nine over Clark, the championship race seemed his to lose.

He started badly but was soon running in the third place he needed to secure the title. Unfortunately for Hill, he was being tailed by Ferrari's Lorenzo Bandini and lead driver Surtees. Shortly before half-distance, whether accidentally or by design, Bandini hit Hill at the hairpin, forcing the champion-elect into the pits to repair damage. Returning to the race out of the points, he could only watch and hope as the race unfolded. Clark had led throughout from pole position and looked set to win race and title. His engine oil supply dictated otherwise, however, and Clark retired on the penultimate lap. Clark's exit allowed Surtees to push through to second place, snatching the title by a point.

Hill was runner-up again in 1965, a year which featured his third Monaco GP win – the one he reckoned to be the best of all. Having led from the start, he dropped 30 seconds with a detour up the escape road on lap 25 but recovered to win by a minute. In 1966, there were no wins and Hill considered that BRM had begun to lose some of their edge. His solution was a return to Lotus, the team that had given him his F1 break, even if that meant partnering with the totemic Jim Clark. Early in the '67 season, Lotus introduced their 49 chassis, mated to the engine that would dominate Formula One for the next 15 years: the Cosworth DFV. Hill used this potent, if flighty, combination to take pole position on the car's debut. Engine trouble forced his retirement, but Clark, who had not driven the 49 before the race, took a famous victory. Hill was unable to match that achievement through the season, yet remained optimistic for 1968, confident that he and Clark would have significant machinery advantage.

And so it proved at the first race of the year in South Africa: a Lotus 1–2, Clark before Hill, was a predictable result and a likely snapshot of the season to come. A four-month chasm to the second championship race in Spain stretched ahead and Clark had entered the Formula Two race at Germany's Hockenheim circuit held on 7 April to stay race-sharp. He was killed on lap 5 in the first of two heats, when his Lotus 48 left the track and hit trees.

The void left by Clark's death was inestimable and nowhere felt more keenly than at Lotus. Magnificently, Hill held the team together through the depths of their tragedy and won next time out in Spain, then again at Monaco. He won once more in Mexico and dedicated the title to a lost leader. The 1968 season encapsulated so much of Hill's champion quality: he married a high level of skill to unbending determination and self-belief. It made for a potent combination.

He won only one more Grand Prix during his long career, fittingly a last hurrah at Monaco in 1969, before slipping from the front rank. By his final season of Grand Prix racing in 1975, Hill was competing with his own team, Embassy Hill Racing, and while he was no longer a force at the age of 46, his indomitable spirit took heart from having found a flashing young talent, Tony Brise, to lead his team. In November that year, they were returning from a test session at the Paul Ricard circuit in France with four other team members. The small plane, piloted by Hill, crashed in fog trying to land near London. All aboard were killed.

OF THE UNITED STATE
GLEN, NEW YORK
6 OCT. 63

DUNLOP
SSO

# JIM CLARK
# WORLD CHAMPION 1963, 1965

**CAREER STATS**

**World title: 1963, 1965**
**Wins: 25**
**Pole positions: 33**
**Fastest laps: 28**

**AT THE VERY TOP OF THE ZIGGURAT, ON** its highest step, there is space only for the greatest of the great. Room enough for four, maybe five, of those who have competed with the utmost distinction in the Formula One World Championship. Jim Clark stands among them. And he stands there quietly, shyly, not seeking acclaim for his achievements, nor recognition of his ability. Had he not been blessed with the most sublime talent for caressing racing cars to perform at their very limit, he would likely have been happy to remain in the Scottish Borders of his birth, farming sheep, living simply.

Fate took a different path, however, carrying this introverted soul to global adulation. No man so quiet ever shouted so loud in a racing car. There was encouragement early on at local rallies and driving trials, where Clark started competing in his Sunbeam Talbot in 1956. An encounter two years later with Lotus founder Colin Chapman at Brands Hatch, where Clark was racing in a loaned Lotus Elite, led to a race contract with the team. Chapman had been impressed by Clark's native talent and by 1960 they were in Formula One together. Clark never drove a Grand Prix for anyone else. It seemed inconceivable that he would.

The partnership between Clark and Chapman transcended any ordinary driver–team-boss relationship. In tandem, their respective, instinctive understanding of what was needed to make a car go quickly – one as a driver, the other as an engineer – elevated F1 performance to a new level. From 1962, when he started winning Grands Prix for Lotus, through to '68, when he was killed in a Formula Two race, Clark was the reference.

Three-time Formula One Champion Jackie Stewart raced against Clark from the mid-sixties and inherited his mantle as the sport's standard-setter. He has no doubts about Clark's skill: 'He was by far the best driver I ever raced against, and I learned everything from him. I don't think he realised what he was doing, it was a completely natural thing for him. It was the smoothness more than anything. He would sometimes say it was all because of the car. But he drove bad cars faster than anyone else, too. I sometimes wonder if he really knew how good he was.'

Clark might have been unwilling to acknowledge his gift, but the score sheet is compelling. In 1963 – his first title-winning year driving the filigree Lotus 25 – he won seven races out of 10, with seven pole positions and six fastest laps. Apart from retirement with gearbox failure at the Monaco GP, he didn't finish off the podium. He was untouchable. His drive at the Belgian GP that year is exemplary of Clark's ability to sustain a level beyond his rivals' capabilities. He started eighth, after troubled practice sessions, but then led by the first corner. The only driver in Clark's orbit was Graham Hill, but after Hill's retirement, Clark went on to win by four-and-a-half minutes! Bruce McLaren, in second, was the sole unlapped runner.

The year 1964 was fraught for Clark, his Lotus-Climax beset by unreliability throughout the year. But he had still placed one hand on the drivers' trophy when an oil leak on the penultimate lap of the title-deciding Mexican GP ended his race. There was no such trouble a year later. Clark and Lotus were once again out of reach as Jimmy eased to six wins out of the first seven races. He missed the Monaco GP (a race he never won) because he was on duty for Lotus at the Indy 500. He won, of course, and – for the first time in America's richest race – in a mid-engined car, the Lotus 38. Victory there and his seemingly effortless superiority in Formula One had fed the Clark legend. He was the cover star of the 9 July 1965 *Time* magazine, which anointed him 'The quickest man on wheels'.

It probably didn't feel that way for Clark during the 1966 F1 season, through which Clark suffered a mix of Lotus chassis saddled with uncompetitive engines. The team were ill-prepared for that year's regulation changes, allowing 3.0-litre engines, and Clark won only once, at the US Grand Prix. For 1967, however, Lotus had an ace up their sleeve in the form of the new Ford-Cosworth DFV engine, around which their new 49 chassis was designed. It won first time out at the Dutch Grand Prix and Clark won three more times that season, taking twice as many victories as anyone else. Unreliability scuppered any hope of a title shot, but for '68, Lotus were looking good. A win from pole with fastest lap at the season-opener in South Africa confirmed pundits' expectations that Clark would breeze to a third title.

Three months later he was dead, killed in a Formula Two race at Hockenheim in Germany. Clark had entered to stay race-sharp during the long gap in the F1 calendar before the Spanish GP. The shock felt after Clark's death extended far beyond the motorsport community, just as it would when Ayrton Senna was killed in 1994. Chris Amon, the gifted New Zealander who raced against Clark in the late '60s, wrote: 'Jimmy's death was the most profound thing that happened to me in my racing career, because I felt if it could happen to him, what chance did the rest of us have? His death touched people who had no interest in motor racing. It got to an awful lot of people. That was the uniqueness of the guy. He was someone very special.'

'When he died,' says Jackie Stewart, 'there was a huge funeral, but full of modesty. Instead of having Graham [Hill] or myself or Jack Brabham or anybody else carry him, it was all Lotus team guys who did it. His family and Lotus. It was exactly in the manner he would have wanted.'

## DAN GURNEY

**A MERE HANDFUL OF AMERICAN RACING** drivers have competed successfully in Formula One, and of the two to have won the world title – Phil Hill (1961) and Mario Andretti (1978) – only Andretti earned household renown. Despite never coming close to winning the world title, the name of Dan Gurney demands inclusion among the American elite as a driver whose speed ranked with the best and whose talent was esteemed by the likes of Stirling Moss and Jim Clark.

Gurney's F1 career lasted from 1959 to '70 and a return of four GP wins, with a championship best-placing of fourth (1961 and 1965), seem scant for one rated by some as the most significant American driver, successful in US racing as well as Formula One. Yet the highs were very high indeed. Most memorable was Gurney's win at the 1967 Belgian GP driving the swooningly gorgeous Eagle-Weslake T1G. The Eagle was the product of All American Racers – Gurney's own California-based motorsport concern – and it was mated in '67 with a 3.0-litre V12 engine manufactured by the English Weslake company, rendering the entry 'Anglo American Racers'. The car's looks and sound alone were deserving of victory and, despite frequent reliability troubles during the season, a win came at Spa-Francorchamps, the most majestic circuit of all. Gurney had profited from mechanical woes for Jim Clark and Jackie Stewart, who ran 1–2 for Lotus and BRM early on, and by flag fall he was in front by a minute. Only a week earlier, he had co-driven the winning Ford GT40 at Le Mans, prompting a celebration that became universal: Dan was the first to spray champagne on the podium. Racing was never again so sweet for a man who had always been determined to forge his own path in motorsport.

Gurney showed his intent in his late teens, home-building a speed-trials racer to compete in the burgeoning SoCal hot-rod and dragster scene. By the late 1950s, his racing efforts had caught the eye of Ferrari USA, leading to a race seat with the Scuderia at Le Mans in '58, then a Formula One drive a year later. Gurney finished second in Germany in what was his second Grand Prix. Another podium that year (third in Portugal) ought to have positioned him well for a future in scarlet, but Ferrari's autocratic ways would never sit comfortably with one so independent of mind and Gurney switched to BRM for 1960 (zero points), before a more fruitful two seasons with Porsche. At the 1962 French GP, Gurney took Porsche's first and only Grand Prix win as a factory team in the dashing 804.

Further success came with Brabham from 1963 to '65, including two wins in '64 and a win-that-should-have-been at that year's Belgian GP, where Gurney retired from the lead on the last lap, out of gas. He quit Formula One after a part-season in 1970 to focus fully on building AAR into a successful racing team and manufacturer over subsequent decades. He died, aged 86, in 2018. Had Gurney chosen a less individualistic career path through the sport, America might easily have had another World Champion.

**CAREER STATS**

**Wins: 4**
**Pole positions: 3**
**Fastest laps: 6**

**CAREER STATS**

**World title: 1964**
**Wins: 6**
**Pole positions: 8**
**Fastest laps: 10**

**AS A SEVEN-TIME MOTORCYCLING WORLD** Champion before he drove a lap in Formula One, John Surtees was never going to be intimidated by the prospect of racing at the highest level on four wheels. Even so, when asked by Lotus during negotiations for the 1961 season who he would most like as teammate, his answer – 'Jim Clark' – showed confidence in the extreme.

It was justified. Between 1956 and 1960, Surtees was almost unbeatable on 500cc and 350cc Grand Prix bikes, earning a reputation for fearlessness and exceptional skill, while riding in the main for the Italian MV Agusta team. Over his full riding career, he won 255 out of 348 races – a winning ratio of better than 73 per cent – and from 1958 to 1960 Surtees became the first rider to win the Isle of Man TT three years in succession. F1 cars would be just another mechanical challenge and besides, as his friend, the 1958 F1 World Champion Mike Hawthorn put it while encouraging Surtees to make the move from bikes: 'Cars stand up easier'.

Duly emboldened, Surtees set about racing cars with characteristic full commitment. He was immediately competitive in the non-championship F1 races entered as a prelude to the World Championship proper. And when he stepped up for a part-season in 1960, he was bang on the pace. Surtees finished second in only his second start at the British GP, well ahead of his more established Lotus teammate Innes Ireland. Then he qualified on pole position and set fastest lap at his next race, the Portuguese GP, having led much of it.

Surtees was clearly no ordinary talent: while impressing hugely in his debut races, he was also wrapping up the 1960 motorcycling World Championships in both engine classes. That was Surtees' final crossover year. He was offered the lead driver's role at Lotus for 1961, before contractual complications scuppered the deal and left him racing a privately entered Cooper.

There was little success for any driver not in a Ferrari that year and 1962 followed in similar vein. Surtees held outline talks with Ferrari for a '62 drive but was unconvinced he would be able to drive at his best in the team's charged political atmosphere. He walked away, having been told 'Mr Ferrari never asks twice', and raced instead with Lola. The partnership showed promise but delivered few hard results. Then came the call from Ferrari. The second call.

Enzo Ferrari had decided a mouthful of swallowed pride was a small enough sacrifice to secure the talents of a racer he had greatly admired in Grand Prix motorcycling. Surtees was enticed by the idea of once again racing for an Italian factory racing team even if that meant separating himself from the blossoming British motor-racing scene. In the book *Lunches with Legends* (2013), he says: '...it isolates you because I'd been a part of what you might call the English contingent, with people like Jimmy, Innes and Roy Salvadori. We were all together piggybacking all the time. Suddenly in Maranello, I felt very isolated. In a way I was Ferrari's link to the outside world, which was largely developing back here in England.'

Surtees wasn't the kind of character to allow a little cultural dislocation to get in the way of the serious business of motor racing, however, and he set about instilling in Ferrari some of the focus they would need to take on fleet-footed newer rivals such as Lotus, Cooper, BRM and Brabham. The year 1963 was patchy, as Ferrari split resources between their F1 and sportscar programmes, but Surtees did take a fine first F1 win at the German Grand Prix. He battled for much of the race with Clark, until an engine glitch slowed Clark's Lotus and allowed Surtees through.

The win was Ferrari's first for two years and proved the value of having a leader of Surtees' calibre to guide the team. The presence of a spiky Brit did not always sit comfortably with such a factional, fiercely nationalistic team, however. While Surtees' relationships with his mechanics were always strong – they recognised immediately the qualities of a pure racer – the likes of team manager Eugenio Dragoni were less swayed. Still, even the most volatile team can contain instabilities if it is successful and in 1964 Surtees would deliver what Ferrari most craved. The bald records tell of drivers' and constructors' titles for Surtees and Ferrari.

Simple? Not in the least. At the final race of the year in Mexico, Surtees (on 34 points) was a title contender with Graham Hill (on 39) and Clark (on 30). This was Hill's to lose – but lose he did, thanks in no small part to the intervention of Surtees' teammate Lorenzo Bandini, whose Ferrari thumped Hill's BRM on lap 31, forcing Hill to pit and fall out of the points. Clark vs Surtees for the title, then, and until the penultimate lap, Clark looked set to win both race and championship. An agonisingly late retirement removed Jim from the reckoning and even then, Surtees had to rely on the Ferrari pits frantically urging Bandini to let his team lead driver past to finish second and snatch the crown. Desperate stuff, but enough to enshrine Surtees' unique position as the only man to have won world titles on two wheels and four.

Despite the triumphs, Surtees never enjoyed a feather bed at Ferrari and he quit, acrimoniously, early in 1966, soon after winning the Belgian GP. He won again that season with Cooper, and once more in 1967 with Honda. They would be his final Grand Prix wins: the tail end of Surtees' F1 career – driving for, and latterly running, his own team through to 1978 – was the inverse of his luminous early years. But it barely dims the legacy of a hugely gifted racer, whose unique sporting record is unlikely ever to be matched.

# DENNY HULME
## 1967 WORLD CHAMPION

**CAREER STATS**

**World title: 1967**
**Wins: 8**
**Pole positions: 1**
**Fastest laps: 9**

**HE DIED AT THE WHEEL. NOT VIOLENTLY,** like so many of his contemporaries, but almost gently, on the 33rd lap of the 1992 Bathurst 1000 saloon car race in Australia. He'd radioed his pit crew complaining of blurred vision – assumed to be the result of heavy rain. Then his BMW drifted left, struck a retaining wall and tacked right before pulling up on the grass. The accident looked innocuous and certainly not severe enough to have caused death by impact. But Hulme, 56, had suffered a fatal heart attack and his last act had been to bring his car to a controlled halt.

He'd have hated the fuss he caused, cringed at being the sudden focus of attention, for Hulme was a man who redefined 'taciturn'. So gruff in adult life that he became known as 'The Bear', he was the product of a certain kind of upbringing, whereby his Victoria Cross-winning father, Clive, believed emotions were better repressed than indulged.

As a teenager, Hulme worked for his father's trucking business around Te Puke, on New Zealand's North Island. Hustling loaded trucks on twisty gravel roads helped Hulme learn some of the wheel skills he would deploy in later life, while the slog of loading and unloading developed the strength and stamina for which he was noted while racing muscular Can-Am cars during the '60s and '70s. He developed a taste for fast driving – often barefoot for better feel – in an MG he'd saved up to buy. His results in local competition earned him backing from New Zealand's 'Driver to Europe' scheme, which would support a year of European competition for 1960. Basing himself near London, he was eased into the racing scene with the help of fellow Kiwi Bruce McLaren, by then already a GP winner. Their friendship would prove fundamental to Hulme's career, although it was with the Brabham team that Denny made his F1 debut.

Hulme worked as a mechanic for Brabham in the early '60s, to help finance his racing. This led to drives for the team in numerous categories, but most significantly in Formula Two, where he raced as teammate to Jack Brabham himself. Non-championship Formula One entries followed before his F1 debut proper at the 1965 Monaco Grand Prix. During that establishing season, Hulme displayed pace and consistency. Fourth place at the intimidating Clermont-Ferrand circuit brought his first points in only his second start, showing he wasn't one to be intimidated by the reputation of either circuit or rival.

In '66, the cards fell in his favour, for Brabham had prepared better than most for the switch to 3.0-litre engines that season, thanks to Jack's connection with the Australian Repco engineering company. Their robust V8 motors were not the most powerful, but reliability and fuel efficiency were a winning hand during this period of technical transition. Brabham took the drivers' title – famously in a car bearing his own name – as Hulme supported with four podium finishes. Their joint haul confirmed Brabham as top constructor.

Roles were reversed for 1967 as Hulme eased to his sole world title. Much like the man himself, the campaign had been unflashy and based on graft, making the most of what was available to secure an unexpected success. Wins at Monaco and Germany's Nürburgring were diamonds among eight podium finishes and, while Jim Clark's Cosworth DFV-powered Lotus 49 was far faster by season's end, Hulme had done enough, sooner, to prevail.

As champion, ill at ease with the accompanying celebrity, Hulme switched to McLaren for 1968, to begin an association that would last through to his F1 retirement at the end of 1974. With Bruce, Hulme found a soulmate and the pair raced with distinction, nowhere more so than on the North American Can-Am scene. There, grappling with bellowing closed-wheel sportscars, Hulme found his true metier. More so than in F1, sheer command of the machine and a capacity to withstand their brutish forces were the keys to success. Hulme was to the manner born.

In 1970, he was due to compete at the Indy 500, but during practice he suffered a horrifying, fiery accident. While lapping at around 200mph, a popped fuel cap allowed methanol to leak over his car which ignited with an invisible flame, engulfing Hulme before he was fully aware of what had happened. In *McLaren the Drivers* (2013), he recounts: 'I was out on track and I saw what I thought was water on the screen. The next lap I saw more and assumed it was rain. On my third lap – boof! The thing caught fire. It was like an oxyacetylene torch. I was damp with fuel and well on fire when I jumped out. My hands had shrivelled to nothing... they were claws, but I finally managed to undo the seat belt.' Car still moving, he jumped, having sustained burns that would keep him in hospital for three weeks and take months to heal.

Worse was to follow during this annus horribilis. Only three weeks later, Bruce McLaren was killed while testing one of his Can-Am cars at the Goodwood Circuit. For a successful, though still young team, the loss of their founder and talisman was a hammer blow. McLaren might have collapsed had it not been for the remarkable fortitude of Hulme in continuing to race, giving the team an invaluable point of focus to carry them through collective grief. Hulme won that year's Can-Am title and finished fourth in the F1 Drivers' Championship, racing often in excruciating pain from hands not yet healed. Removing his racing gloves after driving peeled away unhealed skin, slowing the recovery process by months. Hulme never spoke about his anguish, either physical or emotional, though family members remember him bereft at McLaren's passing.

Hulme continued in Formula One through the early '70s, winning a Grand Prix per season in 1972, '73 and '74. His hunger had gone, however. Chastened by having witnessed death or injury too often, his late-career goal was simply to survive. He slipped away after four laps of the '74 US GP without fanfare, a uniquely reticent champion, whose silent stoicism helped secure the future of one of the sport's greatest teams.

**ON 2 JUNE 2010, THE 40TH ANNIVERSARY** of Bruce McLaren's death, a McLaren M8D Can-Am car was wheeled to the front of the team's McLaren Technology Centre HQ. There, with hundreds of staff gathered around and team boss Ron Dennis in the vanguard, the car's mighty 7.5-litre V8 Chevrolet engine was fired up and revved – hard – till its raucous thunder split the air for miles around. The bellowing tribute could hardly have been more fitting for the team's founder, who was killed in a car very similar to this during a test run at the Goodwood circuit in England, aged 32.

When he died, McLaren had already achieved so much in his brief life; it seemed scarcely possible that such an inspirational force of nature, who once commented 'life is measured in achievement, not years alone', could be gone. His legacy was a team that would win World Championships in the 1970s and become almost unbeatable for periods during the 1980s.

Before all that, Bruce was a brilliant racing driver – one with an acute engineering mind as well as entrepreneurial zeal. That potent blend of attributes meant race driving alone was never going to be enough for Bruce McLaren: after suffering from Perthes disease in childhood, which left him with one leg shorter than the other, he was determined to make the most of all life had to offer, maximising every opportunity.

Born in Auckland to a garage-owning amateur racing driver, Les, there was a degree of inevitability about Bruce's early fascination with cars and his first explorations into motorsport at the age of 14 in an Austin 7, hotted up by father and son. Within three years he had graduated to Formula Two single-seaters and drawn the attention of New Zealand's motorsport officialdom, which deemed Bruce worthy of the country's first 'Driver to Europe' bursary. It was via this route that McLaren arrived at the British Cooper team in 1958 to begin racing in Formula Two. By August, he was lining up to start the German Grand Prix for his Formula One race debut, racing a less powerful Formula Two Cooper, as was then permitted, and finishing fifth overall and first of the F2 entries.

It was some debut and, a little over a year later at the end of his first full F1 season, still racing for Cooper, McLaren became the sport's youngest winner at that point in time, with victory at the US GP aged just 22. The record stood until the even more precocious Fernando Alonso lowered the mark by three months with his 2003 Hungarian GP win. McLaren won again in 1960, en route to second place in the Drivers' Championship behind teammate Jack Brabham, then once more in 1962 at Monaco. But six years passed before McLaren's fourth and final Grand Prix win. By now, Bruce had established his own racing team and took McLaren's first win in Formula One as a constructor at the 1968 Belgian GP. Over subsequent decades, the team Bruce founded would go on to win another 182 (and counting) Grands Prix, along with eight constructors' titles and 12 Drivers' World Championships. How amply it proved his observation that 'it would be a waste of life to do nothing with one's ability. Doing something well is so worthwhile that to die trying to do it better cannot be foolhardy'.

Bruce's ambition for the team was evident that fateful day at Goodwood when rear bodywork detached from his car, making it aerodynamically unstable and sending him out of control into a concrete-reinforced earth bank. He wasn't racing, just testing new developments intended to make his car faster and better. Improving the breed had become intrinsic to Bruce's vision for McLaren as a UK-based version of Ferrari, manufacturing ultra-desirable road cars alongside racing activities. Achieving that goal would require McLaren's creations to be at least as good as anything leaving the Maranello factory gates; as team founder, Bruce felt honour-bound to drive the process – on and off track.

He never lived to see his vision fulfilled, but under the stewardship of Teddy Mayer, then – formidably – Ron Dennis, McLaren flourished into a standard-setting organisation, eclipsed only by Ferrari in sporting eminence. In the hushed entrance galleria of the McLaren Technology Centre, where modern masterpieces of automotive design are fashioned, a line of McLaren's greatest racing cars sit wheel to wheel, bathed in light from the grand curve of the building's uninterrupted glass facade. First among them is a certain strawberry-red Austin 7.

# BRUCE MCLAREN

**CAREER STATS**

**Wins: 4**
**Pole positions: 0**
**Fastest laps: 3**

**ONE LIFETIME SEEMS HARDLY ENOUGH** for Sir Jackie Stewart. Certainly, winning alone could not sate his hunger for a life so full that at times it felt 'like riding a rocket'. Three Formula One world titles, of course; a race-winning record (27 Grand Prix victories) that stood for 14 years before it was eclipsed by Alain Prost; a revolutionary campaigner for better safety standards in motorsport; ambassadorial roles for Rolex, Ford, Moët & Chandon; a high-profile slot as a commentator for ABC in the USA; and then the founding of a race-winning F1 team, Stewart Grand Prix, which lives on to this day in evolved form as Red Bull Racing. All achieved with dyslexia, undiagnosed until his forties.

Where to begin? On a garage forecourt in Milton, Dumbartonshire in Scotland, working the petrol pumps at his father's garage where he would learn, among other skills, an ability to charm and the value of graft that would serve him so well throughout an unparalleled career. It was through a customer who owned fast cars that Stewart was able to taste his first racing laps; quickly he realised the acute eye–hand co-ordination that had already made him an international-standard competitive 'shot' in clay-pigeon shooting, parlayed brilliantly into the precision skills needed to excel on track.

Racing across the UK throughout the early 1960s, Stewart became a regular winner, and by the time of his Formula One debut season in 1965, he was established as a 'coming man', having dominated the '64 British Formula Three Championship. Like other elite F1 Champions, Stewart showed himself to be immediately at ease in the highest echelon. A point on his debut with BRM, a podium for his second race, a win after eight, and third place in the Drivers' Championship... there was little doubt that the motor racing world would be hearing a lot about Jackie Stewart over the coming years.

His first title year in 1969 was consummate: with six wins from the first eight races, driving Tyrrell-run Matra chassis, he had the title in his pocket by late summer. His title defence began promisingly, but faded as the challenge from Jochen Rindt and Lotus came on ever stronger. Tragically, the year would become infamous for Rindt's death at the 1970 Italian GP and his subsequent unenviable record as the only posthumous F1 Champion. Rindt's death robbed Stewart of one of his closest friends in racing and re-confirmed his commitment to improving safety standards. He had suffered his own serious accident at the 1966 Belgian GP, becoming trapped in his car and doused in leaking fuel. He was appalled at the negligible provision of medical care at the track, and over the following years, he campaigned for circuit medical facilities, mandatory full-face helmets and seat-belts, and improved crash-barrier protection.

Stewart's stance made him unpopular with race promoters who were reluctant to take on extra costs, and with critics in the media. But he was unrepentant: 'It was not much fun being portrayed as a loud-mouthed troublemaker set on ruining the spirit of a great sport,' he wrote. 'My response was to talk about safety in a TV interview before a Grand Prix, drive as strongly and as quickly as anybody else, then... start talking about safety all over again.'

The pressure of advocacy had no apparent effect on Stewart's racing capacity: in 1971, he won six out of 11 Grands Prix and almost doubled the points tally of his nearest challenger, Ronnie Peterson. No one else won more than a single race. In a 2012 interview with *F1 Racing* magazine, he reflected on his ability to detach himself mentally from other distractions while at the wheel: 'I was lucky that when I got into the car, I was able to remove all emotion. That was something I learned from shooting. In shooting, once you've missed a target, you'll never get it back. In racing, once you've missed an apex, you can't get it back. I realised that if I removed the emotion, I also drove better races.'

But Stewart, spurred on in part by the need to maximise the returns from his peak racing years in the face of potentially mortal danger, was pursuing numerous extra-curricular opportunities. That year, he began a commentary role with the US ABC network, necessitating a frequent transatlantic commute. In addition, he contested a full 10-round Can-Am Sportscar Championship, raced touring cars and carried out chassis-testing duties for Goodyear and Ford's vehicle dynamics engineers. His 1971 travel tally amounted to 450,000 air miles or 18 full round-the-world tours. Along the way, he contracted mononucleosis and was too exhausted to pick up his champion's trophy. 'The year nearly broke me, and I came very close to retiring at the end of 1971,' he noted.

Ill health plagued Stewart's '72 campaign, which was compromised by a stomach ulcer and enforced absence from the Belgian GP. Stewart still managed four wins, but was beaten to the title by Emerson Fittipaldi, whose five victories and more consistent finishing record for Lotus were decisive. By the start of 1973, Stewart had decided he would quit at the end of the season, having worked out that the last race of the year – the US GP at Watkins Glen – would neatly be his 100th. And with the precise, calculated manner that hallmarked his racing career and later business life, he controlled his year almost perfectly to win his third and last world title.

The dark spirit, then rife in Grand Prix racing, was no respecter of reputations or Hollywood endings, however. During qualifying for the race, Stewart's gifted young teammate and anointed successor at Tyrrell, François Cevert, was killed in a brutal accident. Stewart and team withdrew from the race; he later reflected: 'We saw death up close and personal – and the effects of it on those left behind. That affects your attitude to what you're doing and makes you conscious of trying to make the most of every moment.'

Over the following decades, he set about doing just that: building a lucrative business career around the Jackie Stewart brand and launching (before astutely selling) Stewart Grand Prix. Into his eighties, JYS remains a regular presence at Grand Prix, networking tirelessly and laying daily claim to being the most significant F1 World Champion of all.

**CAREER STATS**

**World title: 1969, 1971, 1973**
**Wins: 27**
**Pole positions: 17**
**Fastest laps: 15**

# JACKIE STEWART
# WORLD CHAMPION 1969, 1971, 1973

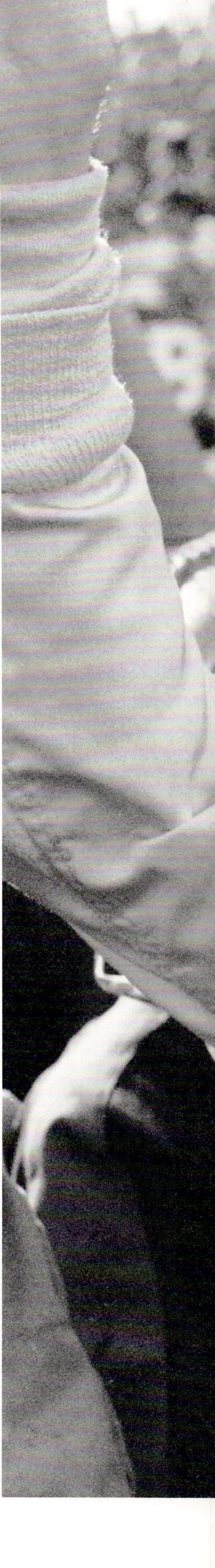

TEAM

# JOCHEN RINDT
# 1970 WORLD CHAMPION

**CAREER STATS**

**World title: 1970**
**Wins: 6**
**Pole positions: 10**
**Fastest laps: 3**

**IN A MAY 1969 LETTER TO HIS BOSS, THE** Lotus founder Colin Chapman, Jochen Rindt shared strong words about the fragility of the cars he was being given to drive. He was writing five days after surviving an accident of shocking violence at the Spanish GP, held at the Montjuïc Park circuit in Barcelona.

*'Dear Colin,*

*I just got back to Geneva and I am going to have a second opinion on the state of my head tomorrow. Personally, I feel very weak and ill, I still have to lay down most of the day. After seeing the new Doktor (sic) and hearing his opinion we can make a final decision on Monaco and Indy.*

*Honestly your cars are so quick that we would still be competitive with a few extra pounds used to make the weakest parts stronger on top of that... Please give my suggestions some thought. I can only drive a car in which I have some confidence. And I feel the point of no confidence is quite near.'*

The Lotus 49Bs of Rindt and teammate Graham Hill were running with the strut-mounted high wings in vogue that season, developed as teams had started to explore the enhancing effect of aerodynamically produced downforce on roadholding and therefore cornering speed.

Lotus were in the vanguard of experimentation and, characteristically, Chapman sought the lightest solution to any technical problem. On lap eight of the swooping track, Hill's rear-wing supports collapsed, causing a crash from which he emerged unhurt. Eleven laps later, the wing supports of Rindt's car also collapsed, causing an accident he was lucky to survive. His letter to Chapman summarised what many drivers of the time were feeling, without having the confidence to air their views. Rindt's predecessor at Lotus, Jim Clark, had been killed in a Lotus Formula Two car a year earlier. Ferrari's Lorenzo Bandini had died in a gruesome fiery accident at Monaco in 1967; Jo Schlesser, driving a Honda, was killed at the 1968 French GP. Rindt was morbidly aware of the risks inherent to his chosen sport.

His feelings were likely heightened by the all-action driving style that was his natural habit. Any Rindt car was usually pushed beyond its comfort zone in a manner that wowed onlookers, while making them fear for the safety of its daring pilot. He had always tested the limits, not only in racing but in life. Orphaned during World War II, he rebelled against the conservative Austrian upbringing enforced by the grandparents who raised him, finding release in his teens by racing bikes, then cars. Rindt was able to fund his first racing forays through the early 1960s with money inherited from his parents' business interests and became noted – even notorious – for his seemingly out-of-control style, on road and track.

He survived, and by 1964 Rindt had graduated to Formula Two. At the 1964 London Trophy race held at Crystal Palace – a round of the British F2 Championship – he announced himself on the international racing scene. Little known outside Austrian and German racing circles before the race, Rindt's name was writ large in the sport's consciousness after beating World Champion and future Lotus teammate Graham Hill to the flag.

An offer to race for Cooper in Formula One duly followed, but Rindt had to suffer through three seasons of largely uncompetitive hardware before making the switch to Brabham for 1968. The Brabham-Repco was a better prospect than anything Rindt had raced before in F1, though the introduction of the Ford-Cosworth DFV engine a season earlier with Lotus had re-set the mark for 3.0-litre engine design. Somewhat becalmed in F1, he was able to keep his racing flame alight with ultra-competitive outings in Formula Two, alongside F1 commitments. There he could remind himself that he was as quick as the best in the right car.

That long-desired 'right car' looked finally to be coming his way in 1969 in the shape of a Lotus 49, as driven to the 1968 world title by Graham Hill. The year did not progress as he might have hoped, however. The speed of the 49Bs was matched only by their propensity for mechanical failure and in the wake of Rindt's near-catastrophe in Barcelona, any prospect for harmonious relations with the team seemed distant. Rindt was showing himself to be quite capable of brilliant performances – dicing for the lead with that year's champion Jackie Stewart for 63 laps at the British GP, before a pit-stop for repairs – but he was yet to win a Grand Prix.

Finally, it came at the US GP, and it was enough to convince Rindt to stay with Lotus for another season. He would lead the team for 1970 and Chapman had promised that the revolutionary new 72 chassis would be a game-changer. And so it proved, although not before teething troubles had been addressed, which left Rindt usually driving the ageing 49 until round five at the Dutch GP. Rindt won easily at Zandvoort, as he would the next three races in succession. He had also won the Monaco GP earlier in the year and led the championship by 20 points with five races to go. For a man who had waited so long for Grand Prix success, who had experienced injury and serial disappointment, this seemed too easy.

Rindt would score no more points in 1970. Retirement from the Austrian GP was followed by a fatal accident in practice for the Italian GP at Monza. He became Formula One's only posthumous World Champion.

**HE MIGHT HAVE BEEN A FILM STAR, HAD** he not been born with petrol in his veins. Instead, the dangerously handsome François Cevert chose to pursue a career in motor racing, initially against the wishes of his wealthy parents but, in due course, with considerable success.

In 1971, racing for Tyrrell as the understudy to Jackie Stewart, he became only the second Frenchman to win a Formula One Grand Prix, picking up the baton laid down by Maurice Trintignant, who twice won the Monaco GP in the 1950s. His victory came at the very end of the year in the US GP at Watkins Glen and a joyful Cevert held both arms aloft as he crossed the line. It was only his 20th Grand Prix in his second F1 season, yet there was a sense that the win had been a while coming. Since joining Tyrrell in 1970, Cevert had quickly learned from the master and was often able to keep up with his illustrious lead driver. Two second places behind Stewart at the French, then the German, Grands Prix helped build momentum; when Stewart began to falter while leading at Watkins Glen, plagued by tyre trouble, Cevert was on his tail, ready to assume the lead.

It was a joyful moment for a young man whose comfortable passage through life seemed assured. A privileged background had allowed François the luxury of being able to fund his early racing adventures with private means and attend the French Winfield Racing School to learn the rudiments of his craft. Clearly talented, he topped his class to win a Formula Three car, in which he contested the 1967 French F3 Championship. Cevert's first season was hampered by his car's poor performance, but switching to a Tecno chassis for 1968 set him up to win the title.

Tecno had been impressed by Cevert's speed and took him on to race as a factory-backed driver in Formula Two in 1969. This allowed François, along with other leading F2 drivers, the chance to compete against Formula One stars in certain races which permitted entries from both categories. Stewart was one of many to notice Cevert's talent and recommended that his team boss, Ken Tyrrell, keep tabs. When Tyrrell's Johnny Servos-Gavin withdrew early in the 1970 season, a call was quickly put through to Cevert, who began his F1 career at the 1970 Dutch GP.

An unforced chemistry flourished between Stewart and Cevert, each benefitting from respective roles as master and apprentice, and they soon became an effective double act on track and firm friends off it. By 1973, with Stewart due to retire at season's end, Cevert was finessing all he had learned in preparation to lead Tyrrell for 1974. Their final race weekend together would be the 1973 US GP, where Cevert was quickly among a group of drivers battling for pole position. It was while chasing top spot that Cevert lost control of his Tyrrell 006 at the Watkins Glen 'Esses' – a fast uphill part of the track with sharp left–right bends. His Tyrrell speared through a gap between two horizontal lines of safety barrier, destroying the car and killing Cevert instantly. His violent death remains one of the most gruesome in Formula One, many drivers admitting to being traumatised by what they saw. To this day, Stewart believes the loss of Cevert robbed France of its first World Champion.

**CAREER STATS**

**Wins: 1**
**Pole positions: 0**
**Fastest laps: 2**

elf
CEVERT

Give a man a Lucky
Marlboro
BRM
GOODYEAR

# EMERSON FITTIPALDI
# WORLD CHAMPION 1972, 1974

**CAREER STATS**

**World title: 1972, 1974**
**Wins: 14**
**Pole positions: 6**
**Fastest laps: 6**

**BLACK-AND-GOLD, THEN RED-AND-WHITE,** from JPS Lotus to Marlboro McLaren, the style was just the same. Languid, rapid and usually hanging the back of his car sideways with fat rear slicks protesting only a little, thanks to the driver's light touch, Emerson Fittipaldi helped define what it meant to be a Grand Prix driver in the early 1970s.

From thick-thatch sideburns to his wrap-around R.Sortonex sunglasses, he looked the part as much as he drove it. And he lived it, too, in all the extremes that went with Grand Prix racing of the age. Fast-tracked into the Lotus F1 squad as third driver at the 1970 British GP, having sparkled for the team's Formula Two entry throughout '69, Fittipaldi placed fourth in only his second race, before suffering the anguish two races later of witnessing his team leader and champion elect Jochen Rindt die in a fatal accident during practice for the Italian Grand Prix. Even during this dark period through to the early 1980s, when F1 drivers were being killed almost every year, Rindt's death was among the most shocking. Flamboyant off-track and on, his skills and speed placed him among the elite and he would win the championship posthumously.

Fittipaldi stepped into the void left at Lotus with an assurance beyond his 23 years. The team skipped the Canadian GP which followed Monza and by the US GP, barely a month after Rindt's accident, Fittipaldi was Lotus' leading driver, teammate John Miles having quit. For the US round at Watkins Glen, Fittipaldi would race for the first time in the dramatic new Lotus 72, a pioneering design which became one of the most successful of the decade. It had proven finicky to develop, sensitive aerodynamically, and also mechanically fragile. But it was quick. Rindt won four times in a 72 pre-Monza and Fittipaldi would win again at the Glen, his result confirming Rindt as champion. Lotus boss Colin Chapman had briefed Fittipaldi pre-race that he had to finish ahead of Ferrari's Jacky Ickx, the only driver still capable of out-scoring Rindt for the title. Young Emerson was equal to the pressure, winning by more than half a minute, after mechanical troubles for his leading rivals.

In *Emmo: A Racer's Soul* (2015), he describes the 'enormous pressure' of being Lotus leading driver and of a sick and sleepless night before the race. Then, elation: 'I still have a very clear vision in my mind's eye of driving around the last corner of the last lap and seeing Colin running onto the track and throwing his cap into the air. I'd seen so many photos of him doing that for Jim Clark and Graham Hill and now he was doing it for me.'

This young Brazilian, so overwhelmed in victory that he found himself temporarily unable to speak any English, had come an awfully long way in a very short time. His route into motorsport was eased by the connections of his father, Wilson, a leading Brazilian motorsport commentator; and teenage racing exploits were sufficiently successful for Emerson to pursue his ambitions in Europe. Fittipaldi shone in Formula Ford and Formula Three, before catching Chapman's eye during his 1970 Formula Two debut season.

While the sight of Fittipaldi's countrymen winning Grands Prix would become familiar over the following decades, his US GP victory later that year was the first for a Brazilian driver. Soon he would become his country's first World Champion, still with Lotus and the 72, but only after a year spent honing its suspension and aerodynamics. In 'D' spec for 1972 and fully fettled, the car was finally realising its potential. Dragging the title from Jackie Stewart, Fittipaldi drove it to five wins, aged just 25 and 273 days, to become the youngest World Champion. The mark stood until 2005, when Fernando Alonso won his first title aged 24.

Emmo might have won again in '73, had not the arrival at Lotus of 'SuperSwede' Ronnie Peterson presented Fittipaldi with rather more of an intra-team battle than he wanted. While his season started brilliantly – three wins and three further podium finishes from the first six races – by mid-season, Peterson was driving ever more strongly and he finished the year just three points behind his notional lead driver, having won four races and set nine pole positions. Jackie Stewart profited from the two Lotus drivers being allowed to race and steal each other's points, to win his third and last title.

Discontented and aware that Peterson was a bit too hot to handle, Fittipaldi accepted an offer to race for McLaren in 1974. It would prove an astute move, for while Lotus lost their performance edge, McLaren's M23 was class of the field. Fittipaldi drove it to three wins and the drivers' title, ably supported by the soon-to-retire Denny Hulme, whose own points haul helped McLaren to their first constructors' cup.

Competitive enough in '75 to finish runner-up to Niki Lauda, Fittipaldi stunned the F1 fraternity by joining his brother Wilson's team for '76, in the process terminating a previously charmed racing career. Over the next five seasons, Emmo achieved only two more podium finishes and a handful of points before quitting the sport, dejected, at the end of 1980. Had that been the end of it, his reputation might have crystallised as that of a brilliant, trailblazing racer whose loyalty to family led to his previously gilded mantle being tarnished. Happily, a resurrection in US IndyCars brought a second chapter of success comparable to the first: two Indy 500 victories and the 1989 title cleansed the wounds of his later F1 years. And, calling time on his front-line career in 1996, he could reflect on having inspired compatriots Carlos Pace, Nelson Piquet, Ayrton Senna, Rubens Barrichello and Felipe Massa to a glorious samba of success.

# JACKY ICKX

**CAREER STATS**

**Wins: 8**
**Pole positions: 13**
**Fastest laps: 13**

**JACKY ICKX MIGHT BE THE ONLY** Formula One driver glad not to have won the world title when the opportunity beckoned. In 1970, driving for Ferrari, he lay second in the drivers' table with two races remaining and was mathematically capable of winning the championship by a point from Jochen Rindt. What the bare statistics do not reveal is that Rindt, champion-elect, had been killed in practice for the Italian GP. Ickx was racing a dead man for the title.

Duty-bound to perform as well as he could for his masters, Ickx won the Canadian GP immediately after Italy and looked favourite to win the remaining US and Mexican Grands Prix. He ran strongly in second place at the American GP behind Jackie Stewart, who would later retire. By then, however, Ickx had encountered mechanical problems of his own – fuel system trouble – which took him out of victory contention, to his overwhelming relief. 'It would have been dreadful to live all of these years with a stolen trophy,' he told *AUTO* magazine in 2016. 'What a chance, what a chance... Jochen deserved it. You do not dream about beating someone who cannot be there to defend himself. It was well written this way. It would not have been normal to forget his accident and lift that trophy. I have no regrets. When I see all I received through these years and to still be alive – you have no right to complain.'

Ickx's association with the Scuderia began in 1968, his first full F1 season and the big break for this gifted young Belgian. He had wowed F1 regulars a year earlier at the German GP, driving a Formula Two car in a field of mixed F1 and F2 machinery. There, despite a significant power deficit, Ickx set third-quickest time in qualifying 20 seconds faster than the next F2 car and beaten only by the F1 entries of Jim Clark and Denny Hulme. His performance around the dizzying and dangerous Nürburgring track was a measure of pure talent, which marked Ickx immediately as one to watch. He swiftly became noted for a fine touch and a feel for track conditions, qualities that were fully in evidence throughout his first Grand Prix victory at the '68 French GP. Ickx was peerless at the challenging Rouen-Les-Essarts circuit, to win by a margin of two minutes in rainy conditions, outshining many established aces. The day was marred by tragedy, however, as the French driver Jo Schlesser crashed on the third lap and died in a fireball, his Honda heavy with fuel.

The manifest dangers of this period in motorsport were top of mind for Ickx during a moment of protest at the start of the 1969 Le Mans 24-hour race. Racing for Ford, he shunned the traditional running start, whereby drivers would sprint across the track to their cars and blast away without tightening safety harnesses. Ickx's lone safety stand was to walk calmly to his car and strap up before setting off – dead last. He and co-driver Jackie Oliver won the race by 110 metres from the second-placed Porsche in the closest-ever Le Mans finish.

Ickx remained a master in sportscar racing through to the 1980s, winning Le Mans six times and enjoying success long after his F1 career had fizzled out with uncompetitive seasons in the latter half of the '70s. Nonetheless, the tug of scarlet pulls hard on his heartstrings, decades after retirement: 'When you have driven once for Ferrari, you have them forever – your heart is painted red.'

Ate Scheibenbremsen
Sicherheit im Auto
KAMEI
Schalensitze
BP
super

# NIKI LAUDA
# WORLD CHAMPION 1975, 1977, 1984

**CAREER STATS**

**World title: 1975, 1977, 1984**
**Wins: 25**
**Pole positions: 24**
**Fastest laps: 24**

**SEEING NIKI LAUDA PROWL AROUND** Grand Prix paddocks in his late-career role as a Mercedes F1 grandee was to connect with an older, darker era of the sport. Not simply because of his advancing years, but because of the scars.

Damaged tissue unhappily grafted all around his eyes and forehead, his right ear burned off, the charred scalp from which only tufts of hair could grow, torched eyebrows... all a legacy of the 1976 inferno from which he was dragged after a crash in his Ferrari on lap three of the German GP, at the fearsome Nürburgring circuit.

The accident, most likely the result of a suspension failure, so nearly killed him: the scars – grim enough externally – reached deeper inside, where inhalation of smoke and petrol fumes had scorched his lungs. The damage might have sapped a meeker man's will to live, let alone race; indeed, Lauda was read the last rites in a Mannheim hospital as recovery seemed impossible in the days after the crash. But as he recalled in his vivid autobiography, *To Hell and Back* (1986), his own force of will wrested him from darkness.

Lauda entered the ill-fated race defending his 1975 drivers' title and dominating the '76 season, having won five Grands Prix to amass a 25-point championship lead, with six races remaining. But surely, after an accident like that, his racing career was over. There was no way he could return, critics opined, although perhaps he might retain his title. Some consolation for a man who had suffered so grievously. Six weeks later, having missed only two races, Lauda was preparing to compete at the Italian Grand Prix. Of course, he wasn't ready. Fluid on his lungs hampered his breathing. His burns weren't healed. But he was there – 'slightly singed' as he described himself, but present. 'I said then and later on that I had conquered my fear quickly and cleanly,' he wrote. 'That was a lie, but it would have been foolish to tell the truth and play into the hands of my rivals by confirming my weakness. At Monza I was rigid with fear.'

One of Lauda's greatest gifts as a racing driver, and in his later business career, was the ability to remove emotion from his thought processes. His cool rationality had been invaluable to a volatile Ferrari organisation when he joined in 1974 and as he forced himself to compete once more, the compelling logic of what he was doing sustained him. 'Some of the newspapers said at the time that I must have burnt out a few circuits in my brain as well, but my chosen course of action was the best I could have taken for my physical and mental well-being.' The handful of points Lauda picked up over the closing races of the season were enough to take the championship fight to the final race in Japan, where his only rival, James Hunt, snatched the title by a point, Lauda having retired after two laps, deeming the monsoon conditions too dangerous. He struck back a year later to secure the '77 drivers' title, before splitting acrimoniously from Ferrari with only two races to go. He had never reconciled himself with the team's decision to sign Carlos Reutemann as his post-accident stand-in.

Two forgettable seasons followed with Brabham, towards the end of which Niki threw down his driving gloves in practice for the Canadian GP and walked away from the sport. Already a hero, a Lazarus figure following his Nürburgring accident, a two-time Ferrari champion, and the definitive mid-1970s driver, Lauda felt he had nothing left to prove in F1. Business was a different matter and long before quitting F1, Lauda had decided to combine his unmatched resolve with his passion for flying by founding his own airline. For a time, Lauda Air served as a channel for his restless energy, but the lure of competition, a fat Marlboro pay-cheque and the persuasive charms of McLaren boss Ron Dennis were enough to tempt him back to the track, for 1982.

Three races in, he won again – at Long Beach – to silence critics with a finality not seen since his '76 comeback. This was an older, wiser Lauda. A stealth warrior, still with the hunger to pursue a third title, even if an edge of his electric youthful pace (nine pole positions in both '74 and '75) had dulled. He was excited, too, by the promise of the TAG-Porsche V6 turbo engine, custom-developed for McLaren and introduced late in '83, at Lauda's insistence. What he hadn't bargained for was the arrival of French hot-shoe Alain Prost as his teammate, who had earned a reputation in his short career as an emerging superstar – perhaps the man to assume Lauda's mantle of greatness.

Their tussle for the 1984 title remains the closest in F1 history, settled in Lauda's favour by a mere half-point. Lauda, characteristically, used guile to hone his car into a race-perfected machine, sacrificing the qualifying battle for race-day advantage. Five wins were his reward, and while Prost took seven, the half-points awarded for the rain-curtailed Monaco GP left Prost short in the championship table. The pupil learned well from the master: Prost dominated in 1985 to take his first title, as Lauda trailed him with just 14 points, although a final win at the Dutch GP brought satisfaction in his swansong season.

Lauda quit racing as a titan of Formula One, to fight new battles with aviation authorities and Boeing as he pursued his airline ambitions alongside executive roles at Ferrari and Jaguar Racing. Latterly, he became a revered member of the Mercedes F1 executive board that guided the team to crushing success with Lewis Hamilton. Ill-health plagued Lauda's final years and he died in 2019, after kidney and lung transplants. His Formula One story, indeed that of his whole life, had been one of astonishing courage allied to unbending resolve. Lauda's place in the F1 pantheon is assured.

**THE TRUE NATURE OF JAMES HUNT'S** demons will never be known; they drove him to a world title and then to self-destruction. Always an edgy competitor and a man who raced as if fleeing his furies, Hunt became a legend during a short, intense F1 career, as much for the operatic on-track drama of his 1976 world title season, as for his incorrigible behaviour off it.

'Master James', 'Hunt the Shunt', 'Superstar', 'the most charismatic man I ever knew' (according to his great friend and rival Niki Lauda) – all appropriate descriptions of a complex, tortured soul who nonetheless was able to channel raging nervous energy into a world-class level of performance.

He had set himself the goal of becoming Formula One World Champion as a teenager and began racing – against his parents' wishes – in a tuned Mini. He progressed, surviving many accidents unscathed, through the junior British racing categories, earning the soubriquet 'Hunt the Shunt' as he raged along. His most notorious clash, at the Crystal Palace British Formula Three race in 1970, was captured by a BBC broadcast. Last lap, last corner, Hunt and rival Dave Morgan collided, putting both out of the race. Morgan came to rest on the right of the pit straight, while Hunt was stranded in the middle of the track with both right wheels of his Lotus missing. Pumping adrenaline, Hunt leapt from his car, strode across the still-live track and marched towards Morgan before punching him to the ground and striding off.

The incident encapsulated Hunt's early race career: fast but wild and volatile, and certainly not the form of a World Champion in waiting. He was a driver constantly on the edge, needing little to tip him over. Race driving didn't come easily to Hunt, in the manner of his champion peers Jackie Stewart, Emerson Fittipaldi and Niki Lauda. Each of those greats possessed spare capacity, an economy of input, a grace to their style, which translated as complete mastery of their machine – almost an artistry. Hunt could make a Formula One car go just as fast as these grandees, but when he did, he was all in.

Perhaps a privileged public-school education, native athleticism and a comfortable home life had led him to expect racing success would come easily. When Hunt discovered that it did not, his hard-wired competitive instinct took over, propelling him into the fray even when a visceral nervous reaction to racing frequently induced vomiting and involuntary shaking before a race. Others less driven might have concluded that motorsport was maybe not for them. It is a measure of Hunt's steel that, despite being agonised by the dangers of 1970s motor racing, he persisted regardless.

Progressing through Formula Two during the early '70s, Hunt made the acquaintance of Lord Alexander Hesketh, a wealthy British aristo who had decided that motorsport looked a fun wheeze. Recruiting Hunt –always 'Superstar' to Hesketh – aligned stars and attitudes perfectly and in combination they began to dazzle en route to Formula One.

Their glory day came at the 1975 Dutch GP, where Hunt resisted 20 laps of pressure from Ferrari's Niki Lauda to take his and Hesketh's first Grand Prix win. The landmark victory silenced those who had dismissed Hesketh as a boozy dilletante. As Hunt combined skill and pluck to hold back a faster car, their battle set the template for what would become one of the sport's most storied rivalries in 1976. Lord Hesketh had decided the party was over at the end of '75, however, despite the win and three further second-place finishes for his Superstar, leaving Hunt, increasingly credible, on the market.

Fortune decreed that, almost simultaneously, double champion Emerson Fittipaldi quit McLaren to join the team about to be founded by his brother, Wilson. McLaren needed a lead driver – and fast. Barely 48 hours after Emerson's departure, Hunt had inked a McLaren contract, setting the stage for a 1976 season sufficiently dramatic for Hollywood treatment as *Rush* (2013), almost four decades later. The précis has Hunt vs Lauda for McLaren vs Ferrari. After nine races, Hunt seemed out of the reckoning, Lauda's points tally of 61 more than doubling Hunt's 26. But everything changed at the notorious German GP, where Lauda suffered a near-fatal accident and sustained burns and lung damage that scarred him for life. His survival seemed miraculous; surely there was no way he would race again that season, if ever. Six weeks later, having missed only two starts, Lauda was preparing to qualify for the Italian GP at Monza, where he would finish fourth.

The points scored there and Niki's podium at the US GP gave him a three-point advantage over Hunt, rendering the finale in Japan a head-to-head shootout. Fuji Speedway was beset by torrential rain on race day and many drivers were reluctant to compete. But start they did, with Hunt sprinting into the lead from second on the grid. At the end of lap two, Lauda pulled into the pits and retired. He shunned the offer of claiming mechanical failure, asserting simply that it was 'too dangerous'.

Circulating in the lead, Hunt was closing in on the title, only for a lap-68 puncture to force him into the pits and resume in fifth place. He charged furiously through the closing laps to finish third – enough to claim the title by a point. Ambition achieved, Hunt began a descent from his career peak. Still motivated in '77, he took three wins from six pole positions, but by mid-1979, after 18 months of uncompetitive McLaren, then Wolf, machinery, he reasoned his way out of the sport. Without hope of success, why race?

Hunt's post-racing life became a frenzied blur of alcohol, drugs and uncertain business ventures, although his F1 commentating role for the BBC earned him global affection. By 1993, he was gone, having died of a heart attack aged 45. A maverick champion, who lived as hard as he raced and only ever on his own terms, Hunt left a unique mark on the sport. His legend burns on.

**CAREER STATS**

**World title: 1976**
**Wins: 10**
**Pole positions: 14**
**Fastest laps: 8**

TEAM

# CARLOS REUTEMANN

**CAREER STATS**

**Wins: 12**
**Pole positions: 6**
**Fastest laps: 6**

**SOME DRIVERS HAVE PLACED TWO** strong hands around the neck of the Formula One World Championship and throttled it into submission: Nigel Mansell, Max Verstappen and Michael Schumacher, for example. Others, none more infamously than Carlos Reutemann, have held the championship in their palms only to let it slip through their fingers like quicksand. His 1981 retreat from a title it seemed almost impossible to lose remains one of F1's most mystifying capitulations. With Williams that year, and long established as a hugely charismatic, mercurial star, Reutemann led the championship by 17 points after nine races, with six remaining. The scoring system then awarded nine points for a win, down to one for sixth place; in the year's best car, Carlos was clear favourite.

That was to reckon without the complexities of this most enigmatic genius. He scored only six more points over the next six races, but even at the season finale in Las Vegas, the title was his for the taking. He flew to a comfortable pole position, three places up from his closest rival, Nelson Piquet. Yet, despite having no obvious technical troubles, in the race he drifted back to eighth, out of the points, as Piquet, almost unconscious from dehydration in the closing laps, scrabbled to fifth and the two points he needed for his first world title. The Las Vegas weekend was 'essence of Reutemann': brilliant and flaky in equal measure.

Reutemann's sheer talent had never been in question. He was on pole position for his first Grand Prix in 1972 at his home event in Argentina, and his long top-team career (Brabham, Ferrari, Lotus, Williams) was studded with diamond days. He won the 1975 German GP at the full-length Nürburgring by 100 seconds and in 1978 took a steely victory over Niki Lauda at the British GP. Reutemann was never, though, a driver on whom to bet the house. At all teams he raced for, other than Ferrari in '78, he bemoaned troubles either with bosses or teammates, never outwardly acknowledging that perhaps his own sometimes brooding presence made him hard to reach.

The '78 Ferrari season was his happiest. Alongside the brilliant tyro Gilles Villeneuve, and in an environment where passionate temperaments were celebrated rather than suffered, Carlos flourished. He won four Grands Prix in a season otherwise dominated by Lotus, who were the first team to successfully harness ground-effect aerodynamics. It was something of a golden moment for Reutemann and who knows what might have been, had Lotus not made their brilliant technical advance.

His move there for 1979 was disappointing, however, as Lotus lost their advantage, but with Williams for 1980, Reutemann was once again back in a front-running car, though contractually bound to drive in support of teammate Alan Jones' title bid. Jones duly became 1980 World Champion and Williams remained comfortably the best team in 1981. Somewhere along the line, though, the 'team order' memo went missing. Neither Williams nor Reutemann had confronted the thorny issue of his supposed number-two status during the off-season. Notionally, he was Jones' wingman, but his speed painted a different reality. He won a non-championship curtain-raiser F1 race at South Africa's Kyalami circuit, then led the season-opener proper at Long Beach before a slip that let Jones through to win.

Undaunted, Reutemann aced the next round at a soggy Rio, in defiance of team orders. His win earned him a team fine and the undying antipathy of Jones. Talking to *Autosport* journalist Nigel Roebuck, Reutemann later explained: 'Jones had reason to be upset. I can't disagree with that. And it did affect our relationship afterwards. I saw the pit signal three laps from the end, and I knew the terms of the contract. But still I was in a dilemma. From the beginning of my career, I always started every race with the intention of winning it, but now I was being asked to give it away, just like that. "If I give way," I thought to myself, "I stop the car here and now, in the middle of the track and leave immediately for my farm in Argentina. Finish. Not a racing driver anymore."'

The bruising fall-out from the race, and of the season as a whole, had wearied Reutemann and he quit at the end of the year, only to make a fleeting two-race comeback at the start of '82. But then he was done, returning to Argentina to pursue a new life in business and politics. He died aged 79 in 2021, status secure as the most vexatious Grand Prix great.

# MARIO ANDRETTI
# 1978 WORLD CHAMPION

**CAREER STATS**

**World title: 1978**
**Wins: 12**
**Pole positions: 18**
**Fastest laps: 10**

**MONZA BLOOD RUNS THROUGH MARIO** Andretti's veins, now, as it did that day in '54 when he watched his idol, Alberto Ascari, race in the Italian Grand Prix. The impression made by Ascari's Ferrari was deep: a scarlet scar across an impressionable teenage mind, indelible even as the Andretti family left their homeland a year later to pursue the promise of The American Dream.

Soon enough, Mario, alongside twin brother Aldo, found his way to the fringes of the dirt-oval scene of Nazareth, Pennsylvania, and began scrabbling, drifting, racing his way to an untouchable future. Dirt ovals became one-mile concrete loops, which became superspeedways. At Indianapolis in May 1965 – the most storied of speedways – Andretti met Lotus team boss Colin Chapman, who was there with his sublime champion Jim Clark, preparing to win that year's Indy 500. Colin made Mario a promise that that year's USAC Champion could race for his Formula One team 'any time he was ready' – an agreement he kept to three years later, ahead of the '68 Italian Grand Prix.

Where else but Monza could Andretti, the most Italian of Italian Americans, have made his late-season F1 debut. He attempted to dovetail existing race commitments with the Grand Prix schedule, shuttling between Indiana and Italy, before succeeding in qualifying 10th for the GP. He then returned to race in the Hoosier Hundred, before jetting back immediately to Europe to make his first F1 start. Bureaucracy, however, found Andretti in breach of a regulation that forbade drivers from competing in more than one major international race within a 24-hour period. It mattered little: on his debut proper a fortnight later at the US GP, Andretti placed his third-entry Lotus 49B on pole and ran second before mechanical failure.

'That car felt very, very good to me immediately,' Andretti recalls. 'Indy cars were much heavier, not as nimble. In the Lotus it was: "Oh, my God, this car is doing exactly what I want it to do".' A blown clutch scuppered his race, but a point had been made. 'I'd wanted Formula One so bad,' he says, 'because that's where my pure love was at the very beginning of my life – it's what drew me to the sport itself. And then Colin being so willing to give me that opportunity... it was golden. And then of course, together, we achieved the ultimate goal of the World Championship.'

A decade passed before that partnership was consummated, during which time Andretti spliced a bountiful US racing career with peripatetic F1 roles – most notably a 1971 Ferrari liaison that brought his first Grand Prix win, in South Africa. By '76, he was back with Lotus, winning the sodden final race of the year, the Japanese Grand Prix – an event best remembered for settling the drivers' title in James Hunt's favour. The win teed Andretti up for a highly successful 1977, driving the aerodynamically advanced Lotus 78. The car was the first in F1 to harness fully the 'ground effect' principle, whereby an inverted wing shape contained within the car's sidepods channeled airflow to produce 'negative lift'. The suction created allowed the 78 to achieve greater cornering speed than its rivals and Andretti, who worked intensively to refine this technical advantage, won four Grands Prix to place third in the '77 Drivers' Championship.

The season was a mere teaser for what was to follow in 1978. Driving the voluptuous Lotus 79, which further refined concepts pioneered in its predecessor, Andretti romped to the title with six wins by that year's Italian GP. Tragically, his moment of greatest triumph would be marred by the death of Ronnie Peterson, teammate and friend. After a fiery start-line accident, Peterson was taken to hospital with leg injuries and while Andretti left Monza as champion, Peterson died overnight, following post-operation blood clotting and a stroke.

In the biography, *A Driving Passion* (2001), Andretti recalls: 'I got up Monday morning with Dee Ann [Mario's wife] and we drove to the hospital. At the tollbooth, the guy said, "Are you going to the hospital?" And I said, "Yes". And the guy said, "Ronnie just died. I heard it on the radio". I was totally devastated. Dee Ann and I had just been talking about his rehabilitation.' Despite the tragedy, Andretti's title was something of a landmark for Formula One. He became only the second American champion and the Lotus 79 confirmed a technical path all rivals would be obliged to follow for the next four seasons.

His F1 career petered out thereafter, hampered by uncompetitive Lotuses and an abortive 1981 season with Alfa Romeo – although there would be one famous last dance in 1982. Already back racing US Indy cars, Andretti was called up for the Italian GP as a Ferrari super-sub, following the fatal accident earlier that year of Gilles Villeneuve and the career-ending injuries to teammate Didier Pironi. Some remember Mario's performance to take pole position as Monza's greatest day. 'I felt very privileged that Mr. Ferrari thought of me,' says Andretti, 'but it was not easy, actually, to adapt, because when the turbo power came on, it was like a charge of dynamite. Then in qualifying, luckily, I just put it in there. I almost had the back-end break loose through the Lesmos... but I kept my foot in and I thought "I hope this is good enough" because I could never duplicate that. It was extremely satisfying.'

Legend cemented, Andretti returned to race in US single-seaters until the mid-1990s, before finally hanging up his helmet at Le Mans in 2000, aged 60. One of F1's true icons, Andretti could still regularly be found turning 180mph passenger laps in a two-seat Indy car late into his seventies...

VICEROY
Mario Andretti
Firestone
FINA
ti benzina
PAGNOSSIN
racing team
2
57

John Player
VALVOLINE
John
Player
Special

# RONNIE PETERSON

**CAREER STATS**

**Wins: 10**
**Pole positions: 14**
**Fastest laps: 9**

**CERTAIN GRAND PRIX DRIVERS ARE** forever associated with a particular car. In the case of Ronnie Peterson, arguably the fastest driver of the early to mid-1970s, that car was the Lotus 72. Dressed in the black-with-gold pinstripes of cigarette sponsor JPS, Ronnie's 72s caught photographers' lenses, just as they made fans catch their breath. Peterson, a driver blessed with God-given car control and immense natural speed, simply drove the wheels off his Lotuses in 1973 and '74, sliding them to wins and pole positions in a manner that paid little apparent heed to the laws of physics.

F1 cars of the era were evolving rapidly, as tyre development progressed in tandem with advances in the understanding of aerodynamic forces. The dual benefit for drivers was more rubber on the road, particularly at the rear of the car, as well as more downforce from bigger wings: in short, more grip. Cornering speeds rose, but the best cars of the period were also forgiving on the limit, allowing the most gifted drivers to slide and drift them on the edge of adhesion, adjusting their cars' attitude with the application of throttle.

No one did this better than Ronnie Peterson – his rivals could only applaud. 'I admired his ability tremendously,' Jackie Stewart told journalist Nigel Roebuck in *Grand Prix Greats* (1986). 'Any number of times, particularly in 1973, I'd follow him into a corner and think, "Oh-oh Ronnie, this time you've overdone it". But he always seemed to get it back somehow... The spectators loved him – he was exciting to watch from where I was, too.'

Peterson's scorecard was proof of his ability. He took nine pole positions in 1973, three times the number of his closest challenger, Stewart, that year's champion. There were also four wins – one fewer than JYS, one more than teammate Emerson Fittipaldi – and third in the drivers' standings behind Jackie and Emerson. Stewart blended speed, consistency and guile to win his third title; Peterson didn't score until finishing third in Monaco, round six.

Ronnie was a multiple winner again in '74, his three victories the equal of champion Fittipaldi, now driving for McLaren, though once again a poor finishing record foiled any attempt at a title shot. Fortune was never Peterson's true ally, despite the abundance of other blessings.

He remained with Lotus in '75 but was unable to compensate for the shortcomings of the 72, which was in its sixth season of front-line service and eclipsed by newer rivals. Disillusioned with Lotus' downturn, Peterson decamped for '76 to the March team, with which he had shown tremendous promise five years earlier by finishing second in the Drivers' Championship in his first full F1 season. Victory at the Italian GP was the stand-out of a season with only one other points finish. An abortive '77 with Tyrrell, driving the six-wheeled P34, left Peterson at a low ebb and prompted reconciliation with Lotus, where Colin Chapman had begun to unlock the secrets of ground-effect aerodynamics.

Partnered with Mario Andretti for '78 and contractually bound to race in support of Mario's world title bid, Peterson showed immediately that his flame still burned. He won twice and finished second four times behind Andretti, leaving the impression that duty, rather than speed, had dictated their placings. Andretti became champion at the Italian GP, with two races remaining. Yet the day of his greatest triumph was tempered with dismay after a start-line accident left Peterson in hospital with multiple serious leg fractures. Andretti would later recall the bittersweet experience of winning the world title at the circuit where he had become entranced by Formula One, while knowing that his friend and rival was receiving emergency medical treatment in a Milan hospital. There was comfort, at least, in the knowledge that Peterson's injuries were not life-threatening.

The hammer-blow came a day later. Peterson had died overnight from fat embolism (a condition whereby fat particles enter the bloodstream) resulting from his injuries. A bronze statue of Peterson in his hometown of Örebro, Sweden, commemorates him driving a Lotus 72.

**IT IS AN UNDERSTATEMENT TO SAY THAT** Jody Scheckter arrived in Formula One with a bang. In only his second race, the 1973 South African GP, he qualified third at his home track, Kyalami, and by lap five he was leading. Scheckter continued to battle at the front until a late retirement from fourth position. Next up was the French GP. He qualified second, led for 41 laps, then clashed with reigning champion Emerson Fittipaldi, who retired, calling Scheckter a 'menace'.

Scheckter had only just begun. His next outing was the British GP at Silverstone a fortnight later. He qualified in sixth place and had just taken fourth at the end of lap one, when he triggered what might still be F1's largest-ever accident. Running wide out of Woodcote corner, Scheckter half-spun at around 160mph, speared towards the pit wall, and bounced back onto the track into the path of his pursuers. The spin caused mayhem, taking 11 cars out of the race, including his own.

He had very quickly developed an unfortunate reputation and was rested for four races. Jody's McLaren deal that season was for five Grands Prix – the team wanted to find out more about this pugnacious youngster before going all-in – and they reckoned he should catch his breath before a return at the Canadian GP. There, unfazed by any talk of his being a liability or a danger to fellow competitors, he qualified third and was fighting over fourth place with François Cevert when they clashed and went out. That Scheckter was quick was not in doubt. But was he too headstrong for his own good? At the US GP two weeks later, he witnessed the aftermath of Cevert's fatal practice accident and, as he later admitted, 'From then on, all I was trying to do was save my life.'

It had been a wild introduction to Formula One and if Scheckter had been determined to get noticed, having battled his way from South Africa to the elite level of world motorsport, he had succeeded. Scheckter had offers for 1974 from Lotus and Ferrari, but opted to drive for Tyrrell, who would be without Jackie Stewart for the first time since 1968. 'Baby bear', a nickname given on account of the similarity in manner between Scheckter and the truculent Denny Hulme (aka 'The Bear'), proved quickly that he had learned a lot in his fledgling year.

He went about stitching together a quietly impressive season that earned him third place in the Drivers' Championship. After 13 rounds and having taken two wins – in Sweden and at Silverstone – he was in the thick of the title fight with Fittipaldi and Ferrari pair Niki Lauda and Clay Regazzoni, before losing ground with two non-scores at the final two races.

The 1975 season was relatively threadbare, despite a popular home win at Kyalami, as Lauda and Ferrari produced a masterclass to sweep to both world titles. Things picked up in 1976, thanks in part to one of the most strikingly adventurous cars ever raced in Formula One, the six-wheeled Tyrrell P34. The chassis was conceived by designer Derek Gardner with the twin aims of reducing drag around the front wheel area, as the smaller wheels would barely protrude above the height of the front wing, and of cleaning the airflow to the rear wing. Unveiled to astonished media ahead of the season, the car was competitive enough to take Tyrrell to third in the constructors' title that year, with Scheckter heading a 1–2 finish at the Swedish GP. Ten further podium finishes suggested Tyrrell might be about to return to the Stewart glory days, but Scheckter had already decided otherwise.

Never enamoured of the six-wheeler, a car he described as 'a piece of junk', Scheckter followed the money for '77 to the all-new Wolf team, founded by Canadian oil magnate Walter Wolf and set to run a single-car entry for Scheckter. It proved an inspired switch as he won the team's debut race in Argentina and followed up with victory at the Monaco GP, then a banner success at the Canadian GP, the home round for the team's proprietor. Only a Lauda-led Ferrari had beaten him and Scheckter's life goal of the F1 world title once again appeared within reach. It seemed logical to stay with Wolf for '78, as no one (save team boss Colin Chapman) had anticipated the paradigm-shifting introduction of the Lotus 79. With their successful harnessing of ground-effect aerodynamics, Lotus left all their rivals, Wolf included, trailing in their wake. Scheckter slumped to seventh in the championship, four podium finishes his scant return.

Then Ferrari came knocking. The 'Old Man', Enzo Ferrari, had long been a fan of Scheckter's abilities; indeed, he had tried to employ the younger, firebrand version of Jody for 1974. Now he was interested in the self-control Scheckter had allied to his native aggression; he already had a rocketship on the books in the form of Gilles Villeneuve. That year's Ferrari 312T4, in which Jody and Gilles contested all but the first two '79 Grands Prix, was not the year's fastest car – that honour went first to Ligier and later to Williams. But it was quick enough and brilliantly reliable, the latter quality being of tremendous value in a period of technical transition for F1. Both drivers won three times and while Villeneuve was almost certainly quicker, he drove to support Scheckter's points advantage late in the season.

Their 1–2 finish at the Italian Grand Prix to win both world titles could hardly have been more perfect. 'Gilles was right behind me all the way and there was still a chance that he could win the title,' said Scheckter. 'But he gave me his word that he wouldn't try to pass, and he had more integrity than anyone else I've ever met.' Mission accomplished, Scheckter retired from F1 at the end of 1980 (only two points scored!) and went on to great business success. Ferrari would wait until 2000 for their next World Champion.

**CAREER STATS**

**World title: 1979**
**Wins: 10**
**Pole positions: 3**
**Fastest laps: 5**

Wolf
PM
PM

**GILLES VILLENEUVE NEVER WON THE** World Championship, yet in a briefly luminous Formula One career, he became one of the most revered drivers ever to have raced. All but his debut Grand Prix, for McLaren in 1977, were driven for Ferrari, guaranteeing a place centre-stage, where he performed for four-and-a-half seasons in a tornado of energy, regardless of the quality of his car.

Much of the spectacle Villeneuve brought to the track could be attributed to his unconventional path to Grand Prix racing. As a speed-obsessed young Canadian, he learned his craft racing snowmobiles on ice tracks, surviving perilous spills and mastering control of a powerful vehicle in low-grip conditions. These high-wire skills would serve Villeneuve well in later years on the frequent occasions when he pushed beyond the limits of his scarlet cars.

He came to Formula One at the relatively advanced age of 27, having been talent-spotted by the soon-to-be World Champion James Hunt, who found himself racing against – and being beaten by – Villeneuve at a 1976 Formula Atlantic event in Canada. Hunt related Villeneuve's talent to his McLaren bosses and within a year Gilles was making his debut for the team at the British GP. By season's end, Ferrari had swooped, dropping Villeneuve into the seat vacated by their newly crowned World Champion, Niki Lauda. There he would remain throughout his too-short career.

Within a year, Villeneuve was a Grand Prix winner, taking a fairy-tale maiden victory in Montreal at the Île Notre-Dame circuit, which would later be renamed in his honour. The win set Villeneuve up perfectly for his role as understudy to Ferrari's anointed leader Jody Scheckter in 1979. Both won three Grands Prix, though Scheckter's greater finishing consistency, along with Villeneuve's respect for team orders, settled the championship in Jody's favour. It was during this year that the Villeneuve racing legend caught light.

At the French GP in Dijon, Gilles and Renault's young buck René Arnoux duelled ferociously over second place, passing and re-passing each other, touching wheels, braking ludicrously late, dancing on the limits of grip and racing etiquette. It was racing at its most raw and mesmerising: the victory of Jean-Pierre Jabouille, 15 seconds up the road, went almost unnoticed.

Later that year, after suffering a rear-tyre blowout while battling for the lead of the Dutch GP, Villeneuve drove his Ferrari back to the pits on three wheels, fighting for control all the way. His effort to stay in the race was futile, even foolhardy, but the swashbuckling heroics had fans swooning. Not that Villeneuve drove like this simply to play the crowd: for Gilles, racing was about competition – winning – above all else. Retiring a functional car on track because of a puncture was for other people. Enzo Ferrari loved his never-say-die racer, referring to Gilles as 'the prince of destruction' while adoring his refusal to accept defeat.

By 1980, Villeneuve was established as F1 box office, and might have hoped for a season of progress after a stellar '79. That year's Ferrari 312T5 was technically outmoded and lamentably slow, however: he scored only six points. Aware they had been left behind by the aerodynamic wizardry of rivals with ground-effect aerodynamics and the growing challenge of turbo-charged engines used by Renault, Ferrari hit reset for 1981 with the introduction of the 126C, powered by their own turbo-charged motor. This inelegant machine, which lacked the cornering speed of the leading cars, held one trump card: power. Even so, only a driver of Villeneuve's lavish gift could have manhandled it to a wildly improbable victory at Monaco, then kept four faster cars behind to win the Spanish GP three weeks later, just staying out of reach at every straight.

Those two magical wins aside, '81 was another season of thin gruel for Villeneuve, though the auguries were good for '82. Engine refinements promised more power with smoother delivery, while Ferrari's recruitment of the talented engineer Harvey Postlethwaite led to a ground-up chassis revamp that would make the 126C2 the Constructors' Championship winner.

Tragically, Villeneuve didn't live to enjoy the success his talents would surely have earned in such a competitive machine. During qualifying for the Belgian GP, his Ferrari clipped another car and became airborne, before disintegrating as it crashed to the ground and throwing Villeneuve to his death. In the wake of the accident, many claimed Villeneuve had been racing in a troubled state of mind and was feuding with teammate Didier Pironi, who he believed had robbed him of victory at the San Marino GP two weeks earlier. The arguments were moot. Formula One's brightest-burning star had been extinguished; the romantic soul of Grand Prix racing forever diminished.

**CAREER STATS**

**Wins: 6**
**Pole positions: 2**
**Fastest laps: 2**

**ALAN JONES WAS THE BARE-KNUCKLE** bruiser no one wanted to meet down a dark alley. The 1980 World Champion elbowed his way to the summit of Formula One, not with the silken assurance of contemporaries such as Niki Lauda, Carlos Reutemann, Nelson Piquet and Alain Prost, but with his teeth buried firmly into their ankles. By his own admission, he was not the fastest, nor the most naturally gifted, but Jones compensated with sheer determination, a will to win and the balls-on-the-line commitment that only an Australian ex-pat 11,000 miles from home can muster. 'When I came to race in Europe, I knew there was no going home for lunch on a Sunday,' he told *AUTO* magazine in 2018, 'so I guess you could say I was pretty determined.'

The son of successful Australian racer Stan Jones, Alan had motorsport in his blood and drifted naturally into the racing scene around Melbourne through family connections and work at his father's garage. The leap to Europe, to test himself against the world's best, was tougher, however. Much like his fabled predecessor Jack Brabham, he had to scrap around the lower rungs of the UK racing scene, finding money and drives where he could. The F1 break came in 1975, driving a privately entered Hesketh at the Montjuïc circuit in the Spanish Grand Prix. He showed enough to earn a full-time F1 ride with the Surtees team for 1976, although the association ended sourly, prompting Jones to head to the USA to pursue his racing ambitions.

It was while stateside early in '77 that he took a career-changing call from the Shadow team, who were seeking a replacement for their star Tom Pryce, killed in a freakish accident at the South African Grand Prix. Jones' season was solid, and a notable first win in an unfancied car at a rainy Austrian GP marked him out as a driver with extra gas in his tank. His own career arc was curving perfectly to intersect with that of the Williams team, rebuilding and on the up after hand-to-mouth first forays into F1.

Both driver and team had been forced to battle for respectability through the hardscrabble badlands of underfunded motorsport and perhaps each recognised steely promise in the other when they came together for 1978. Much like Williams' team boss and founder, Frank, and his chief engineer Patrick Head, Jones was a straight-talking hard ass with little time for anything that got in the way of going racing. All a similar age when they came together in 1978, the trio swiftly gelled and set about taking on the big guns: Frank would find the money, Jones would hustle on track and Head would contribute technical smarts.

The FW06 chassis essayed by Head for '78 was neat and quick. But, without the advantage of ground-effect aerodynamics with which Lotus was revolutionising the sport, front-running pace was a stretch too far for this still-tiny team, running just a single entry for Jones. No matter, the FW07 introduced for 1979 fixed all that, proving to be the best ground-effect car of the year and vaulting Williams to second place in the Constructors' Championship, after four Jones wins and one (Williams' first) for teammate Clay Regazzoni. It was a springboard season for Jones and his newly confident team – the tuned FW07B was 1980's hot ticket. Jones bagged his solo title despite a concerted, though ultimately flaccid, challenge from Nelson Piquet. Williams aced the Constructors' Championship, almost doubling the haul of next-up Ligier.

It would prove the shiniest of Jones's three gilded Williams years. He remained fast and feisty in 1981, enjoying memorable scraps with the likes of Ferrari's Gilles Villeneuve, but the title this time went Piquet's way. Jones's campaign had been scuppered by unreliability; woes that also afflicted teammate Reutemann, whose own title challenge collapsed at the year's final race in Las Vegas.

This was an intensely competitive period for Formula One, the sport blessed with a rich crop of exceptionally talented drivers winning for multiple teams. Jones won his title amid a field in which 17 of the year's 21 competitors were race winners or winners-to-be. He battled Villeneuve, René Arnoux, Prost, Emerson Fittipaldi, John Watson, Didier Pironi, Jacques Laffite and Reutemann. His consistency in a fast car, allied to doughty track skills, were enough to prevail.

He was favourite for the '81 title and reckoned he drove better than in the previous season. But such was the closeness of the competition that back-to-back drivers' titles, which would become the norm 20 years later, were impossible to come by. 'Probably only point three of a second separated the grid,' he says, 'but we didn't really realise how competitive it was, and we certainly didn't think about the danger. When I look back on those cars now, it's just: "Shit, did I drive that thing?"'

Some of the risk inherent to this period of Grand Prix racing arose from the continued development of ground-effect aero. The limpet-like track adhesion of chassis such as the FW07 had driven up cornering speeds, requiring huge commitment on corner entry, and leaving drivers little margin for error once they had aimed their car into a curve. Suspensions became stiffer as cornering loads increased, rendering early '80s Formula One cars ever more unforgiving.

Jones was not alone in becoming disillusioned with the sport's technical direction and was happy to quit at the end of '81, largely unscathed, at a time when drivers still raced against a backdrop of mortal danger. He retired having won what he thought would be his final race, the 1981 Las Vegas Grand Prix (and partied regally, thereafter, according to legend). But after a big-money offer to front the start-up Beatrice Haas team, Jones was back on the grid late in 1985 and through '86. Results were negligible, however, and Jones quit F1 for good at the end of the season, reputation intact as a formidable competitor and early cornerstone of what would become a world-beating Williams team. 'When I went racing, I went racing,' he reflected. 'Head down, arse up... That was me.'

**CAREER STATS**

**World title: 1980**
**Wins: 12**
**Pole positions: 6**
**Fastest laps: 13**

# ALAN JONES
# 1980 WORLD CHAMPION

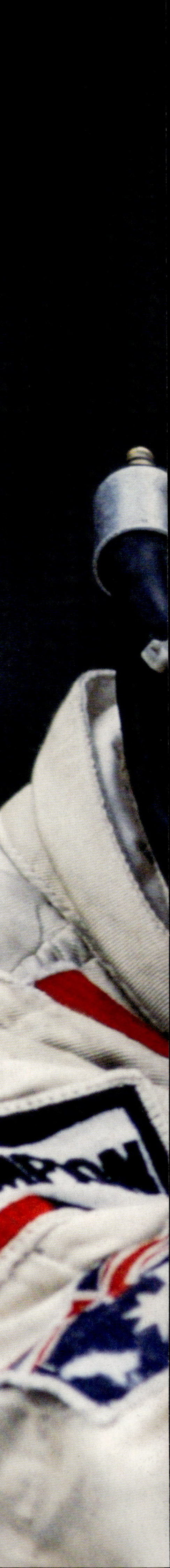

Akai's OkayOK.
Akai's Okay
agv

# NELSON PIQUET WORLD CHAMPION 1981, 1983, 1987

**CAREER STATS**

**World title: 1981, 1983, 1987**
**Wins: 23**
**Pole positions: 24**
**Fastest laps: 23**

**ATOP THE CAREER PEAKS HE'D SCALED TO** win the World Drivers' Championship in 1981 and 1983, Nelson Piquet was, for a time in the early '80s, F1's 'Most Wanted'. Racing with pace and guile for a quick-witted Brabham team, then being run by Bernie Ecclestone, he had twice prevailed during a perilous era, bested a field chock full of talent, and achieved a notable distinction: becoming the first Formula One Champion powered by a turbocharged engine from BMW.

Brabham were always the canniest of racers and, in '83, with a BMW M12 straight-4 engine, they out-smarted wealthier, factory-backed opposition from Renault and Ferrari. Their chutzpah perfectly suited Piquet's waspish style and in his pomp, this golden child of his 'family' team was a match for any rival. He would have been forgiven for looking ahead to a repeat success in 1984.

What he could not have anticipated was that McLaren and their engine partners Porsche were about to re-write the rulebook for efficient chassis-engine integration quite so comprehensively. McLaren smashed both '84 championships, taking 12 wins between Niki Lauda (that year's champion) and Alain Prost, as the rest were left to pick up crumbs. There was consolation for Piquet in flaunting his abilities with nine pole positions, but in race trim the McLaren MP4-2 set new standards. A similar story in 1985, coupled with the stunning emergence of his countryman Ayrton Senna, dulled a little of Piquet's sheen, even – whisper it – raising questions as to whether this glamorous, insouciantly rapid Brazilian was quite the full ticket. Had he lost the edge that hastened the first retirement of Lauda when the two were teammates in 1979? Were his two titles actually, perhaps, a little fortuitous? He'd won in 1981 by a single point after the last-round capitulation of his main rival Carlos Reutemann. And in '83, Prost, driving for Renault, was champion-elect until a late-season collapse in mechanical reliability let a resurgent Piquet through to the title by two points.

Frank Williams, head of the Williams team that had come on ever more strongly during 1985, was not among the doubters. Sensing an opportunity to pluck Piquet from his racing home of seven years, he offered number-one status and the lure of Honda power. Everything seemed peachy, as Peter Windsor, then Williams' commercial director, recalls: 'Nelson came to Williams as a double World Champion who had never had an issue with anything, really, in his life. His contract stipulated his number-one status, a spare car that was always set up for him, the choice of best Honda engine if there was ever a discrepancy between units and first call on any performance-enhancing parts. But he never insisted on the team being obliged to pull his teammate over and let him past if his teammate was ahead. He didn't insist because he had never considered it happening.'

Any notion Piquet might have entertained of an armchair cruise to a third title was about to be exposed as wishful thinking by a rapid Brit with everything to prove and nothing to lose. Step forward Nigel Mansell, a nightmare for Piquet, who had never had to contain such a rude challenge from a teammate, but fantastic for fans who were set for two seasons of no-holds-barred racing between a pair of aces in the sport's fastest car: the fearsome Williams FW11.

Their rivalry raged across 1986 and 1987, with both drivers having their days in the sun. In '86, Mansell's home win at Brands Hatch brought the house down, but Piquet dazzled with a round-the-outside overtake of Senna at Turn 1 of the Hungaroring – a contender for F1's greatest-ever passing move. And so it went on, each taking points from the other until, by the Australian GP finale, Prost, in a lesser McLaren, was able to slip through for the win and title.

The 1987 Williams FW11B put Piquet and Mansell even further ahead of the pack, but intra-team needle pushed both to extremes. Piquet survived a huge crash at race two, the San Marino GP, where he hit the retaining wall at the Tamburello curve at around 180mph. Concussed, he sat out the remainder of the weekend, but he was back at the wheel for round three in Belgium, where he started from P2, though with a lap time 1.39s behind Mansell's pole position. Unbeknown to most, the Imola impact had impaired Piquet's vision and only much later did he reveal that his ability to judge braking distances had been weakened, as had his reading of cockpit instruments. Mansell, meanwhile, crashed out of championship contention with a practice accident at the Japanese GP, confirming Piquet's third title, despite his winning only three Grands Prix to Mansell's six.

The two-year wrestle with Mansell had drained Piquet, so an offer to join Lotus as outright number-one for 1988 was welcome and lucrative. The switch began Piquet's glide from the front rank, however, although he did bag three wins for Benetton over 1990–91, and third place in the 1990 Drivers' Championship showed residual class and pace in the autumn of a long career. A rare triple F1 Champion, Piquet's claim to outright greatness might be questionable, but for a time in the early '80s, he could justifiably be reckoned as the best driver in the world.

**HE WAS THE ICE TO GILLES VILLENEUVE'S** fire at Ferrari in 1981–82. An electrifyingly fast racing driver who succeeded in removing emotion from the intensity of competition, Didier Pironi was nonetheless incapable of escaping the vortex of circumstance that snatched both of Ferrari's stars from the sport within four months of each other, from spring into summer of '82.

Villeneuve died after a monstrous accident during qualifying for the Belgian Grand Prix, still feuding with Pironi in the wake of the San Marino GP two weeks earlier, which Villeneuve believed Pironi had won in breach of team orders. Pironi, dissociating himself from the frenzy that followed Villeneuve's death, won again at the Dutch GP in July and, by the time of the German round at Hockenheim in August, he had carved a nine-point lead in the championship. Driving the year's best car, Pironi was looking increasingly likely to win the drivers' title – his life's ambition.

The dream was shattered during Saturday morning practice for the German GP when he crashed at high speed on a soaking track in heavy rain. Didier's accident was not dissimilar to Villeneuve's at Imola. Pironi's car moved to pass the slower Williams of Derek Daly but was unable to see the Renault of Alain Prost ahead, owing to spray thrown up from Prost's tyres. Pironi hit Prost, launching the Ferrari into the air before smashing back to earth, destroying the car. Remarkably, given the violence of the accident and the catastrophic damage to the Ferrari, Pironi survived, though grievous injuries to his legs ended his F1 career, with four races of the season remaining. Even so, he lost the title by only five points to Keke Rosberg after one of the most volatile seasons in the sport's history.

The calamitous ending to Pironi's pursuit of the F1 title was at odds with the control this privileged, powerfully charismatic man had hitherto exerted over his destiny. Born into material comfort, Pironi studied engineering and might have pursued a career in the family construction business had he not felt the pull of the track and enrolled in the French Winfield Racing School. Graduating as the best pupil of the 1972 class, Pironi progressed through the ranks of French motorsport in tandem with compatriots Alain Prost, Patrick Tambay and René Arnoux, before making his F1 debut with the Tyrrell team in 1978, in which year he also won the Le Mans 24-hour race for Renault.

Two seasons with Tyrrell brought only handfuls of points, though a pair of podium finishes in '79 were enough to pique the interest of the Ligier team for 1980. It was with Ligier that Pironi scored his first Grand Prix win in Belgium, taking the chequer almost 50 seconds ahead of Alan Jones. Pironi's cool-headed approach to racing, allied to an unerring focus on his world title ambitions, made him an ideal replacement for Ferrari's 1979 World Champion Jody Scheckter, who had quit after a desultory 1980 season.

Partnered with Villeneuve for '81, Pironi came up against a teammate who, for the first time in his career, was his equal (or better) in pure pace. Both men struggled with the unruly power delivery and poor road manners of the Ferrari 126C, the team's first turbo-charged machine, though Villeneuve rode the scarlet bronco to two victories, leaving Pironi chasing his shadows. Its 1982 successor, the 126C2, was far more to Pironi's taste, though fate denied him the title that he admitted had seemed 'within touching distance'.

Four years after the Hockenheim accident, Pironi drove an F1 car again, in private tests intended to establish if his legs were sufficiently healed to allow a racing comeback. The outcome was inconclusive and Pironi instead fed his competitive needs by racing offshore powerboats. It was in one of these dramatic machines – Colibri, a lightweight Class 1 design with twin V12 Lamborghini engines – that Pironi was killed in August 1987, along with two crew members, competing off the south coast of England.

# DIDIER PIRONI

**CAREER STATS**

**Wins: 3**
**Pole positions: 4**
**Fastest laps: 5**

Pironi
PIR
HARIBO
Candy
Racing
F1
Marlboro

Marlboro
HOP HAB
Canon
FINNMADE
QUALITY

# KEKE ROSBERG
# 1982 WORLD CHAMPION

**CAREER STATS**

**World title: 1982**
**Wins: 5**
**Pole positions: 5**
**Fastest laps: 3**

**FOR F1 FANS OF A CERTAIN VINTAGE, THE** sight of Keke Rosberg caning a Williams-Honda FW10 at a pace well beyond its comfort zone was as exciting as the sport got. The FW10 was Williams' 1985 car, powered by a turbocharged Honda engine capable of pushing out more than 900bhp when running at full boost. Like all its ilk, the engine delivered way more power than the chassis could comfortably handle, and the shove when it kicked in as the turbos spooled up to maximum revs was akin to riding a rocket for the drivers. Several times each lap.

The likes of Alain Prost, Nelson Piquet and Niki Lauda were the car whisperers of the age, sweet-talking their McLarens and Brabhams to success. Rosberg was the wrestler. With a flamboyant style that relied more on car control than surgical precision, Keke on a flier spelt entertainment, the car's body language screaming dynamic energy. Never was this more obvious than during his bravura performance to take pole position for the 1985 British Grand Prix at Silverstone. Recent Honda upgrades had enhanced performance, reliability and drivability; Rosberg used them all on a slightly damp surface to set a mark good enough not only for pole position, but to post a speed record that would stand for 17 years. His time of 1:05.591s for the 2.93-mile lap equated to an average of 160.925mph – the first Formula One lap to crack 160mph. Truly, the Finn had flown.

The record stood until 2002 when Juan-Pablo Montoya, also driving for Williams, lapped Monza at 161.45mph, in qualifying for the Italian GP. Rosberg was phlegmatic about his achievement, describing it as 'just for fun' – a reaction in keeping with an attitude to motorsport that had always been based on pragmatism. Would the landmark lap mean much for the race? Probably not, Keke reckoned, because Prost's McLaren would likely be stronger in the race. (It was.)

His approach was exemplified by his 1982 title-winning year, a season notorious for fatalities, serious accidents and off-track political rancour. Rosberg had ended 1981 as a driver without portfolio, having quit the Fittipaldi team after a zero-points season. Driving an uncompetitive car without hope of a score – or, sometimes, of even making the grid – had removed any thrill of success from the risk: reward ratio being balanced by all drivers of the period. He had, he admitted, started to feel fear outweighing thrill and decided to stop, see if something better came along.

There was no grand plan to Rosberg's decision; he had simply resolved that he could not continue in the same vein. 'That was a hellish season for me,' he told *Autosport*'s Nigel Roebuck. 'I'd been around a long time and still I wasn't qualifying sometimes. Everything was wrong.' The call, when it came, was from a notable admirer, Frank Williams, though fortune played a role in Rosberg's fate. Alan Jones, Williams' 1980 World Champion, had quit the team at short notice at the end of '81, leaving Williams short of a number one. While Rosberg's stock at the time was low, he retained a reputation for no-nonsense speed, not too dissimilar from Jones' own. He was under no illusions as to the motivation for Williams' call: 'I went to Williams only because Jones quit too late for them to find another top driver. This was the chance of my life, and I knew it.'

Williams were reigning Constructors' Champions when Rosberg signed almost without salary negotiation for 1982. The FW07 series of cars, introduced in 1979 and constantly refined thereafter, had been archetypes of contemporary chassis that combined powerful ground-effect aerodynamics with the compact and efficient 3.0-litre Cosworth V8 engine. By 1982, however, it was clear that this so-called *garagiste* approach would struggle to match the performance of larger, manufacturer-backed teams such as Renault and Ferrari, running more powerful 1.5-litre turbocharged engines. Indeed, '82 would prove to be a fulcrum year in terms of technical development: Rosberg, driving a Cosworth-powered Williams FW08, won the drivers' title, as Ferrari took constructors' honours.

The Ferrari 126C2 was the year's best car and it seemed inevitable that one of its superstars, Gilles Villeneuve or Didier Pironi would become champion. Tragically, Villeneuve was killed in a violent accident during qualifying for the Belgian Grand Prix. Seven races later, Pironi, leading the championship, suffered career-ending leg injuries in another wild accident during practice for the German GP.

Rosberg won only once in his title season, as the rapid development of turbocharging technology made the playing field less than level. The shifting balance of power between turbo- and non-turbo cars contributed to the volatility of a season with 11 winners, none of whom won more than twice. Rosberg's final tally of 44 points seems incomprehensibly low from the perspective of modern-day F1, yet even surviving this period of Grand Prix racing, or avoiding serious injury, was a victory of sorts.

He won a single race again in 1983, brilliantly at Monaco in a still-Cosworth-powered Williams, and once more in 1984 on the streets of Dallas in the thuggish Williams-Honda FW09, finally with turbo power. Only in 1985, in fact, did Rosberg win more than one Grand Prix in a single season: two more street circuit victories, in Detroit and Adelaide, to take his career haul to a modest five. There would almost certainly have been more had he stayed with Williams for 1986, when the brilliant FW11 carried Piquet and Nigel Mansell to nine victories. But as he popped the belts of his McLaren on lap 62 of his final F1 race – the 1986 Australian GP – Rosberg at least had the satisfaction of having led by a country mile. Moreover, his retirement marked the conclusion only of chapter one in the Rosberg–Formula One story…

**CAREER STATS**

**Wins: 7**
**Pole positions: 18**
**Fastest laps: 12**

**A CLASSIC PICTURE FROM 1979 HAS ALL** seven of the French F1 drivers contesting that year's World Championship, posing happily like a gang of Mousquetaires. All of them – Jean-Pierre Jabouille, Jacques Laffite, Patrick Tambay, Patrick Depailler, Jean-Pierre Jarier, Didier Pironi and René Arnoux – were notable talents and all except Jarier were Grand Prix winners. Standing out for his impish smile, a wildness around the eyes and the pose of a photo-bomber, Arnoux looks like the spark that starts the party.

This was a big year for René; he had graduated from a fractured first F1 season with minnows Martini and Surtees to the big time with state-owned factory team, Renault F1. Renault were making waves with their F1 project, having committed to powering their car with turbo-charged 1.5-litre engines against the grain of the 3.0-litre non-turbo motors used by all other teams. Their goal was power – the elusive 'unfair advantage' – and by 1979, Renault's perseverance with this troublesome technology was starting to bear fruit. They entered a two-car team for the first time, Arnoux alongside Jabouille, and the speed of the RS10 started to cause headaches for their rivals. Six pole positions (four–two, Jabouille–Arnoux) were more than any other team achieved as Renault's turbos lit the path for F1 technical development over the next decade. The year also brought Renault's first win with Jabouille at the French GP, though his historic victory – the first for a turbo-charged car in Formula One – was overshadowed by the battle for second place between Arnoux and Gilles Villeneuve.

These two young tigers, both daredevil racers who revelled on the ragged edge of car control, staged a duel over the closing laps that instantly passed into F1 lore. Villeneuve, starting third for Ferrari, leapt into the lead on the opening lap and remained out front for the first 45. Jabouille, knowing he had a speed advantage, passed Villeneuve to lead from lap 46 to the flag, while Arnoux, third and closing, sensed his opportunity. With three laps remaining, he passed Villeneuve – by now struggling with worn tyres – for second place. Arnoux's own car was compromised, however, with fuel system troubles which prevented him from pulling away. The pair passed and re-passed each other as the laps counted down, banging wheels repeatedly, skittering over the track edges in a gloves-off fist fight that stayed just the right side of the rulebook. They crossed the finish line Villeneuve–Arnoux, but more importantly they had authored a passage straight into Grand Prix history.

Arnoux's part in this heroic contest remains the highlight of a career which held numerous other glory days. He kicked on in 1980 to win his first two Grands Prix and out-shine Jabouille as his raw pace came to the fore, but in '81 the arrival of Alain Prost as teammate presented Arnoux with a challenge he could never have anticipated. Prost's devastating blend of speed, intellect and political savvy would go on to make him among the very greatest of all F1 drivers; Arnoux didn't have enough in the locker to compete. On pace alone, in qualifying for example, Arnoux could match Prost, but the all-court game of his compatriot had the edge. After a closely matched 1982 season, during which both Arnoux and Prost took five pole positions and two wins each for Renault, René had wearied of the fraught atmosphere inside the team and joyfully accepted a call from Ferrari for 1983.

The partnership brought out many of Arnoux's best qualities, his head-forward, hard-charging style well suited to the punch offered by the 126C3: three wins, four pole positions and third in the Drivers' Championship his reward. Never again did Arnoux have it so good. Through 1984, he was gradually eclipsed by new teammate Michele Alboreto and he split with Ferrari after the first Grand Prix of 1985. A career coda with Ligier from 1986 to '89 was muted for a driver considered among the very fastest at his peak. Latterly retired in comfort and pursuing interests in luxury watchmaking and historic motorsport, Arnoux remains the second most successful French Grand Prix driver. And still with the impish grin.

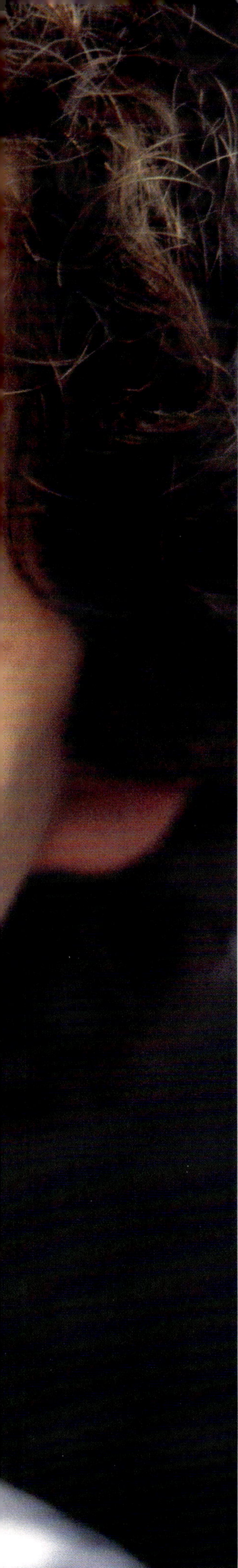

**CAREER STATS**

**World title: 1985, 1986, 1989, 1993**
**Wins: 51**
**Pole positions: 33**
**Fastest laps: 41**

# ALAIN PROST WORLD CHAMPION 1985–86, 1989, 1993

**ALONGSIDE A TINY HANDFUL OF FELLOW** greats, Alain Prost made winning in Formula One look easy. Like Jim Clark and Jackie Stewart before him, Prost married devastating speed with a caressing smoothness and an ability to drift away from rivals as if being pulled, rather than driven towards the finish line.

A multiple winner and championship contender from only his second season, 1981, through to his final, imperious, 1993 title-winning year, Prost was a driver of the highest natural ability, with a calculating mind that earned him the nickname 'Le Professeur', such was the analytical dimension he brought to racing. After a dispiriting debut season with an uncompetitive McLaren, Prost's career leapt forward over the following three years with Renault. He instantly shone as a blisteringly fast driver who rarely dipped a wheel off the track, let alone sullied his race weekend with anything so inelegant as a spin.

Driving like a Rolex, his mastery of machine and the whole process of being a top-line Grand Prix driver meant he could never be a fans' darling in the dashing manner of his early Renault teammate René Arnoux or, later, Keke Rosberg, Ayrton Senna and Nigel Mansell. But that was never a concern: he simply got on with the business of winning Grands Prix and championships.

'People always liked Keke or Ayrton at the time, drivers who expressed their natural talent more in their driving style, rather than with thinking,' he told the FIA's *AUTO* magazine. 'But in my opinion, you can have both. Niki was called "the computer" when he was racing. And why not? People forget that you can also be fast. If you look at all the statistics, you see that maybe Ayrton was very exceptional in qualifying [65 pole positions] but he was really working on that. I worked more on the race set-up, so it makes a big difference. In race conditions with Ayrton, I was never much slower than him. It's just a different approach.'

When he retired in '93, having eased to the title in a Williams FW15C, he was only the second driver to win more than three World Championships and his tally of 51 Grand Prix victories placed him clearly at the top of the pile. So consistent was the level of his performances over 13 F1 seasons, that with only 12.5 more points, he would have been an eight-time champion. He missed out on the title by two points in 1983, half a point in '84, three in '88 (he out-scored champion Senna, before having to drop 18 points under that year's 'best 11' rule) and seven in 1990.

The strength of the opposition faced by Prost en route to those titles was as high as anything offered in the sport's history. His early near-misses were to drivers chasing repeat world titles: Nelson Piquet and Niki Lauda. By 1985, his second year as Lauda's teammate at McLaren, he had learned his lessons from both these masters, and from mid-season was able to stretch away to an ultimately comfortable first World Championship. 'I learned a lot from Niki's approach to the race,' Prost confirmed, 'particularly his mental condition. In 1984 for example, I thought that I was fighting against Nelson Piquet, because most of the time he was on pole or very fast, so I thought that my target was Nelson. But I was wrong, and I learned that it's better to finish fourth and get points and maybe go on to be World Champion.'

In '86, he deployed all his stealthy smarts to snatch the crown at the final race from the clutches of Nigel Mansell and Piquet, both in the faster Williams FW11. The image of Prost jumping gleefully from Adelaide tarmac alongside his McLaren MP4-2C captures a moment of pure joy. 'We won not just as a team that day. It was more like a family.'

Tougher, darker years lay ahead, however, as he and Senna engaged in a mighty and prolonged heavyweight tussle from 1988 to '90. Their '88 season together remains one of the most closely fought intra-team struggles, as they danced on a different plane to the rest in their peerless MP4-4 cars. Prost won seven races, Senna eight; Prost out-scored Senna 105–94, but lost the championship 87–90, as only the season's best 11 scores counted. Prost's third title year, 1989, brought chapter one in a two-part Japanese GP drama, in which Prost and Senna touched and went off at the chicane while battling for the lead. Prost retired, knowing that a non-finish for Senna would give him the title. Senna raged on to win the race, but subsequent disqualification made his efforts futile.

A year later, with Prost at Ferrari, they clashed again at Suzuka, in what many regarded as a Senna revenge attack on Prost. Their high-speed collision resulted in the title going to Senna although controversy around the incident raged then and echoes to this day. The ruthless edge to their rivalry made it among the most compelling ever played out in Formula One, not least because a respect for the other's abilities lay at its heart.

A year after Prost's retirement, Senna sent a poignant message to his former adversary over the in-car radio during practice laps for the San Marino Grand Prix (the race in which he was killed): 'A special hello to our dear friend, Alain. We all miss you, Alain.' Prost's departure from the competitive arena had allowed breathing space between two giants and friendship had begun to flourish. 'Our relationship was really exceptional, you know,' Prost reflected, 'especially compared to what we had when I was racing! And I promise you that I am sure relations would be very, very good, if Ayrton was still with us. There is no question about that.'

Prost went on to become an F1 team boss from 1997 to 2001, though the Prost Grand Prix years were troubled – Prost often looking haunted by the pressures of management despite a peppering of strong results, and the team folded ingloriously. That unhappy episode has done nothing in subsequent decades to dim the lustre of his reputation. The only French World Champion, Prost glitters among the very brightest stars.

**AYRTON SENNA WILL FOREVER BE THE** hero who died in a million front rooms on a Sunday afternoon in May 1994. The shockwaves following his fatal accident echoed across the globe. At the moment of his death, in a violent impact on lap seven of the San Marino Grand Prix, he was among the most famous sportsmen on Earth and Brazil's most cherished son. The state funeral that followed seemed a barely adequate channel for the outpouring of grief that consumed his countrymen.

This three-time champion, revered at home and far beyond, was utterly uncompromising in his approach to racing and had an other-worldly intensity about him. Senna's in-car brilliance and magnetic charisma outside the cockpit enraptured a generation, rendering his accident the 'JFK moment' for Formula One: any fan can recall exactly where they were, what they were doing, when they heard of Senna's passing or, far more shockingly, how they witnessed the accident live on TV.

Senna was racing that year for Williams, Imola only his third start for the team. Previously untouchable through 1992 and 1993 with the technically supreme FW14B and FW15C cars, Williams discovered frailties in the aerodynamically sensitive FW16 chassis entered for '94. The car was fast, but unforgiving. Even a driver of Senna's genius found it challenging. At the season-opening Brazilian GP, Senna qualified on pole position, then spun off while chasing leader Michael Schumacher. Race two, the Pacific GP at Aida, brought another pole, but a first-lap collision and retirement. By the San Marino GP, race three, Senna was feeling pressure to score and peg back Schumacher, who had won the first two races. He duly posted yet another pole position (his 65th) and was leading from a hard-chasing Schumacher when he crashed, fatally.

Thirty years since Imola, Ayrton Senna remains a towering, yet enigmatic F1 reference. Feted for his speed and ruthless dedication to winning, he was nonetheless shunned by many purists for an overly combative on-track style. Ethics aside, by the time of his death he had emerged as the mightiest driver of his era, even against such formidable peers as Alain Prost, Nelson Piquet and Nigel Mansell. None of that famous trio were racing in F1 early in '94. Only the precocious Schumacher seemed to have the full portfolio of skills needed to take Senna on and lead the next generation. Alas, the great Senna–Schumacher rivalry that seemed certain to play out during the mid-90s was glimpsed only for a moment before being snuffed out.

Much like his 'F1 Alpha' successor, Senna arrived into Grand Prix racing with a bang, instantly making his mark. As the hot-shot 1983 champion of British Formula Three, Senna was snapped up by the Toleman team for 1984 and came close to winning the infamously sodden Monaco Grand Prix in his first year. He blended extreme-throttle sensitivity, feel, courage and sheer speed into a devastating package that made it obvious he was a superstar in waiting. As a result, Lotus swooped to secure his services for 1985.

The Senna–Lotus combination became immediately iconic, his yellow helmet highlighted against the black-and-gold livery of his car. It proved immediately effective, too: at the second '85 race, the Portuguese GP, Senna took pole and a famous win, finishing more than a minute ahead of Michele Alboreto, in soaking conditions. That first success provided a snapshot of Senna's career-defining qualities: his balletic wet-weather skills, raw pace, intensity over a race distance and a release of passion in victory. The naked emotional charge Senna brought to the arena marked him out from rivals and was inherent to his complex, captivating persona.

He was electrifyingly quick over his first two Lotus seasons, taking 15 pole positions through 1985–86, although only two wins each year, constrained by the relative fuel inefficiency of his Renault engine. There were two more Lotus wins in 1987, now with Honda power, but it was clear Senna had outgrown the team and was ready to become the F1 standard-setter. The inevitable call came from McLaren, who had snatched Honda engines from arch-rivals Williams and harnessed them to one of the most elegantly effective racing machines ever built, the McLaren MP4-4. That car, driven by the unparalleled pairing of Senna alongside Prost, a two-time champion with McLaren, was the basis of unprecedented F1 domination. Prost and Senna won 15 out of 16 races that year, as Senna edged his teammate with eight wins and 90 points, to Prost's seven and 87. (Prost out-scored Senna 105 to 94, but only the drivers' best 11 finishes counted.) Placing two superlative talents in the same team, with a brilliant car at their disposal and no contractual pecking order, had elevated the concept of Formula One success to a new level. However, it came at a cost.

Throughout 1989, their rivalry took on a harder edge, reaching its peak of intensity at the Japanese Grand Prix. Prost and Senna had blitzed the race, but Senna needed to win to keep his title hopes alive. Entering the chicane at the end of lap 46, Senna tried to pass for the lead. Prost turned in with Senna alongside, they touched and skittered off the circuit. Prost retired, Senna continued after being pushed back on track and finished first on the road, only to be disqualified for missing the chicane. Senna's outrage at this perceived injustice became incandescent and Prost, despite winning the championship, understood it was impossible that he and Senna remain teammates.

Prost joined Ferrari for 1990 and with the duo now in rival teams, their feud raged on. It once again reached a peak at the Japanese GP, where, as title duellists, they clashed immediately after the start. Senna's attempted pass at the fourth-gear Turn 1 was high-risk, but he knew any collision would likely take both out and decide the title in his favour, as it did.

Their Japanese clashes have remained two of F1's most hotly disputed flashpoints over subsequent decades and whatever the merits of either side's arguments, the Senna–Prost contest was as ferocious as anything witnessed in Grand Prix racing, before or since. The two formed a yin-yang of contrasting brilliance and Senna lamented Prost's absence during his 1992 sabbatical year.

Senna's final title, in 1991, was an altogether calmer affair, with only Nigel Mansell providing credible opposition as Williams regathered before crushing all comers through 1992–3. It was with Williams that Senna had hoped to write further chapters of his own F1 legend. Alas, the book closed too soon.

**CAREER STATS**

**World title: 1988, 1990, 1991**
**Wins: 41**
**Pole positions: 65**
**Fastest laps: 19**

# GERHARD BERGER

**CAREER STATS**

**Wins: 10**
**Pole positions: 12**
**Fastest laps: 21**

**A CLUE TO THE CHARACTER OF GERHARD** Berger is given with the choice of framed racing picture hanging above his home office desk. It shows his Ferrari nose-first into the barriers at Turn 1 of the Interlagos circuit, shortly after the start of the 1993 Brazilian GP, with the disintegrating McLaren of Michael Andretti flying above, inches from Berger's helmet.

Not for Berger a celebratory image selected from one of his 10 Grand Prix wins; instead a vivid reminder of motorsport's perils during more than a decade spent in the thick of it alongside Ayrton Senna, Nigel Mansell, Alain Prost, Nelson Piquet and Michael Schumacher. Unlike that quintet, Berger never won the World Championship, nor did he come close to the title: his best championship finishes were distant third places in 1988 and 1994, for Ferrari. But he was always a driver full of fire and commitment, capable of gritty wins and moments of high bravery, usually with a smile on his face and a twinkle in the eye.

A memorable Formula One career was over almost before it started, however. In 1984, shortly after making his F1 debut with the ATS team, Berger was seriously injured in a road crash near his home in Austria. By incredible good fortune, the driver and passenger in the car behind were surgeons. They stopped, realised the gravity of Berger's neck injuries and oversaw his transfer to hospital without aggravating his condition. Fully recovered for the 1985 season, Berger began to make his mark with the Arrows team as a hard-charger who revelled in the barely tamed power delivery of the 1.5-litre turbo engines then in vogue. His first win came in 1986 at the Mexican GP, driving the dramatic Benetton B186, powered by a BMW engine that produced up to 1400bhp.

Berger's memories of taming that generation of F1 car are vivid: 'It was definitely the best time – a time when the driver made the difference. In qualifying, with full boost and sticky tyres, you wanted to brake earlier because you were arriving at the corners so much faster, but you knew also that the tyres were giving you the grip to brake much later. You only had one lap from tyres and engine to get it right. Everything was so squeezed it was mad. The engines would literally melt after one lap putting out 1400bhp and the tyres were completely finished, too. There's never been anything like it. Driving those cars up the hill at Monaco was like being the bullet shot from a gun.'

Berger's gusto earned him a Ferrari ride for '87, where he became a race winner in red by the end of the year, then again, unforgettably, at the '88 Italian GP. This was no ordinary edition of the race: it was the first since the death of Enzo Ferrari during a season dominated by the McLarens of Ayrton Senna and Alain Prost. Monza also seemed to be going Senna's way until a late-race collision with backmarker Jean-Louis Schlesser that left Ayrton in the gravel and allowed Berger through for Ferrari's only win of the year. The joy of Monza's crazed army of Ferrari fans knew no bounds; Berger's place in their hearts was forever secured.

His next race in front of a home crowd was memorable for rather less happy reasons. At the 1989 San Marino GP, on the bucolic Imola circuit, Berger's Ferrari left the track at the fast left-hand Tamburello corner and hit a concrete retaining wall at around 180mph. His car burst into flames and as he sat motionless in the burning wreckage for 20 seconds, it seemed impossible he was not grievously injured. Yet other than cracked ribs and burns to his hands which forced his absence from the Monaco GP two weeks later, he was unharmed and went on to win the Portuguese GP later in the year.

Berger switched to McLaren for 1990, partnering Ayrton Senna; he even managed to outqualify his illustrious teammate on their first race weekend together. Quick though he was, Berger never claimed to be in Senna's league on track and this unforced hierarchy helped the two become friends away from the circuit. As their relationship grew, Berger succeeded in mellowing Senna's monastic approach to racing with occasional pranks such as throwing Ayrton's briefcase out of a helicopter or snatching his car keys while they were stuck in traffic and hurling them into the street. Senna was soon reciprocating with jokes of his own.

There were three wins during Berger's three years at McLaren, and one more for Ferrari during a second spell with the team from 1993 to '95. Over two closing seasons in '96–97, back with the Benetton team that had launched his career as an F1 front-runner, Berger remained a forceful competitor, even as younger rivals such as Michael Schumacher, Jacques Villeneuve and Mika Häkkinen came to the fore. And there was to be one final glory day at the 1997 German GP, where he took pole, fastest lap and win (his last) only two weeks after the death of his father in a light plane crash. Even in his final 210th race, the '97 European GP, Berger finished fourth, less than two seconds behind winner Häkkinen, still pushing. He retired as a hugely popular figure, admitting to exhaustion with the relentless demands of Grand Prix racing. Few drivers have enjoyed careers so long and pugnacious.

**DRAMA FROM FIRST TO LAST: THIS WAS** the Formula One story of Nigel Mansell. Over a career that spanned the technical extremes of ground-effect aerodynamics and the near-untamed power of mid-1980s turbo engines, Mansell was always in the thick of it. Gifted enough to match and beat the great multiple champions of his era (Nelson Piquet, Alain Prost and Ayrton Senna), he was nevertheless somehow always the underdog, even when waltzing to a loftily dominant drivers' title in 1992. The hangdog, flat-cap persona was the legacy, no doubt, of having to wait so long for that title (12 seasons) and an age before that (72 races) for his first F1 win. And this, despite having always been recognised as one of the very fastest.

Talent-spotted by the Lotus founder and team boss, Colin Chapman, Mansell was given his Formula One break late in the 1980 season. But with Chapman's sudden death in 1982, aged 54, Mansell lost his mentor. The subsequent change of team management left Mansell out of favour, though fortuitously placed for a switch to Williams, who were about to begin a period of Honda-powered supremacy.

His first win, at Brands Hatch in 1985, set the tone and from that moment on, he would always be the darling of the British crowd. He won five times on home turf, including the mesmerising seek-and-destroy pursuit of his teammate/nemesis Nelson Piquet at Silverstone in 1987. Perhaps no other driver could have manhandled the fearsome Williams-Honda FW11 and FW11B cars of 1986–87 with quite such thrilling high-wire élan as Mansell.

'Formula One will never get back to that,' he reflects. 'I mean, driving those turbo cars was the most exhilarating, frightening thing that you could do in your life. The Williams FW11B...nothing comes close to that car. Today's drivers will never know what a proper Formula One car feels like. In qualifying you literally had up to 1,500 horsepower. And to have wheelspin in sixth gear down the straight, at 175 or 180mph...you cannot put that into words as a driver. At every single corner you came to, the car was literally trying to kill you.'

A tyre blow-out robbed Mansell of the '86 title at the final race of the season; in '87 he won twice as many races (six) as anyone else but was denied by Piquet's more consistent finishing record. His exploits inspired a fervour in British motor-racing fans not seen before or since: a crushing '92 victory at Silverstone prompted a track invasion of Union Flag-waving fans as Mansell Mania took hold. 'It was humbling,' he recalls, 'because it was so spontaneous. Sometimes there are no words to explain how the British public can actually make you feel – that can't be bought or sold or traded. It was overwhelming and because health and safety then was nothing like it is today, you'll probably never see a crowd like that again.'

Hero-worship for this dauntless British battler had its roots in a foreign land, however. Two seasons (1989–90) spent with Ferrari brought only three wins, but also something precious: the adoration of Ferrari's *tifosi*, for whom he was simply *Il Leone*. 'Those two Ferrari years were just "money can't buy,"' he says. 'To be nicknamed "Lionheart" by the Ferrari fans, and to win the first race out...it can't get better than that. They're beautiful memories.'

Post-title, Mansell's career pivoted, remarkably, to the USA, where he blitzed the 1993 IndyCar title at his first attempt. That unique title double might have been enough to cap any ordinary career – but not Mansell's. Answering the distress call from a Williams team in grief after the death of Ayrton Senna early in '94, he drove in support of the title-chasing Damon Hill and promptly won the season-closing Australian GP!

An ill-starred two-race coda with McLaren in '95 resulted only in headlines about his being too big for the cockpit, but Mansell has infinitely more to cherish: 'In the '80s and early '90s,' he says, 'it was euphoria to compete in F1 and be a part of what was happening. The abundance of talent, the abundance of carnage, the most incredible things that made you go, "How did that just happen?" You had team managers being shot, we raced round car parks in Las Vegas...Formula One did things that you couldn't even think of doing today, so it was an exciting time. I'm so grateful to have been part of it.'

**CAREER STATS**

**World title: 1992**
**Wins: 31**
**Pole positions: 32**
**Fastest laps: 30**

# NIGEL MANSELL
# 1992 WORLD CHAMPION

Marlboro
Canon
CAMEL
Labatt's
RENAULT
elf

Jean Alesi
LUXOTTICA
J. ALESI
WORLD CHAMPIONSHIP TEAM

**CAREER STATS**

**Wins: 1**
**Pole positions: 2**
**Fastest laps: 4**

**FOR A FEW WEEKS IN THE EARLY SUMMER** of 1990, Jean Alesi was the Next Big Thing in Formula One. He had burst onto the scene halfway through the 1989 season, with a stunning fourth-place finish on his debut with the Tyrrell team at the French GP.

Four races into 1990 he had twice finished second in a car less powerful than leading rivals and was racing with an élan and dash that fans – and clamouring team bosses – were finding irresistible. His dynamic driving style carried echoes of the late Gilles Villeneuve and his wheel-to-wheel combat with Ayrton Senna at the 1990 US Grand Prix on the Phoenix street track, and it was this that sealed the deal for any armchair enthusiast in search of a hero.

In only his ninth F1 start, Alesi surged from fourth on the grid to lead into the first corner and remain in front for the first half of the race. By mid-distance, the looming Ayrton Senna had snuck his McLaren past, but Alesi immediately passed him back. 'That's the intimidator being intimidated,' as one commentator noted. It was a classic moment of David-vs-Goliath sporting theatre, which anointed Alesi as a champion of hearts.

More dispassionate team principals could see an exceptional talent whose contract signature they coveted, and soon Tyrrell, Williams and Ferrari all claimed to have Alesi on their books for '91. Ferrari's financial muscle and Alesi's own red-blooded desires eventually held sway and Jean took up a five-season tenure at Maranello, a move abundant with promise. 'You can imagine what it was like at Ferrari,' he told *F1 Racing* magazine in 2011, 'I had the best time of my life because of the passion I had from the fans and the mechanics and everyone. Unbelievable.'

That promise, alas, would remain largely unfulfilled as Ferrari fell behind McLaren, Williams and Benetton during the early to mid-1990s. Flashes of talent were always sprinkled over Alesi's performances, particularly when wet track conditions allowed him to display the acrobatic car control skills he'd learned during teenage competition as a rally driver, before taking up track racing. But disappointment seemed always to stalk Alesi's bravura: at the 1994 Italian GP, he took pole position and led the first 14 laps, before gearbox failure ended his race.

There would, however, be one particular day out of his days with the Scuderia, and it came at the 1995 Canadian GP. At the Montreal circuit named after Villeneuve, Alesi's childhood hero, he took his sole Grand Prix victory in a car carrying the number 27 Gilles had made famous. That year's Ferrari, the 412T2, was a competitive machine, though not the equal of the pace-setting Benetton and Williams entries. For much of the Canadian race Alesi trailed Michael Schumacher's Benetton and seemed set for a secure second place – a result he achieved 16 times in a 202-race F1 career – but on this feted day, Alesi's 31st birthday, fortune favoured him. Schumacher pitted on lap 58 with electrical trouble, allowing Alesi into the lead for a 10-lap run-in to the chequer. He later admitted having to fight back tears when he passed Schumacher in the pits and regather himself for the closing laps. Half a lap after the finish line, Alesi's car slowed, then stopped, out of fuel. A passing Schumacher offered him a lift back to the pits atop his Benetton, where he celebrated wildly, attempting to stand on the Benetton's bodywork as Schumacher cruised home.

The two drivers switched teams for 1996: Schumacher assuming a central role in reshaping Ferrari as a superteam; Alesi, with teammate Gerhard Berger, failing to reach Benetton's 1995 double-championship-winning heights. Alesi's pair of fourth-place finishes in the '96 and '97 Drivers' Championship with Benetton were his best and his career took a slow dive through to 2001 with Sauber, Prost Grand Prix and, finally, Jordan – the team with which he had become Formula 3000 Champion in 1989. His final race, the 2001 Japanese GP, ended after a collision with Kimi Räikkönen who spun in front of him, and Alesi bowed out, waving to the crowd, spectacular to the last.

# MICHAEL SCHUMACHER
# WORLD CHAMPION 1994–95, 2000–04

**FOR A TIME IN THE EARLY NOUGHTIES, IT** seemed Michael Schumacher *was* Formula One. So absolute was his domination, so profound his integration into the most successful Ferrari team ever built, there seemed barely any space for others to breathe, let alone win.

Once Michael and Ferrari found their groove in 2000, taking Ferrari's first drivers' world title since 1979 (Schumacher's third), they never looked back. A brief resumé shows his nine victories in 2000, nine again in 2001, 11 in 2002, a more modest six in 2003 but then 13 in 2004. More than the wins alone was the ruthlessness. The relentless style of the Ferrari winning machine had never been seen in F1 before. Other great champions and teams had left indelible marks, from Fangio and Mercedes in the 1950s, through to Prost, Senna and McLaren in the '80s and '90s. But never like this.

Many elements contributed to the Schumacher–Ferrari phenomenon. His driving abilities were at a level attained by only a tiny handful of others in the sport's history. His stamina and physical fitness sustained an apparently insatiable hunger for victory. And the team built around him was heaving with brilliantly talented and ambitious individuals, such as Jean Todt, Ross Brawn, Rory Byrne and Paolo Martinelli. Funding via Philip Morris was never questioned, while tyre partner Bridgestone were considered integral to Ferrari's performance package, rather than mere suppliers of rubber. There was simply no weakness.

The success in scarlet elevated Schumacher from the status of sporting superstar to global icon and he enjoyed fevered adulation in Germany (he was the country's first World Champion) and Italy. At heart, a humble family man, who might have worked as a mechanic had his gifts not propelled him to another stratosphere, he became a working-class hero to his fans and remains a revered figure of sporting attainment. Admiration was by no means universal, however. The sledgehammer nature of Schumacher's Ferrari success alienated those who relished a little competitive variety in their sporting diet and questions of ethics hovered around Schumacher's on-track behaviour, and that of his team's, throughout his career.

In 1994, his first championship-winning season, the legality of his Benetton car was repeatedly questioned and at the year's final race in Adelaide, the title was decided by a clash between Schumacher and Damon Hill. Critics insisted it was obvious Schumacher had attempted to ram Hill off the road and seal the title, but he was not penalised. Three years on, another last-race title decider, this time in Jerez against Williams driver Jacques Villeneuve: on lap 47 the pair clashed after what seemed a clear ramming attempt by Schumacher. Villeneuve continued, finishing third to secure his only world title, while Schumacher retired and was stripped of second place in the championship.

Fast forward to 2000 and Schumacher was attempting to intimidate arch-rival Mika Häkkinen at 200mph during the Belgian GP. Their fight for victory that Sunday is among F1's most incandescent, as both drivers, in closely matched cars (Ferrari vs McLaren), stretched their limits on a classic, spectacular Grand Prix circuit. As Häkkinen attempted to overtake Schumacher on lap 40, Schumacher moved right, squeezing Häkkinen and forcing him to lift. A lap later, Häkkinen succeeded with a passing move and went on to win the race. Inspection of the cars later showed scuff marks on the left front-wing endplate of Häkkinen's McLaren, sustained during contact with the right-rear tyre of Schumacher's Ferrari.

In 2006, Schumacher was once again at the centre of controversy after the so-called 'Rascasse-gate' scandal. This arose during qualifying for the Monaco GP, when Michael, having set fastest time, deliberately halted his car on track at the Rascasse corner to prevent the challenging Fernando Alonso from bettering his time. Schumacher's actions caused the session to be stopped and his lap times were deleted. Even in his late-career return with Mercedes, the instinct to intimidate lingered. At the 2010 Hungarian GP, Schumacher and ex-Ferrari teammate Rubens Barrichello were scrapping over 10th place when Rubens attempted to pass on lap 64. At 190mph on the main straight Schumacher edged his car to the right, squeezing Rubens to within inches of the concrete pit wall. Barrichello's pass was successful but Schumacher was given a 10-place grid penalty for the next race. Barrichello described the incident as 'the most dangerous thing I've been through'.

Throughout his career Schumacher never explained why he drove with such aggression and any questionable manoeuvres were always defended by his team, never more so than during his Ferrari years. The cumulative taint of these incidents colours objective assessment of Schumacher's achievements and legacy, even as his supporters would rebut any questioning of his greatness – or even of his claim to be the greatest of all time. More constructive, they would maintain, to focus on the sustained brilliance of his driving over 15 years. They would cite how he qualified the unfancied Jordan 191 in seventh place on his debut at the 1991 Belgian GP. Then mention his brilliant first win there a year later. Then they would point to the 1996 Spanish Grand Prix, which Schumacher won for Ferrari in atrocious conditions with a 45-second margin. Or the 1998 Hungarian GP, won with a triple-stop sprint strategy.

Throughout his Ferrari title-winning years, he was simply beyond reach as the performance reference by which all others had to be judged. Retiring for the first time at the end of 2006, Schumacher had won 91 Grands Prix – 40 more than his closest rival, Alain Prost. That record of achievement was surely legacy enough, yet Schumacher was tempted to race for three more seasons with Mercedes' factory team return in 2010. He scored only one more podium during that period before announcing he was stopping for good, aged 43, at the 2012 Japanese GP. Speaking before the race he reflected: 'We are all humans, and we all make mistakes. And with hindsight you would probably do it differently if you had a second opportunity, but that's life.'

Over the course of two decades in Formula One, Michael Schumacher bent the sport to his will more forcefully than any competitor before or since. How bitter his fate, to be laid low by a head injury little more than a year after his safe departure from a hazardous arena.

**CAREER STATS**

**World title: 1994, 1995, 2000, 2001, 2002, 2003, 2004**
**Wins: 91**
**Pole positions: 68**
**Fastest laps: 77**

Marlboro
Marlboro
Formula 1™
AGYDIJ
BUD
Marlboro
Marlboro
Marlboro
MUMM
CHAMPAGNE

elf

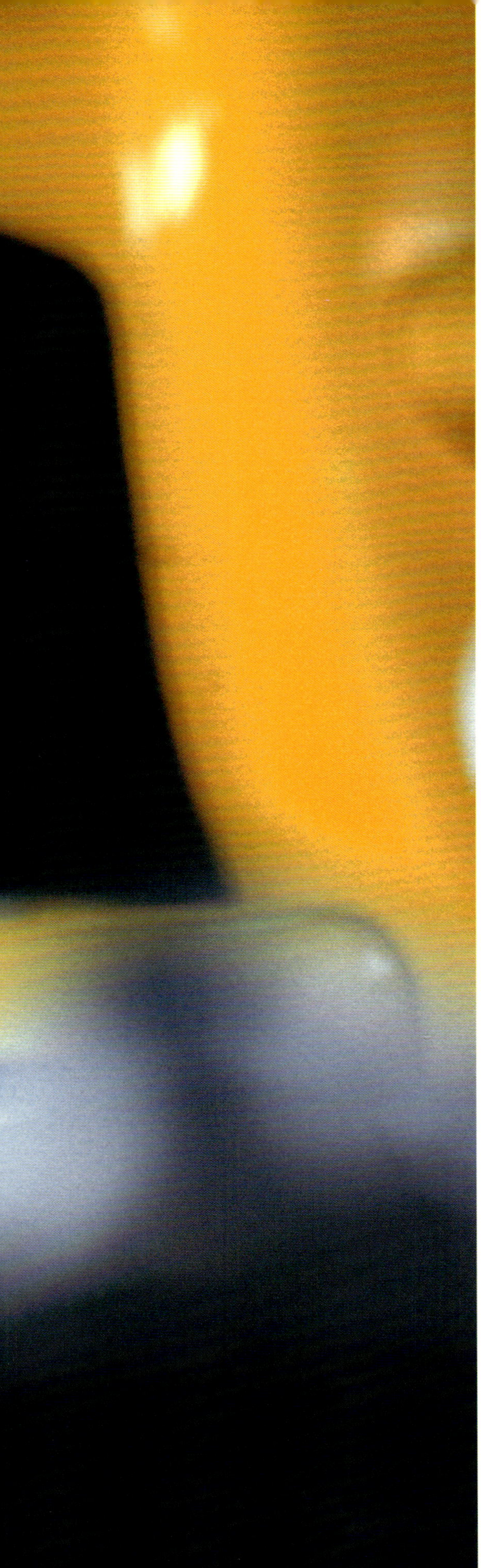

# DAMON HILL
## 1996 WORLD CHAMPION

**'[RACING MICHAEL SCHUMACHER] WAS** more than just not wanting to lose. It was wanting to prevail against a kind of, what I considered to be a rather cynical attitude to the competition.'

It's no surprise that motor racing was more than just a sport for Damon Hill. The son of twice Formula One World Champion Graham Hill, who was killed in a private plane crash, was bound to have a more complicated relationship with the motorsport than those who race without the emotional hinterland of a feted dad. Rejecting the sport completely might have been one choice; Damon opted instead, however, to follow his father's path – though not directly. Racing motorbikes was Hill's first love, but in time he was drawn to four-wheeled competition. Rising through the ranks of British, then international, single-seater racing, he was a late arrival in F1 at the age of 32, driving for the miserably slow remnant of the once world-beating Brabham team. Within a year, however, he was winning races for the mighty Williams, having impressed the team enough in his role as test-driver to be given a chance in the hot-seat.

Another season and Hill was head-to-head with Schumacher for the '94 world title, at the final race of the year. It had been an astonishingly rapid ascent in a Formula One career that spanned only eight seasons. 'It accelerated ridiculously,' he says, 'and you definitely would not say to an aspiring racing driver: "Look what Damon Hill did, that's the way to do it!" I was sucked into the vacuum left by Nigel Mansell' (who quit Williams after winning his title in 1992).

Hill won three races in his first Williams season as understudy to Alain Prost (who cruised to his fourth and final title), but he could not have anticipated the tragic circumstances that threw him into the thick of the '94 title fight. The death of his new teammate Ayrton Senna at the 1994 San Marino Grand Prix elevated Hill to the position of lead driver, pitched against a young, hungry and aggressive Michael Schumacher, driving for the Benetton team. Their tussle that season and through to 1996, when Hill finally prevailed, became one of the most intense F1 had ever witnessed, infused with Anglo–German antipathy and a classic nice-guy–nasty-guy subplot.

Not that Hill bought into the sometimes-hysterical coverage of their sparring: 'I think it was all created by the press,' he says. 'It was no more intense than my own intensity or anyone's intensity when they compete. There was this added dimension to Michael, which was his own body language, attitude, and the fact that he was with a team [Benetton] that seemed to be constantly attempting to try new tricks. That set me up as a kind of "nice boy" who wouldn't dare to dream of doing anything naughty.'

What he won't deny is that he couldn't have chosen a tougher opponent: 'I picked a fight with the wrong bloke. Michael was incredibly talented, incredibly quick, and incredibly smart with the way he went about his competition. You could say I was really his first victim.' Hill felt the hard edge of Schumacher's uncompromising driving ethics many times – most notably during the 1994-title-deciding Australian Grand Prix. The two were separated by only one point before the race – Schumacher ahead on 92 – but their lap-35 collision put both out, settling the championship in Schumacher's favour. Schumacher had clipped a wall just before their shunt and drove his damaged car into Hill's, terminally wounding the Williams. Hill's critics argued he needn't have positioned his car to be vulnerable to a Schumacher swipe; his defenders deemed Schumacher's actions unacceptable. Regardless, the title was Michael's.

Their battle raged on through 1995 and into '96, though by this time Hill had a distinct car advantage in the form of the Williams FW18 – custom-designed around his tall frame. Eight wins from nine pole positions eased Damon to his sole title, but the success wasn't enough to keep his team happy. He split acrimoniously with Williams, landing at the Arrows team for '97, before something of an Indian summer '98 season with Jordan. Hill remembers taking the first F1 victory for Eddie Jordan's team at that year's Belgian GP almost as fondly as he remembers his world title: 'It was brilliant. I'm almost as proud of that as I am of winning the championship,' he says. 'Jordan didn't have the best equipment, but I brought them the focus that they needed. I can honestly say, "I showed them how to win"'.

Self-confessedly 'on my last lap' by 1999, Hill called it quits and returned to the bosom of his family, having earned a legion of adoring fans. 'My experience was that my dad stopped racing and then he died. I had a family, and I didn't want that to happen to them. I'd been very lucky and made it through racing, so it was really a conscious decision to live as long as I could. Although you do become used to a certain level of adrenaline, and it can sometimes be quite difficult to live without that...'

**CAREER STATS**

**World title: 1996**
**Wins: 22**
**Pole positions: 20**
**Fastest laps: 19**

**DAVID COULTHARD HAS BECOME SUCH A** familiar figure in the Formula One community, in the three decades since his race debut, that it's easy to overlook just what a feisty young racer he once was. He was thrust into the Grand Prix limelight in exceptionally challenging circumstances: while still a test driver for Williams early in 1994, he was promoted to a race driver after the death of Ayrton Senna at the San Marino Grand Prix. Reeling from the shock of a loss that was mourned around the globe, Williams entered only one car for the following race in Monaco, but by the Spanish GP, Coulthard was occupying the seat that had been Senna's, with a brief to prove he was worth it.

The pressure was huge for a youngster who had progressed through the junior racing categories showing pace and talent, though never with the starriness of some who burst into the sport like comets. Glitz and glam were never the Coulthard way. A clean-cut, well-brought-up lad from a small Scottish village, he wasn't given to ostentation or braggadocio. Performing on track and doing the right thing for his team and sponsors was much more his style. This approach, learned in part from numerous Scottish mentors, including Jackie Stewart, served him well: Williams held their likeable young racer in great affection and esteem from the get-go and by the end of the season he was finishing in the wheel-tracks of Damon Hill, taking his first podium for second place at the Portuguese GP.

One year on, he was a Grand Prix winner, Portugal once again a happy hunting ground during a season in which he established himself as a front-runner. The win, five pole positions and third in the Drivers' Championship were a highly respectable return in a year otherwise dominated by Michael Schumacher and Benetton. There was something of a clamour for DC's services ahead of 1996 and a switch to McLaren, where he would begin a nine-season tenure, firstly alongside Mika Häkkinen, latterly with Kimi Räikkönen, was duly announced.

Coulthard's McLaren years were the defining chapter of his F1 career. He won 12 times with the team, bookended by victories at the 1997 and 2003 Australian Grands Prix, and while he was never outright number one, he was always more than a number two. He could count blue-riband wins at the British, Italian and Monaco Grands Prix on his palmarès and his victory drive at the 2000 French GP, where he rubbed wheels with Schumacher in a pass for the lead, having earlier flipped Michael the bird as they raced wheel-to-wheel, was a classic.

These two had more than a little history. At the 1998 Belgian GP, which was held in a deluge, Schumacher ran into the back of Coulthard while attempting to lap him and lost his right-front wheel. Both returned slowly to the pits to retire, but a raging Schumacher leapt from his car and stormed into Coulthard's garage screaming 'Are you trying to fucking kill me?'. DC's best championship finish came in 2001, as runner-up to Schumacher, though Ferrari's superiority that year left little on the table for his rivals.

Coulthard remained with McLaren as it made the transition at the end of the season from one quick-but-exhausted Finn, Häkkinen, to a younger model, Kimi Räikkönen. He managed to contain Räikkönen in 2002, another classy win at Monaco being the season's highlight, but the extraordinary pace of early-vintage Kimi soon made him the man with the points. Happily for Coulthard, the budding Red Bull Racing squad made an offer to bring his vast experience to the team, just as his lustre had begun to fade at McLaren. Joining for 2005, DC no longer harboured ambitions to win the world title, but his value to the team beyond the track was immense. The central role he played in bringing Adrian Newey, F1's pre-eminent designer, from McLaren to Red Bull for 2006, amply demonstrated his worth. Newey's leadership of Red Bull's technical department has been the foundation of the team's multiple championship victories in subsequent years. On track, Coulthard was still quick enough to bring Red Bull their first podium finish at the 2006 Monaco GP and even in his final season, 2008, he notched up third place at the Canadian GP – his 62nd and final podium.

Always a driver with his eye on the long game, Coulthard moved seamlessly into a successful broadcasting career the moment he hung up his saltire helmet, as smooth behind the mic as he was behind the wheel.

**CAREER STATS**

**Wins: 13**
**Pole positions: 12**
**Fastest laps: 18**

West
West
Mobil 1
SIEMENS

Castrol
RENAULT
Rothmans
MIRAGE
Rothmans
Rothmans
Castrol
MIRAGE

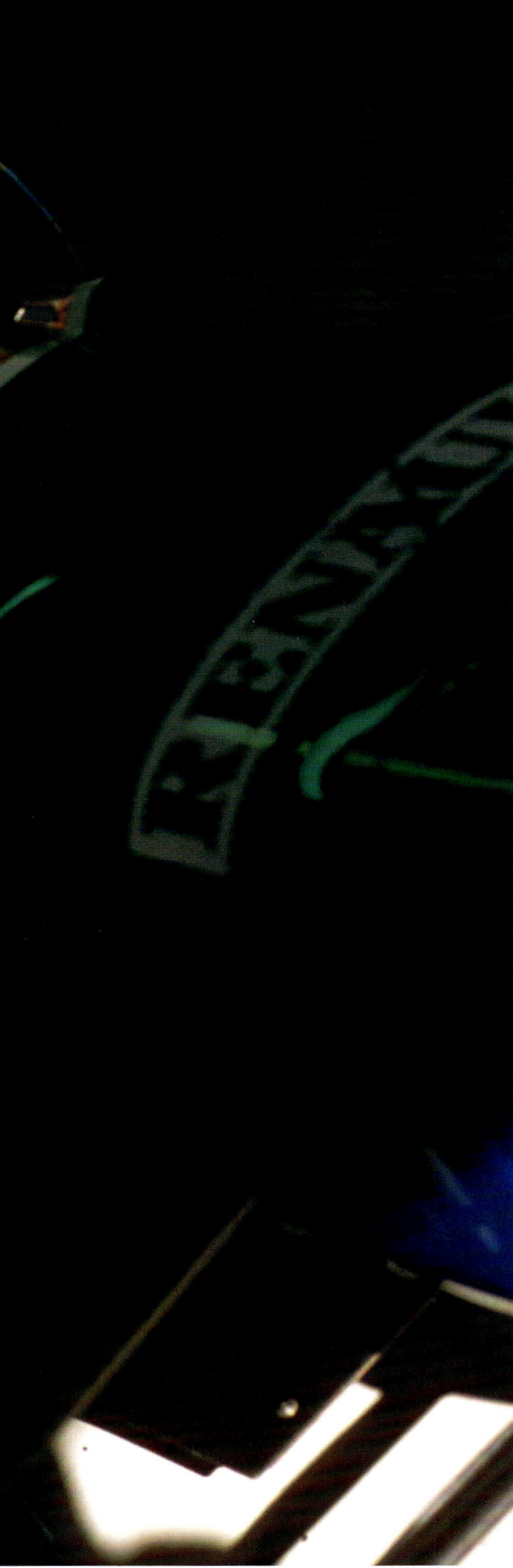

# JACQUES VILLENEUVE
# 1997 WORLD CHAMPION

**CAREER STATS**

**World title: 1997**
**Wins: 11**
**Pole positions: 13**
**Fastest laps: 9**

**HAVING CHOSEN LIFE AS A PROFESSIONAL** racing driver, Jacques Villeneuve's fate was always to be compared to his father. Gilles Villeneuve was one of the fastest, most spectacular and adored of all Formula One drivers. He died in a huge accident during qualifying for the 1982 Belgian GP, flat out, on the limit. His legacy stalked Jacques throughout his racing career: could the son be as good as the father? Would he be so revered? The answer to both those questions is moot, but what is beyond argument is that Jacques won the world title that eluded his brilliant parent.

The expectation surrounding Villeneuve's arrival in Formula One could scarcely have been higher. There was the name, of course, but more significant was the skill and speed he had shown in US racing. In the mid-1990s he was pretty much the hottest ticket in US Indy cars, having moved to the elite category of American racing after learning his trade in Formula Three and Formula Atlantic racing. By '94 he was storming the oval and road courses that made up the Champ Car series, finishing second in the Indy 500 and ending the season as 'Rookie of the Year'. Aged 23, he was The Coming Man.

He followed up in '95 with a champion Indy car season, combining his racing commitments with a Formula One testing schedule for Williams. Spiky, foot usually to the floor, Jacques was just the kind of driver Williams liked, but the team were intent on giving Jacques thorough scrutiny before any talk of contracts. The last driver to leap from Indy cars to F1, Michael Andretti, had been a disappointment, despite a formidable US record, and Williams wanted to be sure this young Canadian charger wouldn't prove to be more of the same.

During a three-day Silverstone test in August '95, Jacques was placed alongside the team's race drivers Damon Hill and David Coulthard. Minor technical troubles prevented what Villeneuve had hoped might be a glory run for fastest time, but Williams had learned enough. They liked the cut of Jacques' jib, and he would race alongside Hill in 1996. The self-possession that marked his character so strongly is evident from his comments in a contemporary test report from *Motorsport* magazine. Asked whether he thought of his father while racing, he answered, 'That's not the reason I'm racing. I don't try to copy him. I don't know if we drive similarly or not, and I never really paid attention to that. I drive like I drive and if it's like him, then great. But if it's not, I like it the way it is anyway'. Whatever Jacques' future held, it would be lived on his terms. Some found him brash, overly self-confident. Others loved the directness of his approach and the intellect he wore without artifice. Fan or foe, none could deny he lived his F1 career centre-stage right from the off.

In his first race, the Australian GP, he qualified on pole position and led the race until five laps from home, when an oil leak slowed him and let Hill through for the win. The authority of Villeneuve's performance was no surprise to those who had been paying attention, least of all to Hill. In his autobiography, Hill recalls Villeneuve declaring, during a pre-season test at the Estoril circuit in Portugal, that he reckoned it possible to overtake around the outside of the fast, 180-degree final corner. He believed its layout was similar to the corners of US oval tracks on which he had excelled. 'I had him down as an over-confident kid who would either come a cropper or learn F1 was more difficult than he had appreciated,' Hill wrote. 'Secretly though I admired his chipper demeanour and the team quickly warmed to him.'

Williams loved Jacques even more when he passed Michael Schumacher around the outside of Estoril's final corner, as promised, on lap 16 of the Portuguese GP later that year, taking third place. The move helped set up Villeneuve's fourth win of the season and kept alive his hopes of winning the World Championship in his rookie season. Hill's victory in Japan two weeks later kept Villeneuve at bay, but by any standard it had been a remarkable debut year. Not until Lewis Hamilton in 2007 would another driver come so close to winning the title at their first attempt. Hill was dropped by Williams for 1997, amid huge controversy, leaving Villeneuve as the incumbent and title favourite in the outstanding Williams–Renault FW19. Counting against him were his relative inexperience and a truly formidable opponent: Michael Schumacher.

The season was frenzied, thanks to resurgent Ferrari and McLaren and a competitive Benetton team. Six drivers won Grands Prix, and the title race, which had see-sawed between Villeneuve and Schumacher all year, went to the final round – the European GP in Jerez, Spain. Schumacher held a one-point advantage going into the race and was leading at the start of lap 47. During the lap, Villeneuve attempted a pass for the lead and was whacked by Schumacher as he went through. The contact sent Schumacher skidding towards the gravel trap and retirement, as Villeneuve went on to third place and the world title. Villeneuve had scorched through his first two seasons like a bleached-blond comet. Never again would he enjoy such success.

Williams waned in 1998 and prompted Villeneuve to make a big-budget switch to the nascent BAR team for 1999. His five seasons there returned only 39 points and his stock collapsed ahead of an inglorious swansong spent between Renault and BMW–Sauber, before retirement in 2006. Late-vintage Villeneuve bore almost no relation to the cocksure daredevil who blitzed into F1 a decade earlier. Better to remember the high times.

# MIKA HÄKKINEN WORLD CHAMPION 1998–99

**MIKA HÄKKINEN FLASHED LIKE A SILVER** blade through late '90s F1, holding at bay Michael Schumacher and a resurgent Ferrari to win back-to-back world titles in 1998 and '99. Häkkinen's '98 McLaren MP4-13 was the most elegant and efficient design of the season, traced by technical ace Adrian Newey to meet regulations that demanded cars be narrower and on grooved tyres – both measures intended to reduce cornering speeds.

In Häkkinen's hands, the Mercedes-powered machine proved devastatingly effective, as Mika, who had taken his first F1 victory only in the final race of 1997, ripped to eight further wins, nine pole positions and the drivers' title, while confirming McLaren as that year's top team. Their momentum carried through into '99, Häkkinen taking another five victories from 11 pole positions, to prevail at the final race with Ferrari edging the teams' battle.

The year 2000 provided another Häkkinen–Schumacher nail-biter as the two greatest turn-of-the-millennium drivers went wheel-to-wheel once more. Their volcanic rivalry erupted at that year's Belgian Grand Prix, where Schumacher, leading and desperate to keep back a faster Häkkinen, attempted to edge Mika off the track on lap 40 at around 200 mph. 'The moment when I tried to overtake him before the end of the race, he was really blocking me very heavily,' Häkkinen recalls. The cars touched at nearly 200 mph, Schumacher's right rear tyre touching Häkkinen's left front-wing endplate. 'And I was shocked because it was not 80 kmph. It was like 300 easily and in those type of speeds, if you lose control, it's guaranteed you will hurt yourself and seriously.'

Häkkinen's response would provide a defining Formula One moment: on the next lap, with a slower Ricardo Zonta separating Häkkinen from Schumacher, Mika passed both drivers at 200 mph into the wet–dry braking zone. 'I suppose that adrenaline is an important part of your performance when it comes to sport,' he reflects. 'But it has to be something that you can control, to be able to make the right decisions. And I was able to turn that moment [the contact] to my advantage. It gave me more courage to be able to say, "Ok, you wanna play the game? Let's play the game."'

Häkkinen understood that passing Schumacher required carrying enough speed through the daunting Eau Rouge corner onto Spa's climbing top straight. But late in the race, with tired suspension and worn tyres, he would not ordinarily have considered it 'flat' (i.e., taken at top speed, with no lift of the throttle). 'But in that moment, I said to myself when I was chasing Michael, "Ok, I'm going to have to do it flat, otherwise I'm never going to have enough speed to be able to overtake him". When I was going through Eau Rouge – I will never forget this – I couldn't believe what a stress the whole machine was going through. I thought it was going to explode, and I was holding the steering as hard as I could to keep the correct line, because if I lost it, I would have flown off I think into the centre of Spa!

'When I actually did overtake, I was still very worried because the inside line was wet, but the racing line was dry and that was the line where Michael was. I thought if he's going to push now, there's no way I can brake as late as he can. I was hoping that he would be so surprised that he was going to brake early, and he would give up. And he did. It gave me just an unbelievable feeling.'

Häkkinen's 2000 title defence ultimately expired in a miasma of engine unreliability, as Schumacher clinched a first drivers' title for Ferrari since 1979, and by 2001 Mika admits that exhaustion hampered any attempt at a championship shot. He won two Grands Prix, in Britain and America, but at the end of the season he was gone, never to race in F1 again despite widely rumoured comeback talks with BAR and Williams through 2003–2004.

While his final two seasons fell short of his title-winning years, Häkkinen's achievement in winning back-to-back championships was all the greater for having beaten Schumacher. His cause was aided in 1999 by Schumacher's absence for six races after a leg-breaking accident at the British GP, but Mika was the only driver Michael regarded as a worthy rival at the turn of the century.

Häkkinen was blessed to still be racing at that stage of his career, having survived an accident at the 1995 Australian GP that left his life hanging by a thread. The '95 season finale was held on the Adelaide street track, where, during Friday afternoon practice, Häkkinen lost control of his McLaren at 130 mph after the failure of the left-rear tyre when approaching the fast right-hand Brewery Bend. Little speed was scrubbed before a brutal sideways impact with the barriers and Mika's head was buffeted violently from side to side in the split-second post-crash.

The impact fractured Häkkinen's skull and he required an emergency tracheotomy to keep breathing. He spent the next eight weeks in hospital recuperating and learning how to restore his balance after disruption to bones in his inner ear. And while his eventual recovery was complete, the crash changed his approach to racing. 'After the accident, my attitude to people changed quite a lot,' he told the FIA's *AUTO* magazine. 'I started looking them in the eye and listening to what they were saying. Before that I was just "Ok, I will keep my foot down on the throttle, I'm the best, I'm going to win every race". But the accident helped me realise, "Oh shit, I have a team around me" and that with the team, we will win.'

And win he did, in a vivid fast-forward couple of seasons that took him from nearly-man to double World Champion. A seven-season wait for the first Grand Prix victory, a near-death experience, the two hard-fought titles... What a ride it had been.

**CAREER STATS**

**World title: 1998, 1999**
**Wins: 20**
**Pole positions: 26**
**Fastest laps: 25**

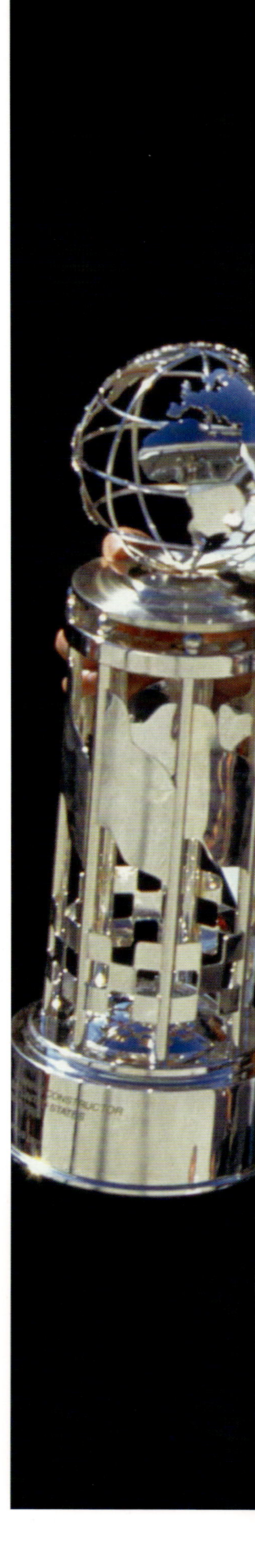

West
BOSS
Mobil 1
BOSS
HUGO BOSS
WARSTEINER
SIEMENS
mobile
West
Hakkinen

Santander
Santander
Santander

# FERNANDO ALONSO
# WORLD CHAMPION 2005–06

**CAREER STATS**

**World title: 2005, 2006**
**Wins: 32**
**Pole positions: 22**
**Fastest laps: 24**

**WHEN THEY LIT THE FURNACE THAT** burns inside Fernando Alonso, they never turned off the gas. He rages to win with an intensity possibly never equalled in Formula One. That was obvious in his first F1 season, aged 19 driving for the minnows, Minardi, and routinely a second or more faster per lap than his teammate in qualifying.

It was obvious 22 years later, at the Brazilian Grand Prix, now driving for Aston Martin, where he beat the faster Red Bull of Sergio Perez to third place by 53 thousandths of a second, having mounted a defensive masterclass. It has always been obvious, in fact, that Alonso would be on the limit, driving to the max, whatever the car, year, or circuit, whoever he was racing against. The ferocity of his winning mindset should, by rights, have secured Alonso more than the two championships that he has. Certainly, once he started winning Grands Prix in 2003, becoming then the sport's youngest winner in Hungary, it seemed that F1 had found its natural heir to Michael Schumacher.

He had to wait a little before his Renault team built a car, the R25, truly worthy of his abilities, but armed with the Anglo–French gem for 2005, Fernando was virtually unstoppable. Once he had taken the title lead by winning round two at the Malaysian GP, he was never headed, despite a strong challenge from the sometimes-faster McLaren of Kimi Räikkönen. Alonso won the championship with two races to spare, his world seemingly perfect, although his comments post-race gave a hint of the flinty mindset and attitude that teams have sometimes found difficult to accommodate. 'I won the championship with maybe not the best car, so I am proud of what I did,' he said. 'The fact that I have taken over the title from Michael Schumacher is a bonus. I came from a country with no tradition in F1. I had to fight my way alone. I have only had the help of two or three people in my career, no more.'

His closing comments carried the barb. A team of maybe 750 Renault F1 staff had contributed directly to their drivers' and constructors' success. Alonso's words were tone-deaf. They could be overlooked because he was a serial winner capable of producing moments of dazzling skill and daring, such as his pass around the outside of Schumacher at the daunting 130R corner on lap 20 of the 2005 Japanese GP. Or his 'thou shalt not pass' closing laps of the 2005 Imola GP, again racing Schumacher. These two giants, one approaching the end of generational dominance, the other seemingly set to snatch Schumacher's baton, would see a lot more of each other in 2006, Alonso's second title season.

After a blip in 2005, when the Michelin tyres supplied to Renault completely outshone Ferrari's Bridgestones, both companies were competitive in 2006, allowing Alonso/Renault vs Schumacher/Ferrari to rumble all season. Two races from the end of the championship, the two were tied on 106 points, before Alonso hammered nails into Schumacher's coffin with a win and a second from the last two races, against Schumacher's sole fourth place. This, Alonso said later, was the sweeter of his two world titles, because he had fought and beaten Schumacher. Winning alone was insufficient for this most competitive animal; to have won while beating the best meant so much more.

As a double World Champion, the youngest ever at the time, Alonso was an object of desire for rival teams. Ferrari courted him before signing Räikkönen to replace Schumacher and he alighted instead at McLaren to be paired with the phenomenon-in-waiting, Lewis Hamilton. The psychodrama that played out at McLaren over 2007 is worthy of the big screen. Against the backdrop of the 'Spygate' scandal, wherein McLaren were found guilty of industrial espionage against Ferrari, Alonso and Hamilton staged a mesmeric head-to-head. Both finished the season on 109 points, with the rookie Hamilton notionally ahead by virtue of having more second-place finishes. Kimi Räikkönen beat them to the title by a single point, much to Alonso's dismay. Had the team focused their efforts on him, an arrangement he believes he was promised, he is certain he would have won a hat-trick title comfortably. This was a very sore point and so poisonous did Alonso's dealings with the team become during the season, he threatened to divulge some of what he knew about the Spygate allegations to the sport's governing body. A relationship that might have delivered so much more was terminated after a single season of a three-year contract, freeing Alonso to return to Renault for 2008–9.

Even here, in a supposedly nurturing 'home' team environment, controversy stalked him, thanks to the team's involvement in the Crashgate race-fixing scandal at the 2008 Singapore GP. Alonso was never implicated in the affair and, controversy aside, his speed on the Singapore streets, and at Suzuka a fortnight later, were a reminder of his formidable racing ability.

He took his talents to Ferrari for 2010, consummating a long-yearned-for partnership. The combination of Alonso's ferocity with the legendary passions of F1's grandee entrant looked to be a match made in heaven – if potentially a volatile one – but once again, his title ambitions were to be thwarted. Alonso's days in scarlet coincided firstly with the impregnable combination of Sebastian Vettel and Red Bull from 2010–13, followed immediately by the Hamilton–Mercedes wonder years. Refusing to be daunted by the challenge of rivals in faster cars, Alonso never gave less than his all to Ferrari. His 2010 and 2012 seasons, finishing four, then three points behind Vettel in the championship, will forever stand as heroic campaigns against the odds. He told *F1 Racing* magazine, '2012 was probably my best season in F1 on a personal driving level, and I definitely believe we deserved that one'. His drive at Valencia, from 11th to first, was an all-time classic.

Four largely fruitless seasons with McLaren followed from 2015 to '18, before Alonso decided to pause, try his hand in some other forms of racing. But back in F1 since 2021, the hunger remains. As he raged through 2023, eight podium finishes and fourth in the championship were his reward. The furnace burns on.

**JUAN PABLO MONTOYA SURFED INTO** Formula One on a wave of expectation so high, it was scarcely possible for one even of his immense talent to ride. He arrived with Williams in 2001, having won the 1998 Formula 3000 Championship and followed up by winning the US Champ Cars Championship in his debut season. The year 2000 was hallmarked by a commanding victory at the Indy 500, where his car control around the mile-long banked oval left onlookers agog.

Formula One was the obvious next step for a racing driver in the classic mould: richly gifted, bold, headstrong and too tough to be intimidated by reputations of rival, circuit or team. Christian Horner, who would go on to become the hugely successful team principal of Red Bull Racing, recalls Montoya insouciantly dipping a couple of wheels off the track to pass him during an F3000 race at Germany's Hockenheim circuit, yet remaining in complete control. It was that moment, Horner believes, that convinced him to abandon ambitions as a racing driver and focus his energies instead on team management.

Montoya's swashbuckling style was evident almost from the start of his F1 career. During his third race, the 2001 Brazilian Grand Prix, he put a sublime move on no less a driver than Michael Schumacher, for the lead of the race. Into Turn 1 on lap three, he out-braked Schumacher, before edging his Williams to the right, leaving Michael with the choice of backing off or hitting Montoya. Schumacher chose discretion, briefly rocked at having received the kind of treatment he was more used to dishing out. Montoya continued untroubled in the lead before being punted out by a tailender, but a marker had been laid down: this was a man to watch – all the more so during a period of growing Schumacher–Ferrari domination.

Juan Pablo's first win was a while coming that season, as he took time to settle alongside incumbent teammate Ralf Schumacher, but a convincing victory was his at the Italian GP – the first for a Colombian driver. Seven pole positions in 2002 further proved his native speed, though no wins followed in a season of near-absolute Ferrari control. All but two Grands Prix went the way of Maranello. Schumacher took the title with 144 points – comfortably more than the combined total of his teammate Rubens Barrichello (77) and Montoya (50), second and third in the table.

In 2003, it was far more open with Montoya in title contention until late in the season, before again finishing third in the table. But this was also the year during which cracks began to appear in the Williams–Montoya relationship. At the French GP, Montoya let fly at his team over the pit-car radio, after a strategy call he believed had cost him victory. Relations were strained thereafter, and Montoya soon agreed a switch to McLaren for 2005. His partnership there with Kimi Räikkönen was a classic fire-and-ice combination, though Montoya was eclipsed by his teammate over the course of 2005. Räikkönen scored seven wins to run Fernando Alonso close for the title, while Montoya managed three victories and a points total barely half of Kimi's (60 to 112).

By the middle of '06, Montoya's disaffection with the strictures of McLaren's internal discipline, and the wider demands of life as a top-line Grand Prix driver, had begun to dim his motivation. Second place in Monaco (where he had won in 2003) was a highlight, but after crashing out of the US GP in round 10, he abruptly quit Formula One to pursue a US-based racing career. Reflecting on his departure, he admitted in *The Red Bulletin* magazine: 'I'd just had enough of F1. That's the truth. I didn't want to stay at McLaren and I definitely didn't want to go to a worse team and run around eighth, tenth or whatever. That made no sense.'

Decisive to the last, Montoya quit Formula One as dramatically as he had entered. The legion of fans, gathered during his brief and often brilliant Grand Prix career, were left to wonder what might have been.

# JUAN PABLO MONTOYA

**CAREER STATS**

**Wins: 7**
**Pole positions: 13**
**Fastest laps: 12**

PHILIPS

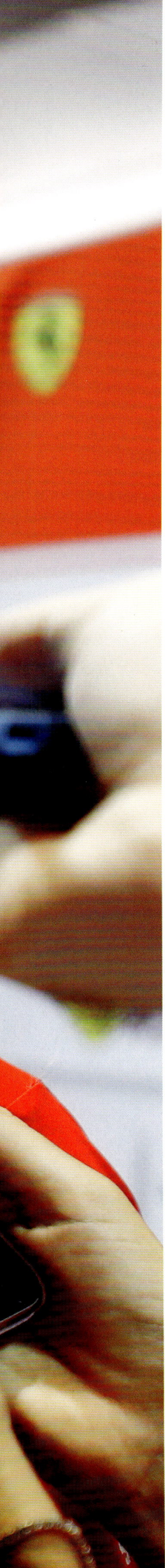

**SO QUICK WAS KIMI RÄIKKÖNEN, THEY** bent the rules to get him into Formula One. The spotty kid from Finland arrived in the UK to race in the 1999 Formula Renault series aged just 20. Just over a year later, he had won the championship and been signed up by the Sauber team to race in F1.

Räikkönen had driven only 23 races in single-seat race cars since stepping up from karts and his inexperience drew opposition from Max Mosley, then president of motorsport's governing body, the FIA. But he had shown so much ability in F1 test sessions, he was allowed to leapfrog the conventional racing ladder through Formula Three and GP2, to spring straight into the top flight. He was that good.

A point's finish on his F1 debut came as little surprise and, throughout 2001, Kimi impressed so widely that McLaren snapped him up to replace their mighty, though exhausted, champion Mika Häkkinen. There, Kimi set about dismantling the career of McLaren stalwart David Coulthard. DC just about contained Kimi during their first season together, later recalling the baby-faced assassin as being 'either very fast or asleep in the back of the truck'. But in 2003, he didn't see Kimi for dust.

Räikkönen was in the thick of the title fight with Michael Schumacher throughout the year and had it not been for a blown engine at the European Grand Prix costing him what looked to be a certain win, he would have been champion. As it was, he finished two points behind Schumi, in a McLaren not in the same league as Michael's Ferrari.

McLaren struggled against an impregnable Ferrari the following season, though 2005 was an altogether different affair. The Michelin tyres supplied to McLaren and Renault were superior to Ferrari's Bridgestones and the title fight swiftly settled into a head-to-head between Räikkönen and Fernando Alonso. They won seven Grands Prix apiece, but Räikkönen, whose season was blighted by unreliability, spent the year playing catch-up after Alonso had established a strong, early points lead. Nonetheless, Kimi once again underlined his pace in the fleet and beautiful McLaren MP4-20. At round four, the San Marino GP, he took pole position with a half-second margin and zoomed away early on, setting a sequence of fastest laps before mechanical failure. His teammate that day, Alex Wurz – subbing for the injured Juan Pablo Montoya – noted: 'That was Kimi special speed.'

He conjured F1 magic later in the season at the Japanese GP, which he won from a 17th-place start. Carving through the field along with Alonso, who had started from P16, Räikkönen was up to second by half-distance. After a late pit-stop he ran second to leader Giancarlo Fisichella by nine seconds with nine laps to go. Surely Fisichella must win? Räikkönen saw it differently. He closed down Fisi with the menace of a Great White and into turn one on the final lap, swept around the outside of the Renault to secure an unforgettable victory.

Japan 2005 was peak Kimi; as his career progressed, some of the quicksilver tarnished. His title-winning year with Ferrari in 2007 was built on the convincing foundation of six wins, although he benefited from the McLaren civil war between Alonso and his rookie teammate Lewis Hamilton, who tore results from each other all year. Kimi edged the title by a single point at the final race in Brazil.

As Räikkönen moved into his second Ferrari season, he ceded primacy to his notionally junior teammate Felipe Massa, who came of age during a stellar battle with Lewis Hamilton for the 2008 drivers' title. A year later, after a mediocre campaign, Kimi was gone, to the dismay of fans who had come to adore his monosyllabic interview style and off-track adventures that included a drunken embrace with an inflatable dolphin during a friend's birthday weekend. It was no coincidence that Räikkönen counted James Hunt as his hero.

A sojourn in rallying cleansed the Räikkönen palate before a return with Lotus for 2012. The car was good enough to carry Kimi to third in the championship with a win and a bucketful of podium places, despite team funding arrangements that could most generously be described as opaque. When the cash ran dry towards the end of 2013, Kimi walked, not content to drive for love but having gifted audiences the immortal in-car quip: 'Just leave me alone, I know what I'm doing.'

Twelve years on from his effervescent debut, Kimi once again took a call from Ferrari, though this time the Scuderia were looking for an exceptional wingman to support Fernando Alonso, then Sebastian Vettel, in their respective quests for the world title. Late-vintage Räikkönen was a different beast from The Iceman whose shimmering speed had once been capable of freezing out any rival. He was a mellower competitor, one who couldn't, for example, quite muster the energy to mount a challenge to the 18-year-old Max Verstappen, en route to his first F1 win at the 2016 Spanish GP.

Still capable of inspiration, such as his pole position lap at Monaco in 2017, latter-day Räikkönen mostly seemed content to let the young guns have their day. His win at the US Grand Prix in 2018 was a last Ferrari flare, before an anonymous three-season coda with Alfa Romeo. Inscrutable to the end, Räikkönen is among the most naturally talented drivers ever to have raced in Formula One – but one who never fulfilled the potential suggested by his extravagant gifts.

**CAREER STATS**

**World title: 2007**
**Wins: 21**
**Pole positions: 18**
**Fastest laps: 46**

# KIMI RÄIKKÖNEN
# 2007 WORLD CHAMPION

**CAREER STATS**

**Wins: 11**
**Pole positions: 16**
**Fastest laps: 15**

# FELIPE MASSA

**FOR 38.907 SECONDS AT THE 2008** Brazilian Grand Prix, Felipe Massa was a World Champion. He had just won his home race, the concluding round of the championship, and half a lap behind him Lewis Hamilton was losing hold of the title that would be decided between them.

Going into the race, only these two could win the championship: Hamilton held a seven-point advantage, obliging Massa to win the race with Hamilton finishing no higher than sixth. Massa delivered, crossing the line to take his 11th (and final) Grand Prix win, as Hamilton slipped to sixth place, a position which would have left him equal on points with Massa, but losing the title on wins during the season: Felipe's six to Lewis's five.

Frantic drama played out over the final half lap. With only two corners remaining, Hamilton passed the Toyota of Timo Glock, struggling for grip on a wet track with dry tyres, to regain fifth place and win the championship by a point. The eruption of joy in the McLaren garage as Hamilton crossed the line was matched only by the twist of anguish at Ferrari, where Massa's consummate victory from pole position nevertheless tasted of defeat. His dignity and poise accepting victory plaudits on the podium, even as he could witness delirious McLaren celebration in the pitlane below, defined him as a champion in spirit, even if not in the final points tally.

Massa had come an awfully long way for a quick-but-wild kid who, in the withering assessment of Jacques Villeneuve, 'couldn't drive in a straight line' when he started with Sauber in 2002. After a ragged first season, Massa spent a year as a Ferrari test driver, learning polish and craft from race drivers Michael Schumacher and countryman Rubens Barrichello, before a racing return with Sauber in 2004–5, still with Ferrari testing duties.

His big break came for 2006 with elevation to a Ferrari race seat alongside Schumacher, and his first two wins in Turkey and Brazil. A highly competitive 2007 followed (three more victories) alongside Kimi Räikkönen, before his memorable 2008 title run. Nine months on from the agony and ecstasy of Brazil '08, racing success was the least of Felipe's concerns as he fought for his life after a freak helmet impact during qualifying for the 2009 Hungarian GP which caused severe head injuries. During the second qualifying session, as Massa approached Turn 4 at around 175mph, a spring weighing approximately 1kg that had fallen from the Brawn car of Rubens Barrichello bounced from the track directly into Massa's helmet, impacting above his left eye. The helmet saved Massa from being killed instantly, but with an unconscious driver, his Ferrari F60 slowed without braking before ploughing headlong into tyre barriers on the exit of the corner.

He was airlifted from the track for emergency medical treatment that saved his life, while he spent several days in a coma. Further operations in Brazil inserted a metal plate into his skull above his left eye socket, where bone had been destroyed. Massa sat out the remainder of 2009, amid speculation that his injury would be career-ending, yet he would prove his doubters wrong. Less than two months after the July accident, he was running practice laps in a go-kart, the healing wound on his left forehead still much in evidence. By February he was once again testing for Ferrari, ahead of his full-time F1 return.

In his absence, the sport had moved relentlessly onward and his outgoing teammate Kimi Räikkönen was replaced with Fernando Alonso, Massa's third World Champion teammate after Michael Schumacher and Räikkönen. As wingman to Alonso, Massa won no more races, despite having a likely victory at the 2010 German GP taken away from him after a team order to let Alonso past. Ferrari's radio communication from the pit – 'Fernando is faster than you' – gained instant notoriety.

Massa's final four F1 seasons were spent with Williams, where he twice helped the team to third in the Constructors' Championship before bowing out with a point in his final Grand Prix, number 269, in Abu Dhabi. It had been a rollercoaster and sometimes glorious F1 career, encompassing triumph and near-tragedy. Massa retired as a much-loved, widely respected grandee.

BRIDGESTONE
BRIDGESTONE
PIAGGIO AERO

# ROBERT KUBICA

**CAREER STATS**

**Wins: 1**
**Pole positions: 1**
**Fastest laps: 1**

**THE LIMIT WAS AN EDGE TO BE EXPLORED** for Robert Kubica, not a zone to be feared. This hammer-hard racer was fearlessly committed and, uncommonly in a notoriously bitchy realm, regarded with universal esteem by his peers.

'He's the best of all of us,' Fernando Alonso once remarked, having witnessed up close the abilities of the first Polish driver to compete in F1 and the first, subsequently, to take a pole position and win a Grand Prix. Those garlands came early in his second full F1 season, 2008, with victory at the Canadian GP vaulting Kubica briefly to the top of the drivers' table and confirming his reputation as a World Champion in waiting. He ended the season fourth in the table, tied on points with Ferrari's Kimi Räikkönen and ruing the decision of his BMW team to channel resources to 2009 car development long before the 2008 title was decided.

His impatience for success, alongside the urgency of his driving style, had been apparent from his earliest races. Kubica finished on the podium at the 2006 Italian GP only three races into his F1 career, but later complained of one or two driving errors over 53 laps, even as onlookers hailed the maturity of his performance. He attacked 2007 with trademark zeal, although that very commitment was to be his undoing. On lap 26 of the Canadian GP, Kubica suffered one of the most spectacular accidents ever caught on camera. Attempting an off-line pass on the approach to the hairpin of the Circuit Gilles Villeneuve, Kubica's BMW clipped the Toyota of Jarno Trulli, ran off the circuit, briefly became airborne, then hit a concrete wall and barrel-rolled across the track, shedding wheels and bodywork before finally coming to rest on its right side against a barrier. Miraculously, Kubica was almost unhurt, suffering only concussion and a sprained ankle, but he sat out the next race, the US GP at Indianapolis, where another super-talented youngster, Sebastian Vettel, made his debut as Kubica's stand-in. It says much for Kubica's resolve that his sole Grand Prix win came at the circuit where he had suffered his mega-shunt exactly one year earlier.

The promise of 2008 was squandered in 2009, as BMW slid from front-running competitiveness to mid-table obscurity; by the end of the season they had gone, citing the global financial crisis as their reason for departure. Kubica was snapped up by Renault for 2010 and showed flashes of dizzying talent throughout the season – nowhere more so than in qualifying for the Japanese GP, where he took third grid spot, behind only the much faster Red Bulls of Vettel and Mark Webber. His race engineer Alan Permane recalled how Kubica reached a hitherto uncharted realm during his best qualifying run: 'Suzuka qualifying in 2010 was a lap like I've never seen from anyone else, ever. He came in absolutely white, having scared the life out of himself. It was unbelievable. It's very clear that Robert was destined for greatness.'

All that bright-burning promise was snuffed out on 6 February 2011, when Kubica crashed during the Ronde di Andora rally in northern Italy, which he had entered to stay sharp over the Formula One off-season. On the rally's first stage, Kubica's Skoda Fabia clipped a poorly secured metal barrier, which peeled backwards against the car's movement, cutting through its nose and bonnet and passing the engine to enter the cabin and slice into Kubica. The barrier almost severed his right arm, inflicted multiple fractures on his right leg and pelvis and rendered him helpless, almost bleeding to death.

Desperate medical attention saved his life, though it seemed Kubica's racing days were done. Only three days before the crash, he had set fastest time at the first pre-season F1 test, amid rumours that he had already signed to join Ferrari for 2012, partnering Fernando Alonso. That tantalising prospect was destined to remain out of reach, although Kubica did battle through six years of rehabilitation to test again for Renault, then Williams, in 2017, before a full-time F1 return as a Williams driver in 2019.

His Lazarus-like comeback earned Kubica even greater respect than he had enjoyed before his injury, but Formula One is too cruel an arena for fairy tales: he scored only a single point in 2019 and called time on his F1 racing career after cameo drives with Alfa Romeo in 2021. He stands as one of the sport's greatest lost talents

**BRITISH MOTOR RACING CROWDS HAD** witnessed innumerable moments of high skill and drama at their home Grand Prix weekends since the inaugural Formula One race at Silverstone in 1950. Lewis Hamilton gave them another in 2006 to match any that had gone before.

He wasn't quite in F1 that season, though the sense of anticipation about his impending graduation hung heavy in the air. Everyone knew that this kid, on his way to winning that year's GP2 title, had something very special. And on lap nine of the GP2 sprint race supporting the Grand Prix, he flaunted all of his gifts. Approaching the high-speed swoops of the Maggotts/Becketts corners, at around 170mph, Hamilton was closing fast on Clivio Piccione and Nelson Piquet Jr, squabbling over second place. Before they even realised what was happening, Hamilton had ghosted to the right into Maggotts, then taken a fearsomely tight line through Becketts, kicking up the dust on the inside kerbs to exit, having passed both drivers. Piccione had to lift to avoid an accident; Piquet, discombobulated, ran wide over the grass as Lewis powered ahead and up the road on his way to win from an eighth-place start. It was a stunning smash-and-grab, executed with fearless commitment and total control. Hamilton was gone before his victims even knew he'd arrived.

His moment of brilliance carried the mark of genius and the McLaren F1 team, who had nurtured Lewis through junior racing categories, knew that space had to be found for him in their F1 line-up. By happy coincidence, Juan Pablo Montoya was about to waltz from his McLaren seat back to racing in the USA, creating a vacancy for Hamilton alongside Fernando Alonso, who would also be new to the team for 2007, though as reigning double World Champion.

The most astonishing debut season followed. Over the course of 17 races, Hamilton matched Alonso point-for-point to end the year tied on 109, both having won four races plus eight more podium finishes. Kimi Räikkönen won the title by a single point, with Hamilton pipping Alonso to the runner-up spot, thanks to more second places (five, to Fernando's four).

McLaren's commitment to treating both drivers equally had made two worlds collide. Hamilton refused to play a subservient role to Alonso, insisting he be judged on speed, not notional status. Alonso, unimpressed, was convinced he'd been duped and returned to his Renault alma mater for 2008. Lewis powered on, now clearly McLaren's number one, and a world title was his prize. Once more he fought to the very last gasp of the championship, this time against Ferrari's Felipe Massa. The manner of Hamilton's first title win, being confirmed only a few corners from the finish line of the last race of the year, passed instantly into legend. Champion by a point, Hamilton became (then) the youngest F1 champion, aged 23 and 300 days.

In two breathless seasons, he had established himself as probably the outright fastest driver in F1 and he had done so without any of the caveats attached to the likes of Ayrton Senna (Hamilton's idol) and Michael Schumacher before him, both of whose on-track behaviours attracted periodic scorn. Hamilton might have been expected to dominate post-2008, but the Hollywood script took a twist. In 2009 came the Brawn–Button phenomenon, then from 2010–13 Sebastian Vettel and Red Bull pulverised their opposition.

There were periods during these seasons when Hamilton seemed distracted, particularly in 2010, when he began to distance himself from his influential father, Anthony (who had managed Lewis's early career), and mingle in celebrity circles. His bold fashion sense, and the ease with which he blended into the worlds of music and film, made him a magnet for media attention. But it troubled traditionalists, who preferred their racing drivers less clean of cut, perhaps carrying the whiff of gasoline, not cologne. For these critics, Hamilton always had an answer on track. Only three times in his 17-season (to date) F1 career has he been out-scored by a teammate and never has he been beaten to a world title in equal machinery.

The sheer accomplishment of Hamilton's driving ability and racecraft are hard to deny. He has almost always been devastatingly fast, in any conditions, rarely makes mistakes and has never resorted to intimidatory tactics to achieve a result. His stats are a sledgehammer of achievement. At the end of the 2023 season, Lewis stood equal with Michael Schumacher for the number of titles won – seven – and comfortably topped the table for Grand Prix wins (103) and pole positions (104). And aged 39, he is still racing with no indication of imminent retirement.

The great bulk of Hamilton's racing success has come with Mercedes, where, from 2014 to 2021, he led the team to eight consecutive constructors' titles. He did so as the first winning Black driver in Formula One. For much of his career, Hamilton avoided questions about race or ethnicity, despite having been subject to racism since his days as a young karter. His stance changed dramatically in 2020, when he became a vocal advocate of the Black Lives Matter movement, explaining that supporting a cause beyond motorsport had renewed his motivation to keep racing and campaigning from a global sporting platform.

Activism brought new gravitas to Hamilton's already pre-eminent position as the world's most famous racing driver. It simultaneously fuelled critics who would have preferred him to 'just drive'. Not that Hamilton had much time for naysayers while continuing to set the bar for voracious pretenders such as Max Verstappen. Their titanic scrap for the 2021 title showed that Hamilton had lost none of his speed or hunger, and while Max stole the show through 2022–23, Hamilton insists it is only a matter of time before Mercedes equip him with a car to fight for title number eight. Is all of this enough to make Hamilton the GOAT (Greatest Of All Time)? No answer is definitive. But who, past or present, could claim to be better?

# LEWIS HAMILTON
# WORLD CHAMPION 2008, 14–15, 17–20

**CAREER STATS**

**World title: 2008, 2014, 2015, 2017, 2018, 2019, 2020**
**Wins: 103**
**Pole positions: 104**
**Fastest laps: 65**

INEOS
INEOS
INEOS
Hewlett Packard Enterprise
PETRONAS
LEWIS

# JENSON BUTTON
# 2009 WORLD CHAMPION

**CAREER STATS**

**World title: 2009**
**Wins: 15**
**Pole positions: 8**
**Fastest laps: 8**

**IT WAS DURING THE PENULTIMATE** pre-season test of 2009, at the Circuit de Catalunya near Barcelona, that the cat leapt from the bag. Jenson Button and Rubens Barrichello, refugees from the axed Honda Formula One entry and now paired at a Brawn GP squad scraped from the remnants of the Honda collapse, sat pretty at the top of the timesheets: first and second for a team brought back from the dead.

A handful of the photographers and journalists present on the final day's running sprinted to their laptops to place bets, with insanely long odds, on Jenson or Rubens becoming 2009 champion, and on Brawn winning the constructors' title. Those brave enough to commit that March week would be handsomely rewarded come November.

Barely three months later, the F1 season had taken on a mirage-like quality. Button had won six races out of seven, streaking away from the field like a latter-day Jim Clark – all smoothness and precision – to lead the Drivers' Championship with authority. The performance of the lightly sponsored BGP 001 seemed scarcely believable and, sure enough, the double diffuser aerodynamic solution used at the rear of the car's underbody was protested by several rivals. The Williams and Toyota teams, who had also developed their chassis around double-diffusers, found themselves similarly subject to protest, but the designs were declared legal and early-season results left to stand.

Button and Brawn took advantage of the situation while their rivals played catch-up, and the points buffer they established proved essential for their eventual success, as a lack of finance began to tell against the might of McLaren, Ferrari and Red Bull, all of which won Grands Prix in the second half of the season. But a battling drive from 14th to fifth at the Brazilian GP was enough to secure Button's sole drivers' title with a race to spare. The scenes of rapture that greeted the result were as unconfined as any witnessed in the sport's history. Particularly touching was the tearful embrace between Button and his father, John, who had supported his son's racing since the earliest days and who remained a constant, pink-shirted presence throughout Jenson's F1 career.

Perhaps they had begun to fear the title would never come, for just as Button's World Championship triumph had been the unlikeliest imaginable, so had his F1 career as a whole failed to follow the script. He burst onto the F1 scene in 2000, fresh from a strong season in Formula Three, blessed with a calling-card smoothness and delicacy of touch in mixed-weather conditions that marked him out as a driver with an unusually cultured skillset. Tests for both the Prost and Williams teams duly followed.

As a fluff-chinned 20-year-old, he stopped the show by qualifying third for the 2000 Belgian GP, while unwittingly establishing himself as something of a media darling. His charms failed, however, to win over his next boss, Flavio Briatore, who infamously withered that Button 'would never be a World Champion'. After two trying years at Benetton, Button had at least developed some of the resilience he would call on later in his career, as his obvious talents serially failed to find a happy match with a competitive team.

Joining BAR-Honda in 2004 promised a breakthrough, as Button clocked up 10 podium finishes and posted his first pole position to finish a respectable third in the drivers' table. It was his (and others') misfortune that year to come up against a superlative Ferrari, which won 15 out of 18 races – 13 of them scored by Michael Schumacher in his pomp.

The following season was tarnished by a fuel tank illegality scandal, but finally, after 113 attempts, Button won his first Grand Prix in famous style at Hungary's Hungaroring circuit in 2006. To say the win had been a long time coming does no justice to the sense of expectation that had surrounded Button since his debut. Routinely heralded as the 'next big thing', at least in the partisan British press, his career up to that point had failed to live up to the hype (never more so than during an interminable contractual tussle between Williams and BAR throughout 2005). On this day in Hungary, however, he was imperious, winning by more than 30 seconds from 14th place in mixed conditions to which his soft skills were perfectly attuned. The win was also Honda's first in F1 as a factory team since 1967.

A strong finish to 2006 seemed to have set Button up well for 2007, but the two seasons that followed came close to terminating his career. He scored only nine points across 2007–08 and – far worse – the global financial crash of 2008 allowed Honda a blameless exit from an apparently doomed F1 project. It was from these ashes that team principal Ross Brawn dragged the essence of a race team and agreed a deal to buy the rump operation from Honda for a nominal fee. Crucial to the team's viability was an engine deal agreed with Mercedes, which supplied a top-line motor to what would prove a front-running chassis. Cue Valhalla.

Even a season as charmed as 2009 ended with a sour note, however. Contractual discord between Button and the team resulted in his exit for McLaren, as Brawn were snapped up by Mercedes to metamorphose into 21st-century Silver Arrows. The move was complicated by the presence at McLaren of Lewis Hamilton, unquestionably the most precocious talent to have alighted in Formula One for a generation.

Some pundits predicted a drubbing, but over 2010–12, Button edged his vaunted teammate by 672 points to 657. Those stats reveal nothing of their true relative performance and even the most ardent Button fans wouldn't claim he had Hamilton-matching pace. He had, though, flourished in a true top team and found some kind of professional serenity late in his career. And it was with McLaren that Button remained, through to his final full season, 2016, despite the team's fall from front-running pace. While never the outright fastest, Button can claim to have possessed as refined a touch as any F1 great and to have co-authored maybe the most unforgettable title run of all.

**FOR SO LONG, SEBASTIAN VETTEL'S WAS** the perfect F1 career. He started out winning a point on his race debut, making him the sport's then-youngest scorer, aged 19. A starring role six races later at the 2007 Chinese GP saw him finish fourth in the unfancied Toro Rosso. Then, barely a year later, a first victory – at Monza of all places – for the local team and everyone's favourite underdog (still 'Minardi' for those with long enough memories). Immediately onwards – almost before he'd arrived – to the big time with Red Bull Racing where he won his third race with the team.

Vettel was simply one of those drivers for whom every star aligned. And as a racer, at this stage of his career, he had the lot. His outright speed was devastating in the nimble, grippy, Red Bull RB5 and that searing pace earned him immediate de facto lead driver status, despite his tender years and the freshest of faces. Like some kind of vacuum-packed Insta-Driver, he was just ready: ready to lead, ready to win and, as the world was about to discover, ready to wipe the floor with the opposition.

Viewed in sum, his four consecutive titles from 2010 to 2013 elevated him to all-time great status, his stats bearing comparison with the likes of Juan Manuel Fangio and Michael Schumacher. In 2011 and 2013 he seemed effortlessly dominant: 11 wins from 15 poles, then 13 from nine. At the end of both those seasons, he enjoyed crushing margins of more than 120 points to his nearest challenger.

The years 2010 and 2012 told somewhat different stories. In the first of those, his teammate Mark Webber and Ferrari's Fernando Alonso ran him close; both were ahead of Vettel in the standings before the season-closing Abu Dhabi GP, yet Vettel prevailed to win both race and title. Alonso and Webber had both suffered from tyre and traffic problems, while Vettel's run from pole had been almost trouble-free. Still only 23 (and 134 days), he became the sport's youngest-ever champion. It set the tone. Despite a teary-eyed post-race press conference, which revealed what a young man he still was, the steel and relentlessness of his driving carried the hallmark of a natural-born winner.

One of the keys to his speed, identified early on by his race engineers, was a great feel for his cars' behaviour under braking, which enhanced his corner entry. Vettel also proved exceptionally adept at exploiting the rear-grip benefits offered by exhaust-blown diffusers. These intricate constructions would sometimes require drivers to use the throttle counter-intuitively in order to increase exhaust output and, in effect, suck the back of the car closer to the ground. The ease with which Vettel adapted to the new requirements highlighted not only skill, but intelligence in being able to identify and maximise an edge. He wasn't shy of playing intra-team politics to his advantage either, as Mark Webber repeatedly found to his cost when crossing swords with the team's favourite child.

Vettel's 2012 Championship was a far more close-fought affair. The Red Bull RB8 was less dominant, both McLaren and Ferrari provided stern opposition, and his battle with Alonso raged until the Brazil finale. This dramatic race gave evidence of a raw hunger for victory that wasn't always possible to discern in Vettel's frequent pole-to-flag wins. Having been tipped into a spin at the start, he recovered from 22nd to sixth, to snatch a third title already half-grasped by Alonso.

Red Bull reset the playbook for 2013, unleashing the RB9 as the ultimate iteration of a concept pioneered with the RB5 in 2009. Harnessing the 2.4-litre Renault V8 engine, sophisticated electronic throttle mapping and an aerodynamic package that tested the limits of the regulations, the RB9 represented the definitive manifestation of the high-revving non-turbo F1 cars, before their enforced redundancy under subsequent hybrid-engine technical regulations. With this machine and its predecessors, Vettel and Red Bull had created a partnership worthy of Schumacher–Ferrari or Clark–Lotus comparisons: it was almost impossible to think of one without the other.

Had Vettel's career ended there (unlikely, having become a four-time champion aged only 26), he would probably be regarded as an unalloyed legend of Grand Prix racing. Over the following seasons, however, the once-impregnable image of this charismatic, funny and hugely successful driver became more nuanced. The first question marks were raised by his performance in 2014 against his hot-shot young teammate Daniel Ricciardo. Fresh as the Fremantle breeze that had carried him from Western Australia to Europe, Ricciardo blew into Red Bull Racing and set about blowing up Vettel's reputation. Ricciardo's speed and athletic driving style had been obvious throughout his preceding seasons with Red Bull's junior team, Scuderia Toro Rosso. No one expected him to take three victories that year to Vettel's zero and to place third in the Drivers' Championship with 238 points to Vettel's 167.

Vettel – Red Bull's golden boy, the chosen one – suddenly, unthinkably, looked off the pace. And if Red Bull's slump was in part explained by the excellence of Mercedes in the new hybrid-engine F1 era, harder to fathom was Vettel's deficit to Ricciardo. Some pondered whether he had deliberately taken a dive, to allow an easier exit from the team and smooth his path to Ferrari, for whom he would drive between 2015 and 2020.

A rapid German champion leading F1's most storied team... We'd been here before, but unlike Michael Schumacher, whose Ferrari years helped bring the team its greatest success, Vettel never scaled such heights with the Scuderia. Fourteen wins and twice second in the Drivers' Championship behind Lewis Hamilton were no mean return, but Vettel's days of sweeping rivals aside were done. Another extremely rapid young teammate, Charles Leclerc, furrowed Vettel's brows through 2019–20 and it was perhaps with relief that he accepted a graceful descent out of F1 with Aston Martin for his final two seasons (2021–2).

Still only 35 when he announced his F1 retirement, Vettel bowed out as a hugely respected statesman with eyes set on pastures beyond motorsport. His title-winning years had etched his name in Formula One's tablets of stone... but with an asterisk.

**CAREER STATS**

**World title: 2010, 2011, 2012, 2013**
**Wins: 53**
**Pole positions: 57**
**Fastest laps: 38**

# SEBASTIAN VETTEL WORLD CHAMPION 2010–13

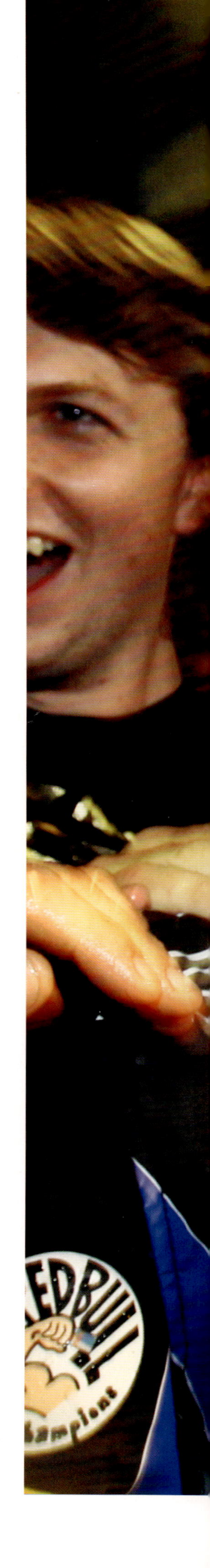

MUMM
MUMM
Red Bull
MOBILE
TOTAL
Red Bull

P ZERO
PETRONAS
QUALCOMM
UBS

**ASHEN FACED, LOOKING SICK TO THE** stomach and overwhelmed by conflicting emotions, Nico Rosberg prepared to face the media after winning the 2016 Formula One World Championship in Abu Dhabi. Voice choking, he uttered: 'I don't want to have to go through that ever again! I was very, very glad it's over. The feelings in that battle with Max during the race were unbelievably intense. There was pressure from behind and pressure in front. It was crazy. And Lewis was massively quick all year. It's incredibly tough to beat him. It will take some time for all those feelings and emotions to settle and come out.'

Rosberg had just succeeded in a quest no other driver had ever managed and maybe never will: beating Lewis Hamilton to a Formula One title in identical machinery. It was the pinnacle of his 11-season F1 odyssey, and his final struggle had been excruciating. He and Hamilton had arrived at the season finale both in a position to win the title. Amid myriad permutations, if Hamilton won, Rosberg had to finish no lower than third to be champion.

One–two finishes were common that season for Mercedes but, still, both had to deliver. Hamilton did, by dominating from pole. Rosberg had a torrid evening. First, he had to pass Max Verstappen for second place, in order to avoid becoming mixed up in others' pit-stop strategies and falling out of title contention. Then he had to endure Hamilton, leading, teasing him like a cat with a mouse. In the race's latter stages Lewis began to lap around three seconds off his true pace. The effect of this was to back Rosberg, in second, into the pursuing Sebastian Vettel and Verstappen. This was brutal racecraft from Hamilton: staying just far enough out of reach to avoid being passed, but reversing Rosberg towards two hungry rivals who could push Nico down to fourth. Hamilton first, Rosberg P4 would have made Lewis champion and crushed Rosberg.

That didn't quite happen, but the torture of the closing laps said much about the nature of relations between the two Mercedes drivers during their seasons together from 2013 to 2016. Hamilton's status as F1's primus inter pares was hard to dispute at this time. No team orders existed at Mercedes but by 2016 he was already a three-time champion and the team's totem. Except Nico Rosberg didn't quite see it that way. Brilliant though Hamilton unquestionably was, for Rosberg he held no fear. Their careers had overlapped since childhood karting days. They had won the GP2 title in consecutive years (Rosberg 2005, Hamilton 2006), each graduating to F1 a year later as GP2 Champion. Rosberg spent four years with Williams, before joining Mercedes as teammate to Michael Schumacher in 2010. He didn't win a Grand Prix until 2012, while Hamilton had exploded into F1 as a fully formed superstar in 2007 and never looked back.

As far as Nico was concerned, however, at Mercedes Hamilton was fair game. Over their four seasons in silver, Hamilton usually had the upper hand, but Nico never made it easy. He was the son of 1982 World Champion Keke Rosberg, one of the feistiest F1 racers ever, and no son of Keke's would be a pushover. In 2013, their first Mercedes season, Hamilton edged the points, but Rosberg had two wins to Hamilton's one. Then Lewis got busy. In 2014, he won 11 races to Rosberg's 5; 2015 was 10–6. In both years Hamilton was never out of sight, but always out of reach.

A defining moment in their rivalry came at the 2015 US GP. Rosberg had the upper hand in qualifying and looked the likely winner until a late-race Safety Car period closed the pack up and gave Hamilton a chance to pass for the lead. A small mistake on lap 48 allowed Hamilton through for the win, which delivered his third title. Rosberg seemed dejected, offering the thin excuse of 'a gust of wind' as the reason for his error. Deep down he knew he'd been thumped.

A lesser driver might have capitulated after two seasons of Hamilton drubbings; Rosberg, by contrast, mined his inner resources. He recognised that in wheel-to-wheel racing Hamilton was superior and approached 2016 determined to be more robust. Early in the season, at the Malaysian GP, he put an uncharacteristic wheel-banging move on Kimi Räikkönen, having also clashed with his Ferrari teammate Vettel; in Abu Dhabi, when a mistake would have blown his title shot, his pass on Verstappen was executed with exquisite precision. He had searched inside and out for any advantage – or, at least, any way to reduce a deficit.

During the brief August break from racing, Rosberg stopped cycling as part of his fitness regimen. The change allowed him to lose 1kg in muscle mass from his legs, a saving which translated into a lap-time gain of 0.04s and which he credited with helping him to pole position for the Japanese Grand Prix: 'My smaller leg muscles got me on pole [by 0.013s], and that messed with Lewis's head, so he messed up the start. I finished first, he finished third, and I had the points lead that I needed to be able to cruise home with second places.'

He did indeed finish second behind Hamilton at the four concluding 2016 races, although to say he 'cruised' in Abu Dhabi rather understates the agony of his experience. It was clear in victory that he had squeezed every last drop of speed, spirit and skill from himself to beat Hamilton, having come to understand that nothing less would do. Rosberg's title win did benefit from Hamilton's worse reliability record that year, though to suggest Nico was a lucky champion would sell him very short indeed. Sebastian Vettel, who had a ringside view of the Mercedes battles from the cockpit of his Ferrari, observed: 'In my point of view, you don't win a championship by luck. Over the course of the year, you collect a lot of points and sometimes you have a good season, sometimes it's bad. [Abu Dhabi] was Nico's day and it's a sign of respect to give him that.'

That Sunday in Abu Dhabi was Nico's last as a Formula One driver. Spent, he retired five days later, having achieved something quite remarkable.

**CAREER STATS**

**World title: 2016**
**Wins: 23**
**Pole positions: 30**
**Fastest laps: 20**

# NICO ROSBERG
# 2016 WORLD CHAMPION

**CAREER STATS**

**World title: 2021, 2023, 2024**
**Wins: 54**
**Pole positions: 32**
**Fastest laps: 30**

**BORN LIKE A BULLET, THERE WAS LITTLE** doubt Max Emilian Verstappen would grow up to be a racing driver. The son of Jos Verstappen, a notoriously combative '90s F1 pilot, and go-karter Sophie Lumpen, he was whizzing round the backyard on a mini-quad bike aged two and driving a kart by four. Ten seconds later, or so it seemed, he was testing a Formula One car as a young star of Red Bull's driver programme and on 15 May 2016, he won his first Grand Prix, aged 18!

His epochal achievement sliced two-and-a-half years off the mark for the youngest Grand Prix winner, held by Sebastian Vettel. Fortune favoured him that day, as the Mercedes pair Lewis Hamilton and Nico Rosberg took each other out on lap one. Still, he out-shone his rapid teammate Daniel Ricciardo and beat two Ferraris with the assurance of a veteran. Not bad for a kid driving his first race weekend for Red Bull Racing, after his fast-track promotion from the Toro Rosso junior squad. Critics who'd dismissed Verstappen as too young for F1, or at least not ready to race, suddenly looked foolish. Max had just owned F1's future.

It was already obvious that Verstappen was the coming man. In his 2015 debut season with Toro Rosso, he quickly became a points-scorer and finished the season comfortably ahead of his teammate and fellow rookie Carlos Sainz. But even one genetically selected for greatness couldn't know it all; an almighty accident at the Monaco GP – head-on into the St Devote barriers – was the kind of shunt that would have killed ambitious young hot-shots in previous F1 generations.

Verstappen had been on a charge for tenth place and the final points position. He was gaining places by tailing the faster Ferrari of Kimi Räikkönen, but on lap 62 came across the Lotus of Romain Grosjean on the fast run into Turn 1. Instinctively, he launched an out-braking move, but as he edged to the right, Max's left-front wheel clipped Grosjean's right-rear, ripping the front suspension from Verstappen's car and spearing him into the barriers. It was a misjudgement, pure and simple – one born of supreme confidence and a misguided belief in his invulnerability. Clearly, there were still errors in the Verstappen code and his edgy, uncompromising driving style started to ruffle feathers. Grosjean described Max as 'too aggressive' after the shunt and Verstappen was penalised five grid places for the next race.

There were echoes of Senna and Schumacher in Max's speed, track manners and generally haughty air. Both those past greats burst rudely into F1 and raced against supposed elders and betters without a care for reputation. And like them both, Verstappen was uncompromising in his pursuit of F1 success. The manner and pace of his driving even briefly prompted a clamp-down on manoeuvres in the braking zone that became known as 'the Verstappen rule'. This was just the kind of notoriety that allows the most talented drivers to intimidate rivals on a plane beyond pure driving ability, and Max knew it. After one spat with Räikkönen, he reflected: 'As racing drivers you always have those moments when it gets a bit heated but then you start from zero again. When you're new they always try to be hard on you. If you're a good, quick new guy there's more attention on you. And when you start to beat the established big guys, they don't like it. I was on the limit but you always have to find a limit with everything.'

The influence of his hard-edged, though less-talented, father was evident in every Max utterance. 'My dad always told me, "you have to be as fast as you can straight away within five laps,"' he told *F1 Racing* magazine in 2017, 'and I always did because in formula racing you always have to be on it straight away'. Singular, focused, there was little room for anything beyond motor racing on Planet Max. Downtime was racing in e-sports; his partner Kelly is the daughter of three-time F1 World Champion Nelson Piquet.

Quickly he established himself as the golden boy of Red Bull Racing, despite the considerable presence of Daniel Ricciardo as teammate. Ricciardo managed to contain the Verstappen force of nature throughout 2016–17, but by 2018, the team's gravitational centre had shifted. The inevitable flashpoint came at the Azerbaijan GP. On lap 39, battling over fourth place, Ricciardo speared Verstappen from behind, under braking for Turn 1, putting both out of the race. Red Bull later airbrushed the clash as 'a racing incident' and both drivers could have been deemed at fault: Ricciardo for braking too late, Verstappen for weaving while decelerating. Privately, Ricciardo felt the team would always sway Max's way and he left for Renault at season's end.

Through 2019–20 Verstappen brushed aside junior teammates, while having to watch Mercedes' Lewis Hamilton ease to sixth and seventh world titles. By 2021, however, Max finally had a car to take on the Mercs and after a titanic, season-long scrap with Hamilton, he won his first World Championship. There had been high drama along the way: a 51G crash at the British GP and a Monza clash that left Verstappen's car perched perilously on top of Hamilton's. The title, indeed, was only decided on the last lap of the final race, after a late Safety Car call that secured Verstappen's victory.

A driver so polarising was never destined to win his first world title in a straightforward manner, though titles two and three, which followed almost unopposed in 2022 and '23, were studies in team–driver symbiosis. Verstappen's 23 haul of 19 wins from 22 starts, with only one non-podium finish, was almost comically dominant. Purists might have recoiled, but Verstappen's essay in excellence rewrote the script. What lies next for the Dutch master is uncertain after season-ending comments that he 'would not be around forever'. Should he continue in similar vein, all records will tumble.

ORACLE
Mobil 1
viaplay
BYBIT
JUMBO
GIVES YOU WINGS
GIVES YOU WINGS
Hard Rock
Mobil 1
ORACLE
Red Bull

*Theatres of dreams, as essential to the fabric of Formula One as the cars and drivers themselves.*

# CIRCUITS

Shell Oils
CAMPARI
Marlboro McLa

# SILVERSTONE ENGLAND

**SPEED. SILVERSTONE HAS ALWAYS BEEN** about speed. The self-styled 'Home of British Motor Racing' thrills drivers with its high-speed nature – corners such as Maggotts, Becketts, Club, Stowe, Woodcote written into fable.

Motor racing began there in 1947, when the site of a former RAF base in Northamptonshire in England found a new purpose as a wide-open space where fast cars could be raced. By 1950, with a remodelled layout, Silverstone was hosting the inaugural Formula One Grand Prix, attended by King George VI.

To date it has hosted 58 Grands Prix and is one of only four venues from the original championship still on the F1 calendar. Through the decades, its swooping curves have staged innumerable moments of high drama, none more electrifying than Nigel Mansell's epic comeback charge to beat Nelson Piquet in 1987.

**MONZA, LA PISTA MAGICA, IS FORMULA** One's grand theatre. The atmosphere conjured by this majestic circuit set in parkland north of Milan is unrivalled, almost tangible. Much of its captivating energy is conveyed by the legions of Ferrari fans – the *tifosi* – who arrive every September to worship the home team and its gladiators. There is also the crackle of danger, a knowledge conveyed through generations that Monza is a circuit where accidents have consequences. Wolfgang von Trips died here, chasing the 1961 title, in an accident which also killed 14 spectators. Jochen Rindt, 1970 champion-elect, was killed in practice for the race; and Ronnie Peterson died after a start-line accident in 1978.

Monza first hosted a Grand Prix in 1950, a round of the inaugural Formula One World Championship. It has hosted the Italian GP every year since, with the sole exception of the race held at Imola in 1980. That lineage makes Monza part of Formula One's very fabric: its thread of darkness shot through scarlet is the purest essence of Grand Prix racing.

# MONTE CARLO MONACO

**THERE IS NO CIRCUIT MORE INTRINSIC TO** the glamour of Formula One than Monaco. The sinuous track on the streets of 'a sunny place for shady people' remains an unrivalled challenge of driver skill and a victory there is coveted above all others.

Monaco's racing history dates back to the pre-F1 era of Grand Prix racing and its current layout remains substantially the same as the one used for the first Monaco GP in 1929. Its own legend is intertwined with that of the many racing greats, such as Ayrton Senna and Graham Hill who mastered it, but also with those who have failed.

Alberto Ascari survived a plunge into the harbour waters almost unhurt during the 1955 race; in 1967 Lorenzo Bandini was terribly burned after crashing at the chicane and being trapped in his blazing Ferrari. He died three days later. Archaic though Monaco's layout might seem by the standards of modern Formula One, its allure remains undimmed.

ERMÈS
HERMÈS
SEV MARCHAL
BP

BP
TOILETTES
STOCK
STOCK
STOCK
STOCK
STOCK
LUCAS
CASTROL

# SPA-FRANCORCHAMPS BELGIUM

**EAU ROUGE. POUHON. BLANCHIMONT.** The mere mention of these corner names at the Spa-Francorchamps circuit is enough to make racing enthusiasts experience a vicarious thrill. They're the gems in one of Formula One's crowning glories – a classic road-racing circuit that featured in the original 1950 calendar and which survives to this day in adapted form, soul intact.

The original Spa-Francorchamps track was a 14-kilometre monster draped across the Belgian Ardennes, whose dramatic undulations dictated the circuit's character, much as the Eifel mountains forged the Nürburgring. For 1983, following a long hiatus after the original Spa circuit was deemed too dangerous, a revised configuration was introduced – only half as long, but retaining the character and challenge of the original loop. In both layouts, Spa was feared and revered in equal measure: only the best could win there.

It was no coincidence that Jim Clark was unbeatable at Spa from 1962 to '65; Ayrton Senna won five times between 1985 and '91; Michael Schumacher won six races out of 11 between '92 and 2002; then Kimi Räikkönen won four out of six between 2004 and 2009. The key to a successful Spa lap is momentum and flow; embracing its rollercoaster nature is the path to victory. The most gifted drivers, those able to pirouette on the highwire between joy and despair, have always flourished. For the rest? There are always other circuits.

# NÜRBURGRING GERMANY

**NO CIRCUIT USED FOR FORMULA ONE HAS** presented drivers with a greater challenge than the Nürburgring Nordschleife. Although not used for Grand Prix racing since 1976, its fearsome legend still towers in the sport's history like some dark monster from a forgotten time, spoken about only in hushed tones. The sheer length of the track, more than 14 miles, was daunting enough. More intimidating still was the endless variety of corners (150-plus) packed into its length, gradient change, a rough, bumpy surface and the possibility of weather variation during a lap.

Built over two years from 1925 to '27, in Germany's mountainous Eifel region, the Nürburgring was envisioned as a showcase for the German auto and construction industries. It first hosted Formula One in 1951 and remained a fixture on the calendar, with occasional exceptions, through to 1976. When Jackie Stewart won there in 1968 in wet conditions, he described it as 'the green hell', but steeled himself to produce the greatest drive of his career. 'It was like flying an aircraft in bad weather without radar,' he wrote in his autobiography *Winning Is Not Enough* (2007). 'The conditions would be hellish on any circuit, but nothing less than terrifying at the Nürburgring, with its undulations and many fast bends and slow, tight corners. Little streams on the track are almost impossible to see in the shadows of the trees, but you know they are there soon enough as the car aquaplanes in water that feels two inches deep.'

Always a venue that filled drivers with trepidation, it was also a place where the very greatest could demonstrate their mastery. Juan Manuel Fangio's 1957 victory there was another to rank alongside Stewart's in '68. In 1961, Stirling Moss produced a virtuoso performance to win ahead of the faster Ferraris. Niki Lauda's near-fatal accident during the '76 race spelt the end for the track as a Formula One venue, however. Even before the Lauda inferno, drivers had protested against the level of risk, boycotting the track after the 1969 race and forcing the German GP to move to the Hockenheim circuit while modifications were made. It returned for 1971, though its inaccessibility and the impossibility of raising safety standards over a full-lap distance made it out of step with shifting attitudes towards risk. The Nürburgring Nordschleife remains an active circuit beyond F1, still red in tooth and claw.

RCHAL
ENERGOL
BP
PAVILLON
Andre LAMBERT
ENERGOL ENERGOL
BP
REDEX DUNLOP
DUNLOP DUNLOP
DUNLOP

# REIMS FRANCE

**ONE OF THE MOST CELEBRATED FRENCH** Grand Prix circuits is easily stumbled across driving through the country's Champagne region. Made up of public roads, the Reims-Gueux track is less than 100 miles north-west of Paris, and can be driven along, in part, as the D27. It passes the original, well-preserved pit buildings which once witnessed the likes of Mike Hawthorn, Juan Manuel Fangio and Jack Brabham blasting wheel-to-wheel down its wide-open straights.

One of the six European tracks on the original 1950 race calendar, Reims was a deceptively simple, wickedly fast track that favoured power and speed. A layout that was little more than two straights connected by a swooping back section encouraged slip-streaming as cars ran nose-to-tail, the driver behind hoping to be sucked forward in the draft of the car ahead and tow past. Then it would be a question of who was bravest on the brakes.

A regular F1 venue through the 1950s, Reims hosted its last Grand Prix in 1966. Its unique flavour is still easily sampled.

# YAS MARINA ABU DHABI

**RISING LIKE A DESERT MIRAGE ON THE** edge of the Persian Gulf, Yas Marina Circuit is the very expression of a 21st-century Formula One facility. Pristine and with immaculate, spacious working environments for teams, officials and media, it is beyond rational criticism. Soulless? Of course – but how could it not be, given its apparition from once-empty sands. A classic track? Not in the least, by comparison with the glories of Monza, Spa and Monaco.

Yet in the years since its glitzy arrival on the Formula One calendar in 2009, the Abu Dhabi Grand Prix has developed a charisma of its own, thanks in part to the championship-deciding season finales it has hosted. A teary Sebastian Vettel became F1's youngest champion there in 2010. In 2016, Nico Rosberg was squeezed in a Hamilton–Verstappen vice before emerging as that year's champion. Then in 2021, Yas hosted among the most dramatic finales the World Championship has ever witnessed: Lewis Hamilton versus Max Verstappen in a title shoot-out that wasn't decided until mid-way through the final lap (see Chapter 5: Rivalries). Formula One purists find Yas hard to love, but its measurable excellence has made it hard to ignore.

TIHAD
Choose Well.

Marlboro
Marlboro
Marlboro
Marlboro
Marlboro
Marlboro
Marlboro
COURTAULDS
Shell
8
GOODYEAR
GOODYEAR
GOODYEAR

# SUZUKA JAPAN

**NO CIRCUIT IN FORMULA ONE HAS EVER** received quite the veneration accorded to Suzuka. Others might be feared, respected or perhaps celebrated for their proximity to a lively city. Suzuka is simply adored by drivers.

They can thank Dutch circuit designer John Hugenholtz for their pleasure. He was commissioned by Honda in the late 1950s to design a track that could be used for road car development as well as racing. His entrancing, fluid, figure-of-eight ribbon was the result. Almost 30 years passed before Suzuka was included on the F1 calendar in 1987, the two previous Japanese Grands Prix having been held at the Fuji circuit. Since then, it has been present almost without interruption, hosting some of the sport's most memorable moments.

There was drama from year one, as Nigel Mansell crashed out of his 1987 title bid having overcooked it through the demanding Esses section. In 1989 and '90, Alain Prost and Ayrton Senna came to blows, settling the championship via car-to-car contact. More recently, the 2005 edition of the race was hailed in many quarters as one of the greatest ever Grands Prix, during which Kimi Räikkönen and Fernando Alonso flew through the field to win and finish third.

There is unquestionably also a dark side to Suzuka, one sometimes disguised by the joyous enthusiasm of the fans who throng to every Grand Prix. Its intoxicating thrills have lured many drivers into serious accidents, none more so than the eventually fatal impact suffered by Jules Bianchi during the 2014 GP. Suzuka races have also frequently been assailed with extreme weather conditions, adding meteorological hazard to an already challenging topography. Nonetheless, its popularity among the Grand Prix fraternity is assured. If Formula One was not already blessed with a Suzuka, it would have to invent one.

# INTERLAGOS BRAZIL

**FORMULA ONE PASSION FLOODS FROM THE** massed grandstands of Interlagos, fuelling a fever that's approached only by Monza's *tifosi*. Sometimes fans are drenched with fire hoses to cool their ardour. They seem not to care, enthusiasm remains undimmed.

Well might they adore Grand Prix racing; since the '70s, exploits of Emerson Fittipaldi, who became Formula One's youngest champion in 1972, Brazil has produced a series of champions and winners, none more feted, of course, than Ayrton Senna. And Interlagos is where fans come to worship, at a track built on the outskirts of São Paulo in Brazil.

Dating from 1940, Interlagos was originally a demanding five-mile long course that began hosting Formula One in 1973, a race won by Fittipaldi. Safety concerns led to the track being dropped from the F1 calendar at the end of the 1980 season, while a full remodelling was carried out prior to a return for 1990. Curtailed to a more modest 2.7 miles, Interlagos 2.0 retained the character of the original and remains a favourite among drivers, thanks to multiple challenging corners and fairground-style elevation change.

Already celebrated for home wins by Carlos Pace and Senna, as well as Fittipaldi's two in 1973–74, Interlagos gained racing immortality when it hosted the breathtaking finale to the 2008 World Championship. Felipe Massa won the race, his second Interlagos victory, crossing the line with enough points to have won the championship. But half a lap behind Massa, his only title rival, Lewis Hamilton, made a pass for fifth place, with only two corners remaining, gaining him the points he needed to snatch the title.

It was among the most dramatic season conclusions ever seen in Formula One. If any circuit was worthy of such a finale, it was Interlagos.

MICHELIN
RENAULT
MICHELIN
15
J.P. JABOUILLE
elf
RENAULT elf
15

# MARINA BAY SINGAPORE

**EXPECTATIONS WERE MIXED WHEN THE** addition of the Marina Bay Circuit to the F1 calendar for 2008 was announced. Would this be just another too-tight street track, held in sweltering conditions and destined to be unloved, instantly forgettable? Sceptics were swiftly confounded. Staged under lights as the first Formula One night race, and with a dynamic configuration that encouraged incident, the Singapore GP was a hit from the off, uniquely atmospheric – though destined for immediate, unsought notoriety.

The memorable first edition will forever be recalled for the 'Crashgate' race-fixing scandal. It centred on Renault driver Nelson Piquet Jr, whose lap 15 accident prompted a safety car that worked to the advantage of his team's lead driver, Fernando Alonso, who went on to win. A year later, Renault were found guilty of having instructed Piquet to crash deliberately and fix the result. Team boss Flavio Briatore and senior engineer Pat Symonds were both banned and Renault issued with a suspended disqualification.

The controversy added a certain frisson to the race's reputation and in subsequent years the travelling F1 circus approached Singapore with a degree of expectation: usually there would be some kind of incident to generate headlines and the on-track action was often intense. Photographers and TV crews came to love it, too. The 1,600 floodlights adorning the circuit allowed the creation of images never seen before in Formula One.

# ICONS

*The movers, shakers and star-chasers who have shaped Formula One's past, present and future.*

**MYTH AND MAN, FABLE AND LEGEND**, 'Ferrari' evokes a thousand stories and a million emotions rooted in motor racing. Enzo himself towers above any pretender to his eminence as the greatest figure in the history of Formula One, and the contribution made by the team that bears his name to Grand Prix racing is beyond measure.

Longevity plays its part: no other team has contested every World Championship season, and only Mercedes can also trace its origins back to the early 20th century. Blood and death are also woven deep into the Ferrari tapestry, that macabre strand adding a dash of ghoulish magnetism.

The man with hooded eyes that witnessed tragedy and triumph across 90 years was born in Modena to hard-grafting parents whose family metalwork business manufactured parts for the Italian railway and auto industries. Enzo and his older brother Alfredo were immersed in the world of heat and flame and noise throughout their childhood, but the death of their father, Alfredo Sr, and Alfredo himself, within months of each other when Enzo was 18, led to the collapse of the business and the surviving Ferrari male was left adrift with little formal education.

Enzo served briefly in World War I and tried, unsuccessfully, to find a job with FIAT in Turin when hostilities ceased. Undeterred, Enzo continued his search for employment in the city at the heart of the fast-growing Italian motor industry. Restless ambition and a deep-seated desire to race cars led him by fortune and persistence to the CMN car bodies business, where he took up a role as test driver. Finally behind the wheel, Ferrari was able occasionally to enter races and, having shown talent, establish himself as a driver for Alfa Romeo. Competing alongside luminaries such as Antonio Ascari and Giuseppe Campari, Enzo came to realise that while his driving ability was high, it was not at the level of these natural-born superstars and that his future in motor racing lay in managerial and organisational roles.

He threw himself into work for Alfa Romeo, becoming a leading dealer of their road cars, while keeping his racing flame alive. Working under the aegis of the main company, he formed a racing division, Scuderia Ferrari, in 1929. Enzo swiftly demonstrated the benefits, both to his own ambition and to Alfa's costs, of out-sourcing racing activities entirely and it was in this guise that independent Ferrari racing operations began in 1933, exclusively running Alfa Romeos.

The relationship with the parent company lasted until 1939, when a rift between Enzo and his automotive alma mater led Ferrari to become a fully independent manufacturer and supplier of racing components. Wartime bombing of his Modena factory forced relocation to Maranello, 10 miles away, where the Ferrari legend began to evolve. In 1947, the first Ferrari car, the 125S, rolled from the factory floor, carrying cues that live on to this day. A sophisticated engine – a V12 of only 1,500cc – had been central to the car's design. It was intended to race and beat competitor machines, especially those from a now-bitter rival, Alfa Romeo. And it was painted rosso corsa.

Victory at Le Mans in 1949 was an early headline success for Ferrari and when the Formula One World Championship was inaugurated in 1950, the Scuderia were ready – although not for the first round of the championship, the British GP, where an argument over appearance fees kept the Scuderia away. Ferrari's willingness to play hardball with race and championship organisers would be a constant of the team's racing participation over the following decades, the tone set from the top. Enzo Ferrari was never willing to take another's lead or be told what to do, let alone what his team's presence might be worth.

At the next Grand Prix, in Monaco, Scuderia Ferrari were on the grid, but a year would pass until the first F1 win, for José Froilán González, at the British GP. The rotund Argentinian, nicknamed 'The Pampas Bull', finished more than 50 seconds ahead of compatriot Juan Manuel Fangio, driving for Alfa Romeo. In Brock Yates' *Ferrari – The Man. The Machines* (2019), Enzo recalled: 'I cried for joy. But my tears of enthusiasm were mixed with those of sorrow because I thought today I have killed my mother.' Twelve years after his acrimonious split with Alfa, Ferrari's emotions towards his former employer remained conflicted.

Ferrari and Alberto Ascari battled Alfa Romeo and Fangio throughout '51, losing out at the final round in Spain, but through 1952–53, after Alfa's competition withdrawal, they dominated with the Tipo 500. Ascari's titles were the first for a Ferrari driver and in both years the team would easily have won a Constructors' Championship, had it been awarded. Fangio became the second Ferrari World Champion in 1956, followed by Mike Hawthorn in 1958, although a constructors' title did not come until 1961. In the ensuing decades, Ferrari continued to amass race wins and world titles: to date, 243 Grand Prix victories, 16 Constructors' Championships and 15 drivers' titles.

Sportscar success ran in tandem to the F1 accolades: 10 Le Mans wins stand alongside countless victories in every major endurance racing championship. All the while, Ferrari road cars were being manufactured, the profits from which were channelled to racing, Enzo's true passion. Central to the sporting achievements was Ferrari's conviction that the car, and in particular its engine, was the foundation of success. Grimly aware of the dangers of motor racing, having witnessed the deaths of many friends and rivals in competition, Enzo found it more comfortable to focus on mechanical certainties, rather than the vagaries of human emotion.

Accordingly, he prevented himself from becoming close to drivers; Gilles Villeneuve, with whom he developed an almost paternal bond, was a rare exception. Legend has it that when Eugenio Castellotti was killed during a private test of the Tipo 801 in 1957, Ferrari's first response after being told of the fatality was to enquire about the car. Later that year, during the Mille Miglia road race, Alfonso de Portago lost control of his Ferrari 335 at around 175mph, following a tyre blowout. Portago was killed in the accident, along with co-driver Edmund Nelson and 10 spectators. At no point did Ferrari consider altering his life's path. It is no coincidence that he entitled his memoirs *Le Mie Gioie Terribili* (1962) – My Terrible Joys.

The Scuderia's competitiveness ebbed and flowed, decade by decade, though with two sustained periods of excellence. In the mid-70s, with Niki Lauda as lead driver and Luca di Montezemolo as sporting director, Ferrari held an advantage over the cluster of fleet-footed British teams vying for top spot. Twenty-five years later, in the Michael Schumacher–Jean Todt era, Ferrari established a level of domination never previously seen in F1.

Enzo Ferrari had long passed by the time this generation were carrying the torch – he died in 1988 aged 90. Just under a month later his beloved scarlet cars finished 1–2 in the Italian GP at Monza, taking the only non-McLaren win of the season. His had been an extraordinary life, driven by an unquenchable passion for red racing cars. A self-described 'agitator of men', who loved to pitch rival drivers against each other, Enzo Ferrari could be an uncomfortable acquaintance, an unforgiving master. Nonetheless, his legacy is the most bewitching racing team the world has ever known.

# ALFRED NEUBAUER

**THE MERCEDES FORMULA ONE TEAM OF** 1954–55 was so far ahead of their rivals, they competed almost in a league of their own. Armed with the immaculate W196, shimmering in silver and leagues ahead of the opposition in both ambition and execution, they achieved nine wins from 12 starts across those two seasons.

Just as significant as the technical advantage was the professionalism brought to team operations by the perfectionist rigour of team manager Alfred Neubauer. He was prototypical in the role, having created the template for it while running Mercedes' pre-war Grand Prix efforts, commanding superstars of the day Rudolf Caracciola, Dick Seaman, Manfred von Brauchitsch and Hermann Lang. Neubauer was steeped in the culture of the early 20th-century German auto industry, working with armoured vehicles during World War I and becoming acquainted with Ferdinand Porsche, who employed Neubauer when the war ended. After a move to Daimler-Benz, he rose through the ranks, creating for himself the role of 'racing manager'.

A burly Austro-Hungarian, Neubauer drank as hard as he ate and was variously described as a taskmaster, domineering and overbearing – all attributes ideal for his chosen position, the more so in a carefree time that pre-dated computer-age organisational optimisation. But Neubauer was more than a crude disciplinarian. He was gregarious, fun-loving and possessed a feel for racing and drivers' needs. As early as 1926, he pioneered a system of signalling with flags and pit-boards to inform drivers of their position in a race. His method, simple and effective, was a forerunner of the pit-to-car radio communication now ubiquitous.

The exploits of the pre-war Silver Arrows, Mercedes versus Auto Union, loom large in motorsport lore, but it is for his leadership of Mercedes' racing division in the 1950s that Neubauer is best remembered. In his 1960 autobiography *Speed was my Life* (*Manner, Frauen und Motoren* in the German original), he writes passionately about Mercedes' motorsport return in the '50s: 'I'm never likely to forget May 2nd, 1952, the day my second youth began, the day Mercedes-Benz returned to motor racing for the first time since 1939. I was in my element again. Organising, planning, juggling with schedules and stop-watches, keeping the mechanics on their toes and never letting my three protegés [Caracciola, Lang and Karl Kling] out of my sight.'

He was also a leader capable of inspiring great affection, with particular fondness and respect for drivers, possibly because his own early endeavours in the cockpit had forced him to acknowledge his limitations as a sportsman. Stirling Moss, quoted in *Motorsport* magazine in 1999, recalled Neubauer with particular affection as 'a sympathetic, but hard-faced man'.

'He was very strict, but he had a wonderful sense of humour,' Moss added. 'I think he really loved his drivers and took great care of them. His attention to detail was fantastic. Before I signed for Mercedes, they invited me for a test drive at Hockenheim. After a good session in the W196 I came in with a lot of dirt on my face – brake dust which had been blown into the cockpit from the inboard front drums. I was greeted by a mechanic in pristine white overalls with a towel over one arm, offering me a bowl of hot water and a bar of soap!'

Neubauer's organisational zeal was allied to vigorous defence of Mercedes' corner in political disputes of the day and deft manoeuvring in the driver market: when trying to entice Fangio to spearhead Mercedes' Grand Prix return, he used guile as well as Deutschmarks to influence the champion's thinking. At a non-F1 race weekend in Germany during 1953, Neubauer secured Fangio a coveted suite in a local hotel, also enlisting the Mercedes team doctor to help treat the conjunctivitis with which Fangio had been afflicted. Following the race, Neubauer found Fangio stranded at the roadside alongside his broken-down Alfa Romeo. He was able to offer Mercedes' factory services to repair Fangio's car and loan a German machine as a replacement for Fangio's stricken Italian auto. 'The upshot of all this,' wrote Neubauer, 'was that Fangio gained enough confidence in me and Mercedes to sign on the dotted line'.

He was far from starry-eyed about drivers, however, and would bring them into line if he felt their actions were not in the team's best interest. In 1955, Moss became one of many forced to yield to his boss's authority. Neubauer had become concerned at Moss's insistence on following Fangio so closely in races that the slightest error by either driver could have brought disaster for both. Moss's reasoning was that only by running in Fangio's wheel-tracks could he hope to learn from the master. Neubauer countered: '"But I always thought you considered yourself a better driver than Fangio. In that case you've got nothing to learn from him." Moss flushed to the roots of his hair and turned away. But from that moment on he stopped shadowing Fangio.'

Mercedes' Formula One success in the mid-1950s was consummate until a notorious accident at Le Mans in 1955 brought their motorsport activities to a shuddering halt. Pierre Levegh, racing in Mercedes' parallel sportscar programme, crashed fatally in a catastrophic accident that killed 83 spectators. The disaster prompted Mercedes' withdrawal from motorsport, remaining absent as a 'works' F1 team until 2010.

Neubauer's time at the helm of one of the sport's great racing organisations was curtailed sooner than he would have wished, though the pursuit of perfection evident in Mercedes' modern Formula One activities owes a debt to Neubauer's earlier ambition. As Moss observed in 1959, 'It is hard for me to believe he has retired. I am sure his strong personality still pervades the racing department as it did for so many years'.

R75

# COLIN CHAPMAN

**IF A FORMULA ONE TEAM CAN POSSESS** sex appeal, then Colin Chapman's Lotus had it. The cars conceived by his fizzing, electrified, engineering mind were original, daring, brilliant, disastrous, dangerous... sometimes all of these things. But they were never ordinary. Never like anything else.

Chapman, born in 1928, was steeped in the giddy experimental energy of the post-war British aircraft industry, having studied engineering and briefly joined the Royal Air Force, before being lured by the nascent British motor-racing scene of the late 1940s. Early tinkering focused on modifying road cars with high-efficiency cylinder-head designs and enhanced suspension. Soon enough he was designing his own machines, having founded Lotus Cars, always with the mantra of 'adding lightness'. This signature philosophy often gave Lotus a competitive advantage, while rendering the cars fragile and prone to mechanical failure.

A keen racer who made it to the fringes of Formula One in the '50s (though without actually starting a race), Chapman had an unerring, instinctive feel for what a driver wanted from a racing car, namely responsiveness, balance, accuracy and precision. Through the '60s and '70s, the best Lotus F1 cars gained their advantage from chassis designs that achieved higher cornering speeds. This was as true of the Lotus 25, which pioneered monocoque construction in 1962 and carried Jim Clark to an apparently effortless 1963 world title, as it was of the Lotus 79, the first fully fledged ground-effect F1 car that eased Mario Andretti to the 1978 world title, with teammate Ronnie Peterson in his wheel-tracks.

The Chapman approach stood in marked contrast to that of Ferrari (or, much later, Renault, Honda, BMW and Mercedes), who believed that more power (engines) was the route to success. Chapman's riposte? A more powerful car might be faster in a straight line, but a lighter, more efficient, nimbler car would be faster everywhere. Validation of Chapman's approach came first with the Lotus 25, then with its successor the Lotus 33, both of which conveyed Clark to world titles. Along the way, Clark swept to victory at the 1965 Indy 500 in a Lotus 38, a cousin of the 33. The win was the first for a rear-engined car and precipitated technical change in US oval racing, much as the 25 and 33 had altered F1's course.

Two years later, working with his chief désigner Maurice Phillipe, Chapman hit another home run with the Lotus 49. This dramatic, initially unruly machine had been designed around the new Ford-Cosworth 3.0-litre V8 engine and the combination of Lotus chassis excellence with a genre-defining motor changed the game. Nothing came close to the 49 for sheer speed and it remained a race winner until 1970, adopting the colours of tobacco sponsor Gold Leaf along the way – another Chapman innovation.

The 49 should have been the car that carried Clark to a third and perhaps a fourth world title, but he was killed, driving for Lotus, in a 1968 Formula Two race at Germany's Hockenheim circuit. His teammate Graham Hill became that year's World Champion, as Lotus won their third teams' title. Chapman's passion for flying and aircraft engineering became manifest as the 49 was modified with aerodynamic wings during its lifetime. During 1969, the 49B cars of Hill and Jochen Rindt were equipped with aerofoils mounted on tall struts more than a metre above the main chassis, where they produced downforce in exactly the opposite manner to the lift produced by an aircraft wing. The innovation was effective, but deadly. When both Lotuses crashed out of the '69 Spanish GP after strut failures, Rindt wrote furiously to Chapman, urging him to make his cars a little stronger, heavier and safer.

Rindt's protestations were prophetic. At the Italian GP the next season, driving another of Chapman's radical designs, the Lotus 72, he was killed in an accident resulting from the apparent failure of a brake component. Despite the tragedy, the 72 went on to become an iconic F1 Lotus, winning over five seasons thanks to continual refinement and innovations, such as side-mounted radiators, which soon became universal.

The hyperactivity of Chapman's mind was the spark of genius that fired his team's brilliant creations through the '60s and '70s, but which also made him infuriating to work with. In an interview with *Motorsport* magazine, leading engineer Tony Southgate, who worked at Lotus in the mid-1970s, recalled: 'He was a great one for whizzing in, whizzing round the factory, and whizzing out again. I used to call him "The White Tornado" on account of his hair. He was a very impressive bloke – but you always had to be on your guard, it was a total madhouse.'

The proximity of madness and genius brought despair alongside joy. Seeking a successor for the 72, Lotus conceived the lamented 76, yet its inadequacies led Chapman and his engineering team, including the eminent Peter Wright, to embrace the unproven field of ground-effect aerodynamics in the Lotus 78 and 79. The results were sensational: Mario Andretti and Lotus recorded a title double in 1978 and ground-effect designs ruled F1 until they were banned at the end of 1982. Ground-effect was Lotus' last great F1 innovation and the team spent several seasons in the doldrums after the high of '78. Chapman's energies were by now divided between racing, Lotus' road car division and his involvement in the notorious DeLorean sports car scandal; little wonder the race team lost its edge.

When Chapman died of a heart attack in 1982, aged 54, rumours swirled that his demise had been faked to escape financial calamity, that he had somehow disappeared before being framed. True believers cared little for such conjecture; they had seen F1 legend being written by the greatest drivers at the wheel of Lotus cars. There had never been a race team like this. After Chapman's death, there never would be again.

# BERNIE ECCLESTONE

**FOR THE BEST PART OF 40 YEARS FROM** the early 1980s, Bernie Ecclestone held Formula One in the palm of his hand. As controller of the sport's commercial interests, its deal-maker-in-chief, and the man who spotted the potential to turn Grand Prix racing into a global sporting phenomenon, he ruled F1's empire from his HQ at 6 Princes Gate, London. His famously lean Formula One Management (FOM) operation was central to all of the sport's global commercial dealings, controlling aspects such as sponsorship, track signage, hospitality arrangements, TV deals, circuit negotiations, prize money, and paddock access.

Ecclestone and FOM did not do this alone, of course. One of the keys to Ecclestone's success over many decades was his ability to manipulate other key stakeholders such as governing body FIA (with whose president Max Mosley he enjoyed a near-telepathic relationship), team principals, major car manufacturers, country presidents (step forward Vladimir Putin) and billionaire entrepreneurs, such as Dietrich Mateschitz. To all these suitors he was able to sell the allure of Formula One as something impossibly glamorous and desirable. It could be a platform via which a luxury brand might burnish its profile, or where an automaker might demonstrate sportiness and technical leadership. A state or kingdom such as Singapore or Bahrain might wish to use Formula One as a means of positioning itself on the world stage; others, maybe Russia or Saudi Arabia, might desire a softening of the image. Ecclestone could always be amenable, so long as the price was right.

Understanding the value of an asset was a skill Ecclestone had learned early as a post-war dealer in the motorcycle and car trade. It was said he could walk into any showroom, take a glance, and calculate the value of the hardware on show almost instantly and with unerring accuracy. That acumen, combined with a native understanding of his customers' desires, placed him at a competitive advantage in all his dealings. He was uniquely positioned to understand the value of what he controlled and what a prospective buyer might be willing to pay for a slice of it. Special partners – the Monaco Grand Prix, Ferrari, one or two teams of long standing – were always given a preferential deal by Ecclestone. Newcomers would be expected to pay top dollar.

Ecclestone's rise from modest beginnings as a trawlerman's son is one of the great tales of self-made success. Having amassed income through his motor trade and property dealings, he was on the fringes of Formula One by the late 1950s, as an occasional competitor and the manager of Stuart Lewis-Evans, a promising young British driver who twice finished on the podium with Vanwall in 1958. Lewis-Evans' death, after being badly burned at the '58 Moroccan GP, led to Ecclestone's withdrawal from the racing scene for a number of years, before re-emerging a decade later as manager of Formula Two's hot-shot Jochen Rindt.

By 1970, Rindt was a Formula One superstar, heading for the world title with Lotus. His death during practice for the Italian GP wasn't enough to prevent him from winning the title posthumously. Ecclestone was by now embedded in F1 and in 1971 he bought the Brabham F1 team, which he set about transforming into an ultra-slick operation from its base on the outskirts of South West London. Like many entrepreneurs, Ecclestone had a sharp eye for talent and promoted a young Gordon Murray to become chief designer, allowing his creativity free rein, while running elite drivers including Carlos Reutemann, Niki Lauda and Nelson Piquet. As team principal, Ecclestone showed an unyielding perfectionist streak, once reputedly ripping a telephone from a factory wall because its untidily hanging cable offended his eye.

It was with Piquet that Ecclestone-era Brabham truly flourished in the early '80s, Nelson winning close-fought titles in 1981 and 1983 and establishing himself briefly as the sport's number-one driver.

Peak Piquet coincided, however, with Ecclestone's growing interest in what he had identified as F1's untapped commercial potential. As a key player in the Formula One Constructors' Association (FOCA), a body comprised mostly of the UK-based F1 teams, he eventually secured the right to negotiate the sport's global TV deals. This was the power-play that propelled Ecclestone from being wealthy and influential to the position of near-absolute control over F1, exercised through FOM, that he enjoyed through to the late 2010s. Having sold Brabham in 1988, Ecclestone focused solely on F1 commercial activities, driving the sport through a period of unprecedented growth to the point where it could command global prime-time audiences measured in the multi-millions and charge race-hosting fees of $50m or more.

Ecclestone's gift for playing one party against the other, while maintaining a carefully cultivated aura of menace-laced mystique, made him a billionaire many times over and virtually untouchable as 'Mr Formula One' until well into his eighties. Often overlooked was the deadpan twinkle he brought to his dealings, as he ran rings around slower-witted opponents. (Once questioned how many people worked for FOM, he quipped: 'About half of them'.)

Purists objected to some of Ecclestone's methods, for example his embrace of lucrative state-backed new circuits, while beating up on relatively impoverished venues such as Silverstone (in 2002, he described the British Grand Prix as 'a country fair masquerading as a world-class event'). So long as the dollars kept rolling in, however, few insiders voiced serious complaint, despite the many and varied controversies in which Ecclestone became embroiled. Even a reign so imperious eventually had to end: Ecclestone's demise came as Liberty Media bought a controlling interest in the Formula One Group in 2017, ousting him as CEO.

Under American ownership, F1 has continued to boom, and despite throwing the occasional hand grenade from a position of enforced retirement, Ecclestone has kept his opinions about the sport's less elitist new direction largely to himself. From his lofty perspective, he is doubtless content that no single individual has had – or ever will have – a greater influence on Formula One.

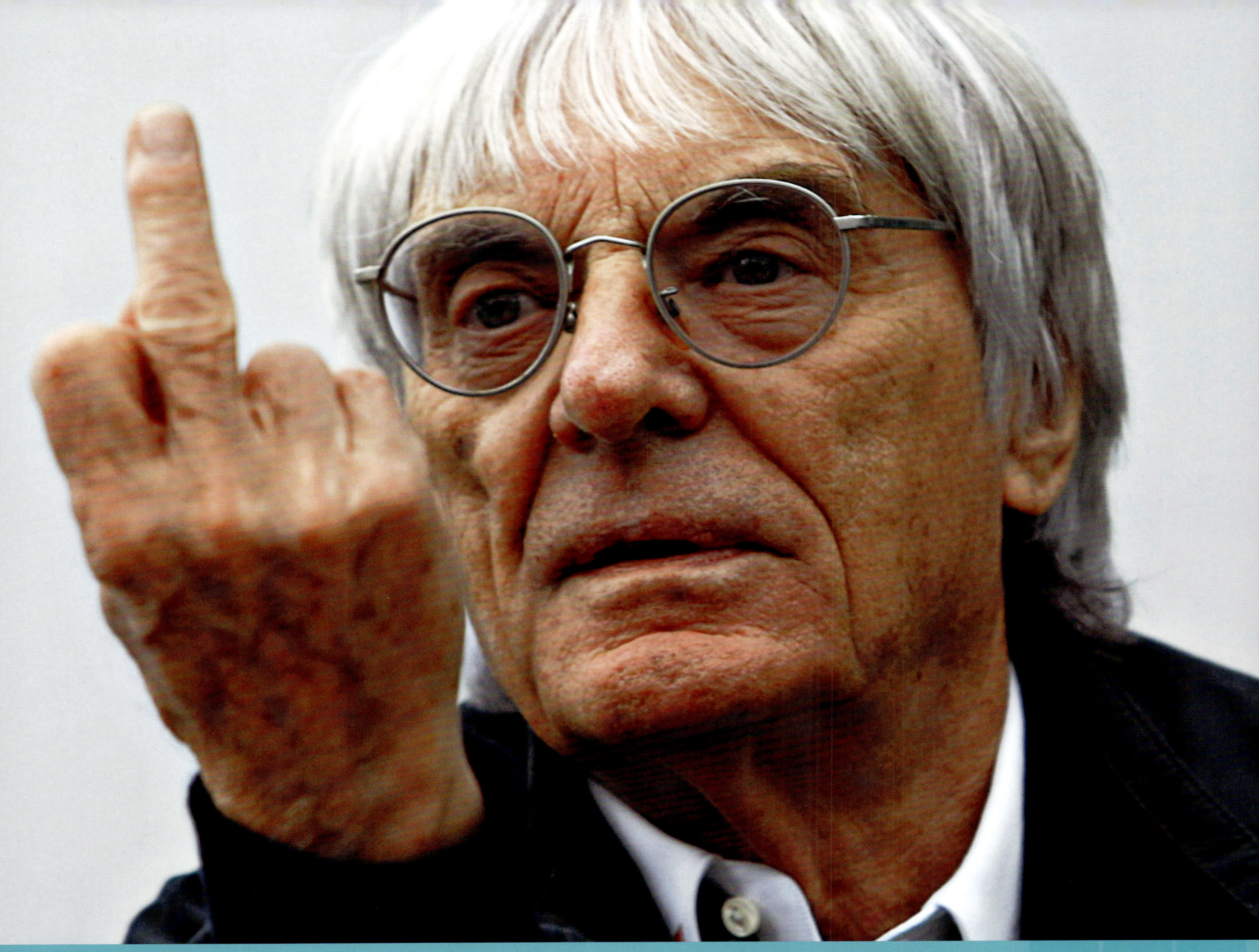

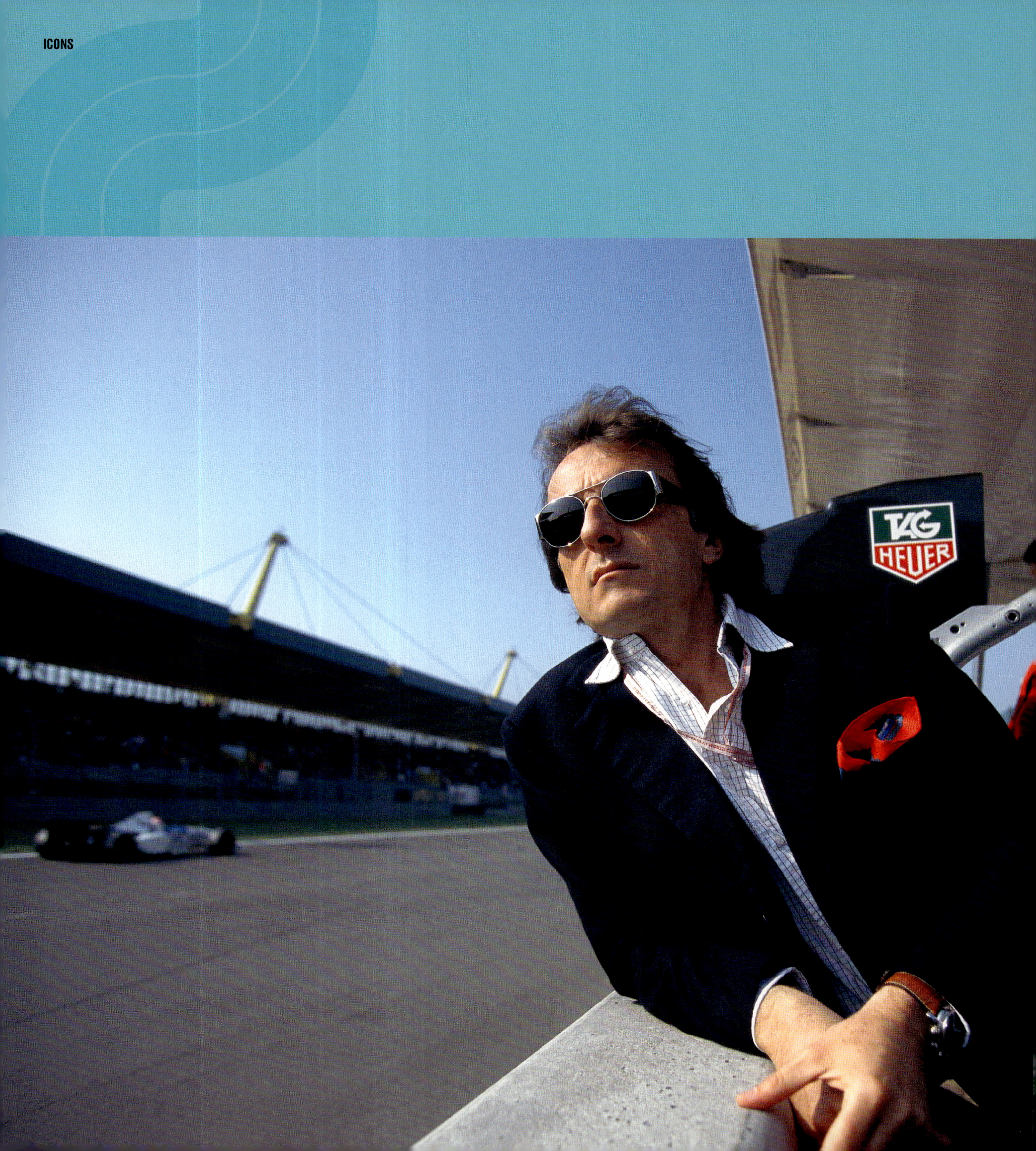
TAG
HEUER

# LUCA CORDERO DI MONTEZEMOLO

**THE ITALIAN GRAND PRIX AT MONZA** possesses an atmosphere like no other. There are fans, there are ghosts, there is late-summer sun hazing through the treetops of the wooded parkland near Milan, in which the Autodromo is located. The source of this febrile mood is, of course, Ferrari, the team whose scarlet presence through 75 years of Formula One has contributed beyond measure to the sport's allure. Ferrari happenings matter and over any Italian GP weekend, rumour upon rumour swirls around the Scuderia, never more so than when Luca di Montezemolo is in town.

This is the man who saved Ferrari – not once, but twice – and who is therefore feted in his homeland only marginally less than the Pope. Before his departure as Ferrari chairman in 2014, Montezemolo's arrival at the Grand Prix, invariably Monza in latter years, would make media fizz with expectation that the great man might express words of significance. Whether or not his words merited such accord was moot. Luca Cordero di Montezemolo had spoken. Axiomatically his utterances were of the utmost importance.

To understand why he enjoyed – and still enjoys – such exalted stature in Italy, the clock must be rewound to the early 1970s when Ferrari were at a low competitive ebb in Formula One. In 1973, they managed not a single Grand Prix victory, nor even a podium finish, and slumped to a flaccid sixth in the constructors' table, scoring 12 points. Champions Lotus scored 92. Something had to change, so Enzo Ferrari took a gamble. He had become aware of a young rally driver, reputedly of aristocratic lineage, called Montezemolo, who had mounted a spiky defence of motorsport's worth during a live-audience TV show. Impressed by the youngster's pluck, Ferrari tracked him down and offered Luca a job as his personal assistant. Within months Montezemolo, barely out of law school, had been promoted to manage the F1 team, aged only 26, allowing Enzo to escape what he described as 'the prison of engineers'.

This was no position for a wallflower. Within Ferrari, the F1 team manager's role was among the most coveted, offering huge opportunity but also the risk of career calamity. It was Montezemolo's good fortune to be righting the ship at a moment when two other stars were also seeking to make their mark. One was the tyro Niki Lauda who had joined Ferrari after a disappointing 1973 with BRM, scoring only two points. The other was Ferrari's technical savant, Mauro Forghieri, who was acutely aware of the need for a return to front-line car performance.

In their own departments, each went about setting higher standards: Montezemolo for team management, having restructured race operations; Lauda, who formed a formidable driver pairing with Clay Regazzoni, and Forghieri on the technical front, delivering the 312B3-74, which became a race winner and vaulted Ferrari to second in the constructors' table. The turnaround was dramatic and even better days lay ahead. For '75, Forghieri penned the 312T, his masterpiece. An increasingly assured Lauda steered it to the drivers' title, his championship being confirmed at Monza, where Regazzoni won the race. After an almost impossibly perfect day, on which a Ferrari World Champion was crowned for the first time since 1964, even the Old Man was reduced to tears. Montezemolo recalls hearing the voice of his boss cracking with emotion on the other end of a phone line when they spoke post-race. Ferrari repeated their championship success in '76 and Lauda would likely have won a second drivers' title without his fiery, near-fatal accident at the Nürburgring. Another title double came in '77.

Having overseen such a heady return to form, Montezemolo's place in the Ferrari firmament, and the wider Italian business community, was assured. Numerous prestigious roles followed, including his stewardship of the committee organising Italy's hosting of the 1990 football world cup.

He was lured back to Ferrari in 1991, three years after Enzo's death, this time with a brief to return lustre to both racing and road car activities. Much as Ferrari had once entrusted his beloved race team to Montezemolo, so Montezemolo hired a thrusting young Jean Todt to lead the Scuderia back to World Championship success. The 1990s turnaround was a little longer in coming than the 1970s chapter, but once the likes of Michael Schumacher, Ross Brawn and Rory Byrne had been hired, success began to flow until it reached a torrent from 2000 to 2004. During this period Schumacher and Ferrari were unstoppable as they romped to five consecutive title doubles.

Montezemolo's role in racing was not hands-on during this period – he delegated those duties to his exceptionally able lieutenants – but he remained intimately involved in wider F1 political dealings, fighting as hard as he ever had for Ferrari's interests. His exit in 2014, after board-level power struggles, was unseemly for a man of powerful charisma and with high regard for orderly presentation. Nonetheless, Montezemolo's position as the most significant figure in Ferrari's history, after Enzo Ferrari himself, is beyond reasonable argument.

**HE WAS THE RACER'S RACER. A MAN SO IN** love with Formula One that even a broken neck suffered in a 1986 road accident, which left him quadriplegic, couldn't slow him down. Frank Williams, whose legendary F1 team still bears his name, was enraptured by the sport from first to last: 'first' being days spent marooned in a Scottish boarding school reading copies of *Autocar* and *The Motor*; 'last' being his death in 2021, having overseen the growth of Williams from a two-bit customer team entering hand-me-down cars for drivers who could pay for the ride, to an all-conquering Grand Prix behemoth that won nine constructors' titles, 114 Grands Prix and produced seven World Champions. And counting. Hard to imagine, on the far side of that victory roster, that Frank was once derided as 'wanker Williams', so impoverished were his racing endeavours. 'Sir Frank Williams', as he became in 1999, was altogether more respectful.

Williams' first forays on to the racetrack began in 1959, after scraping together £400 to buy an Austin A35, fitted with A40 parts to increase performance. He entered saloon car races and began making racing friends, one of whom – the unrelated Jonathan Williams – invited Frank to support his European racing campaign. There would be no salary, just food and tented accommodation, but this was the break, the portal to the magical world of continental motorsport that Williams so craved. Frank had a natural talent for languages, his skills in French, German and Italian helping him to barter and trade his way across Europe, incrementally amassing enough resources to fund an entry into the 1969 F1 World Championship.

Ever canny, Williams had come across a Brabham BT26 in identical spec to those raced by the works F1 team, being used for hill-climb events. £5,000 and a dab of FW charm later, the owner had parted with the chassis and Frank was ready to go racing with the talented brewing heir Piers Courage at the wheel. Their first season together brought unimaginable success for a team owner who thus far had survived on little more than his wits: from 10 starts, Courage twice finished second and twice fifth. High times indeed, but a desperate low was to follow. Five races into the 1970 F1 season, Courage was killed in an accident at the Dutch GP. The loss was keenly felt throughout the F1 fraternity, but Williams admitted in a 2015 interview with the FIA's *AUTO* magazine that he never considered quitting. 'I was deep in it, in every sense of the word. I had to keep going. I suppose I was born with a certain dollop of irresponsibility and in those days it was easier. And I was always... what's the word... "optimistic" about the future, so I thought I would stick at it a bit longer.'

Frank Williams Racing Cars scraped through the early to mid-1970s, before Frank eventually sold a majority stake in the team to Canadian oil baron Walter Wolf. This appeared to be the end of Williams as a Formula One entrant, but Frank was several steps ahead. He had already engaged the services of a gifted, determined engineer named Patrick Head and they went racing as Williams Grand Prix Engineering in 1977, using an off-the-shelf March chassis.

Behind the scenes, Head was busy designing the FW06, a neat and elegant car with which Williams would enter the 1978 Championship as a constructor for the first time. The FW06 drew many admiring glances and established a platform on which Head could develop the FW07. A rigorously engineered masterpiece, the FW07 finally made Williams a winner at the 1979 British GP and continued as a Grand Prix-winning car through to 1981.

With the FW07 and combative Australian lead driver Alan Jones, Williams were transformed from also-rans to title contenders almost overnight. Jones was 1980 World Champion; Williams won back-to-back constructors' titles in 1980–81. 'Patrick did a fantastic job for himself and for Formula One and for Williams,' Williams told *AUTO* magazine. 'I mean, he made the company, not me. I was pretty handy at finding the dosh – but on the back of his success and beautiful cars.'

After the early 1980s breakthrough, Williams were a force throughout the decade. Their partnership with Honda from 1984 to 1987 produced era-defining turbo cars, the FW11 and 11B, in which drivers Nelson Piquet and Nigel Mansell competed no holds barred. Williams' mantra that teammates should always be allowed to race each other further endeared the team to a growing legion of fans.

It was during this period that Williams suffered the accident that might have killed him, on the eve of the 1986 season, while returning from a testing session at the Paul Ricard circuit in France. He recalled: 'I remember [team manager] Peter Windsor, who was in the car with me, saying, two minutes earlier: "Frank do you always drive like this?" We were late for the plane. And he was actually saying in a nice way: "For fuck's sake, slow down", which I didn't, and I lost it and went off and we ended upside-down in a ditch, car on its roof, with my head supporting the roof.'

The team built by Frank survived the incapacity of their talismanic leader and adapted to his altered, wheelchair-bound presence at team HQ and at races. Rarely did he speak about the life-changing accident; never did he let it stand in the way of his ambition for Williams. 'It will only make him more dangerous, with fewer distractions,' noted arch-rival Ron Dennis, head of the McLaren team, soon after the accident – and he was right.

Williams were the team to beat for much of the 1990s, having formed a harmonious engine partnership with Renault and recruited the brilliant young aerodynamicist Adrian Newey. The team won serial world titles in the 1990s, while also enduring the loss of Ayrton Senna in one of their cars. Williams last won championships in 1997, since when competitiveness has ebbed and flowed, even as the approach to racing and stubborn independence have endured. Under new ownership, the Williams name remains proudly above the door and on the F1 entry list. Their founder and number-one fan will surely be looking on, eternally 'optimistic' for the future.

CHAMPION
SIMPSON
WILLIAMS
GRAND PRIX
ENGINEERING

NACIONAL
RHEOS
BOSS
MEN'S FASHION

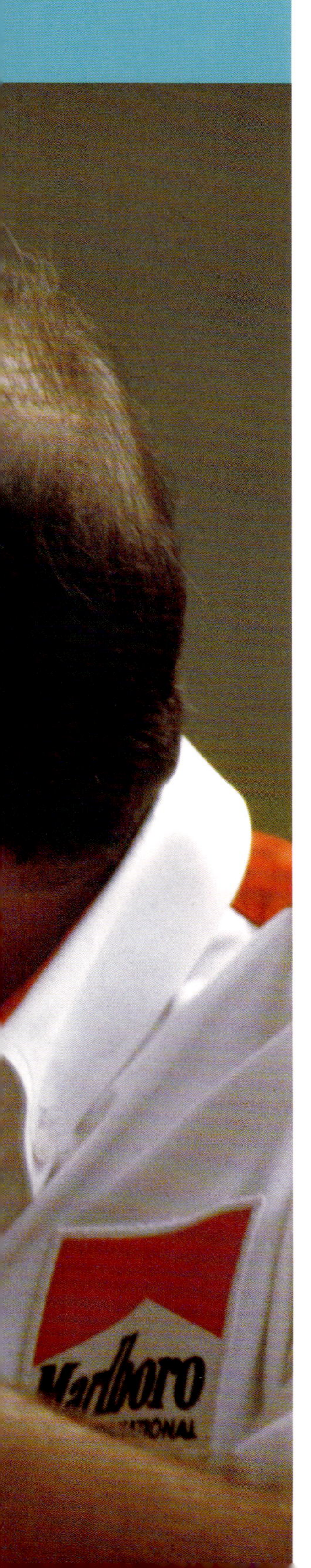

# RON DENNIS

**IN THE EARLY 1980S, RON DENNIS,** as the boss of McLaren International, rewrote the Formula One team playbook. A product of the vibrant 1960s British motor-racing scene, learning his trade as a mechanic to the likes of Jochen Rindt and Jack Brabham, Dennis was a successful Formula Two team owner by the mid-1970s, his sights fixed on F1.

The arcs of his own burgeoning Project Four race squad and the waning McLaren F1 team intersected in 1980, when he became part of McLaren's management structure with the backing of sponsor Marlboro, before assuming full control in 1981. By then, Dennis had already prised the highly rated engineer John Barnard from a successful US racing career to spearhead the design of a new generation of McLaren F1 car. Barnard's resulting MP4-1 successfully pioneered the use of carbon-fibre as the primary chassis material, prompting a revolution in F1 construction that remains in place to this day. The car was a Grand Prix winner in its first season, and its success, along with the enhanced crash protection offered by carbon-fibre build, encouraged Niki Lauda out of retirement to partner John Watson for 1982. Together, they helped McLaren to a close second in the Constructors' Championship; only two seasons earlier the team had languished near the bottom of the table.

The Ron Dennis effect was impossible to ignore: bold recruitment of top talent, commercial acumen, a ferocious will to win and his driven, perfectionist streak had quickly remade McLaren the title contenders they had been in the mid-1970s. Very soon they would be the team to beat.

By 1982, turbocharged engines were beginning to supersede the previously dominant 3.0-litre non-turbocharged motors. In 1982, Ferrari were the first team to win a constructors' title with a turbo engine; a year later Nelson Piquet became World Champion in a BMW turbo-powered Brabham. Sensing the sea-change, Dennis convinced Porsche to design and build a custom V6 turbo engine, tailored to Barnard's exacting packaging requirements. The project was funded by the TAG group, owned by French–Saudi businessman Mansour Ojjeh, who would become a long-term McLaren investor.

The first TAG turbo McLarens ran at the end of '83 and by 1984, with Alain Prost recruited to join Lauda, this prototype Dennis F1 superteam was set to dominate. McLaren's rivals were not ready for the onslaught of obsessively assembled firepower that Dennis unleased that year. The MP4-2 chassis was an early Barnard masterpiece; the TAG-Porsche V6 offered power, reliability, fuel efficiency and the lean dimensions insisted upon by Barnard to help optimise aerodynamic efficiency. Lauda and Prost, meanwhile, were as strong a duo as had ever been paired in F1. Little surprise McLaren annihilated the opposition, logging 143.5 points – more than the combined total of Ferrari, Lotus and Brabham in second, third and fourth. Lauda edged his third and final title by just half a point from Prost, who went on to win consecutive drivers' titles in 1985 and '86.

Williams, with Honda engines, eclipsed McLaren in '87 but for '88, Dennis once again demonstrated his ruthless genius by snatching Ayrton Senna from Lotus and Honda from Williams, to join design ace Gordon Murray, poached from Brabham. With Prost still in place, a formidable McLaren arsenal crushed all rivals, winning 15 out of 16 races to set a standard arguably not matched to this day. Dennis-led McLaren had changed the game and they continued to set the standard as the '80s became '90s, with a run of four consecutive driver-team title doubles through to 1991.

The team Dennis had built was reckoned by outsiders to be austere, too corporate, though that perception was at odds with the experience of staffers who became fiercely loyal to the organisation and spoke of a deep camaraderie. The team's image was shaped to a considerable extent by the character of Dennis himself. A complex man of exceptional intelligence and ambition, some found him hard to warm to. Yet Dennis' emotional waters ran deep. He would speak of the 'actual pain' he felt at losing and was capable of great generosity and outbursts of unexpected humour. Motor racing was not a casual enterprise for Dennis: the sport was burned into his soul. McLaren's method and accomplishments were the manifestation of Dennis' demands.

After the peaks of the Senna–Prost years, McLaren's success tapered in the mid-1990s, as the team sought an engine partner to replace Honda. Mercedes proved to be the answer, starting a partnership in 1995 that endured to 2014. Through this period, McLaren became champions again in 1998 and won drivers' titles with Mika Häkkinen (1998–99) and Dennis' prodigy Lewis Hamilton (2008). Mercedes investment was also instrumental in the building of McLaren's dazzling HQ, the McLaren Technology Centre, opened in 2004. Dennis became a figure of increasing eminence and power throughout this time, as McLaren attracted the cream of driving and technical talent to its glittering doors.

There was also darkness, however. The 'Spygate' affair of 2007, which centred on McLaren illicitly obtaining technical designs of chief rival Ferrari, resulted in a $100m fine being issued by governing body FIA, and the team stripped of 218 constructors' points – enough to have won the constructors' title.

As he approached his third decade at the helm, Dennis began to hand control to his deputy, Martin Whitmarsh, and while McLaren remained highly competitive on track in the early 2010s, they were outgunned by the financial might of Red Bull, Ferrari and Mercedes' own F1 team. Behind the scenes Dennis became locked in a struggle for control of the McLaren organisation, by now encompassing road car and advanced technology divisions, which resulted in his being ousted late in 2016 after a legal dispute.

It was a bitter exit for a man who had devoted his life to McLaren, but Dennis' legacy was the creation of a team which took Formula One into new realms of professionalism and the enduring loyalty of many who worked with him most closely.

# MAX MOSLEY

**AN IRON FIST INSIDE AN IRON GLOVE.** This was Max Mosley and Bernie Ecclestone between 1993 and 2009, with Mosley as president of motorsport governing body the FIA and Ecclestone heading Formula One's commercial operations as the head of Formula One Management (FOM). Between them, they oversaw dramatic growth in F1's global audiences and revenue, while also making transformational changes in the safety standards of a once-deadly sport. Frequently controversial, often deliberately and even mischievously so, they tag-teamed as the toff and the barrow boy to devastating effect. Woe betide those who stood in their way during more than three decades at, or near, the helm of Formula One.

Mosley's favoured modus operandi as FIA President was to use his mind as a weapon, skewering opposing positions with rigorously thought-through arguments and an edge of cruelty to those he deemed beneath him. The mental agility was learned in part through legal training as a barrister, though also gifted via a remarkable genetic inheritance: he was the son of British fascist leader Oswald Mosley and the aristocratic socialite Diana Mitford. Max was not destined to live an ordinary life.

In his twenties, he worked as a barrister, as well as engaging in varied political activities and competing as an amateur racing driver. Often dismissive in later years of his sporting efforts, Mosley rose to Formula Two and in the late '60s, shared grids with many established or future stars. The high death toll of the sport at that time framed Mosley's thinking about motorsport, however, and sparked the reformist zeal that marked his later safety crusades.

Having reached his limit as a driver, Mosley poured his energies, and some of his own cash, into establishing the racing car manufacturer, March. The team took its name from the surname initials of each of the five founders, Mosley being the 'M'. Established with huge ambition, March burst into the 1970 F1 season with considerable initial success. Jackie Stewart won the 1970 Spanish GP in a March 701 entered by Tyrrell, helping March finish third in the Constructors' Championship. The initial promise fizzled away over subsequent years, however, despite two more F1 wins, and Mosley sold his stake in the company at the end of 1977 to focus on his growing interest in the sport's political dynamics.

Since entering F1 with March, Mosley had been part of the Grand Prix Constructors' Association and, later, the Formula One Constructors' Association (FOCA). Through these bodies the relationship between Mosley and Ecclestone grew and strengthened to the point where, in the early 1980s, they were able to take on the established grandees – the FIA plus manufacturer teams including Ferrari and Renault – in a fight for overall control. The outcome of the high-stakes confrontation was a document known as the Concorde Agreement, under which F1's regulatory matters would remain with the FIA, while Ecclestone-led FOCA controlled commerce. By 1993, when Mosley was elected FIA President, having spent a decade in and out of motorsport, he and Ecclestone were effectively in complete control of F1. One presidential perk brought singular delight. Ecclestone, knowing that Mosley enjoyed a view of Big Ben from the balcony of the FIA's London office, would call his friend to ask: 'What's the time, Max?'

Moments of levity aside, Mosley's years as president were marked by a confrontational, even autocratic, style which, in Mosley's own view, was essential if he were to achieve the motorsport and road safety goals he had made it his mission to deliver. After the death of Ayrton Senna in 1994, in the wake of which the very future of motorsport was called into question, Mosley acted swiftly to cut the power and speed of Grand Prix cars, also amending circuit layouts to reduce hazard at certain corners. He cared little for the objections his actions would sometimes trigger. Mosley believed teams were incapable of acting beyond their own self-interest and that it was the duty of the governing body to act for the sport's wider benefit. His manner ruffled feathers in an arena overflowing with alpha males, not least those of McLaren team boss Ron Dennis. He and Mosley shared a mutual antipathy, which peaked during the 'Spygate' scandal of 2007. An FIA-led investigation into the affair found McLaren guilty of having illicitly obtained technical information from Ferrari, for which McLaren were fined $100m. It was said at the time that Mosley's personal dislike of Dennis was responsible at least in part for the size of the fine.

Beyond motorsport, Mosley used the broad remit of the FIA presidency to drive road safety campaigns – notably the pioneering work on automobile crash safety standards that became Euro NCAP. Adopting well-rehearsed methods from Formula One, Mosley overcame resistance from motor manufacturers objecting to the increased costs of improved safety standards, by simply refusing to countenance their arguments.

Provocation ran through Mosley's 16 years as FIA President; even in his fourth term, he revelled in baiting F1's manufacturer teams with calls for cost-capping and restrictions on engine technology. As the end of that four-year period approached, Mosley hinted he might stand once more for re-election, but a 'sting' by tabloid newspaper *News of the World*, showing Mosley engaged in compromising sexual activity, ultimately prevented him from remaining in office. Far from crushing Mosley, the newspaper roused him into a pugilistic offensive against media intrusion, in which activity he remained engaged until ill-health began to sap his strength. In May 2021, after a terminal cancer diagnosis, Mosley took his own life with a shotgun, seeking control to the last.

GTX
LAPS

FUJI-TV
Marlboro
tic tac
L'ORÉAL

**HE WOULD SIT, POISED, INTENSE, COILED** inside, ready for action, saying little, watching everything. Acutely alert, profoundly intelligent. This was Jean Todt as head of the Ferrari Formula One team during its most successful period, fielding the world's media. He was ready to defend, keen to rebut or attack a notion he found disrespectful or stupid. Formidable, pugnacious, even faintly intimidating despite his diminutive stature. Always with Todt came the sense that he would do whatever it took to serve what he perceived to be his team's best interests. As Ferrari's Formula One team boss from 1993, through to his departure in 2009 as a special adviser, having been CEO, passion for the Scuderia coursed through his veins.

He had been similarly invested in his previous role as head of Peugeot Talbot Sport, where he oversaw rallying and sportscar programmes that brought victories and titles at Le Mans, on the Paris–Dakar rally and in the World Rally Championship. Todt had been appointed at a time of financial struggle for the French manufacturer, and motorsport success was seen as a means of re-establishing credibility and driving road car sales. He brought to the role his keen intellect, relentless work ethic and a competition background as a World Championship-winning rally co-driver, blending those qualities to become a prodigiously accomplished motorsport manager.

As Todt was peaking at Peugeot in the early '90s, Ferrari were at a low ebb. They had lost technical direction and, since the acrimonious departure of Alain Prost in 1991, they had been without a recognised ace driver. Ferrari's CEO Luca Di Montezemolo, who had himself turned around a rudderless Ferrari in the mid-1970s, recognised that a similar fix was needed. He turned to Todt with the simple brief to 'make Ferrari great again'. History confirms that Montezemolo picked the right man for the job, but what he could never have anticipated was quite how successful Ferrari's F1 team would become on Todt's watch.

Todt's first major play was to poach Michael Schumacher from the Benetton team, where he had won consecutive drivers' titles in 1994–95. Having Formula One's best driver would give Ferrari the perfect benchmark, Todt reasoned. If Ferrari were slow, it would certainly not be the driver holding them back. In his first Ferrari season, 1996, Schumacher helped deliver three race wins, to finish third in the Drivers' Championship. Of greater significance, his transfer paved the way for key Benetton lieutenants to follow, notably technical director Ross Brawn and chief designer Rory Byrne. This triumvirate had been the foundation of Benetton's rise to prominence through the early 1990s and they set about replicating their winning method at Ferrari.

With Todt's blessing, Brawn sought to harmonise working relationships between Ferrari's often factional engine and chassis departments. Both he and Todt believed that Ferrari's in-house resource should be delivering far better results. By 1997, Todt's labours, and those of the team he had assembled, were starting to bear fruit. Schumacher fought for the drivers' title until the last race of the season at Spain's Jerez circuit, where his attempt to drive eventual champion Jacques Villeneuve off the track cost him a season's worth of points – though they still counted in the Constructors' Championship, allowing Ferrari to finish second.

Another second place was secured in the '98 teams' table, before Ferrari finally won the title in 1999 – their first since 1983. The wait for a drivers' title was even more prolonged: when Schumacher finally secured the 2000 crown, he became the first Ferrari World Champion since Jody Scheckter in 1979. What followed was unprecedented: Schumacher and Ferrari won title doubles through to 2004, giving a total of six consecutive championships for Ferrari, five for Schumacher.

Throughout this period, Todt was totemic as a team chief. His support for Schumacher during many on-track controversies was unwavering, his commitment to the team absolute. In a 2005 interview with *Autosport* magazine, he noted: 'Keeping the team winning is my satisfaction, making my people happy. And I do feel that the people who work at Ferrari are my people. I feel like a godfather. This is a company with a soul and with one heart. The others will never achieve that.'

Todt stayed with Ferrari for another four years, overseeing a transition from Schumacher to Kimi Räikkönen (who won the drivers' title in his first Ferrari season, 2007), while handing over many of his own team responsibilities. By March 2009, Todt had exited, having overseen Ferrari's greatest-ever period of F1 success, but he was far from finished with motorsport. Later that year, he became president of motorsport governing body the FIA, in which role he sought initially to calm the turbulent waters left behind by his more overtly political predecessor, Max Mosley. During his three terms in office, Todt oversaw the introduction of a landmark safety feature in F1 and other single-seater racing series, the halo head protection device. He was also instrumental in the foundation of the first global all-electric motorsport series, Formula E.

Less confrontational than Mosley, Todt's fixity of purpose and political nous were equally strong. In 2018 he told *F1 Racing* magazine: 'You know if you have influence, you don't need to say that you have influence – it's clear! Have you ever seen powerful people saying "I'm powerful!"? It's obvious. So, let's say I don't care about that. What I do care about is what the final achievement will be. And the final achievement will correspond to what we want.' Jean Todt's ability to get 'what he wanted' enabled him to forge a storied career in motorsport. Ferrari will be forever in his debt.

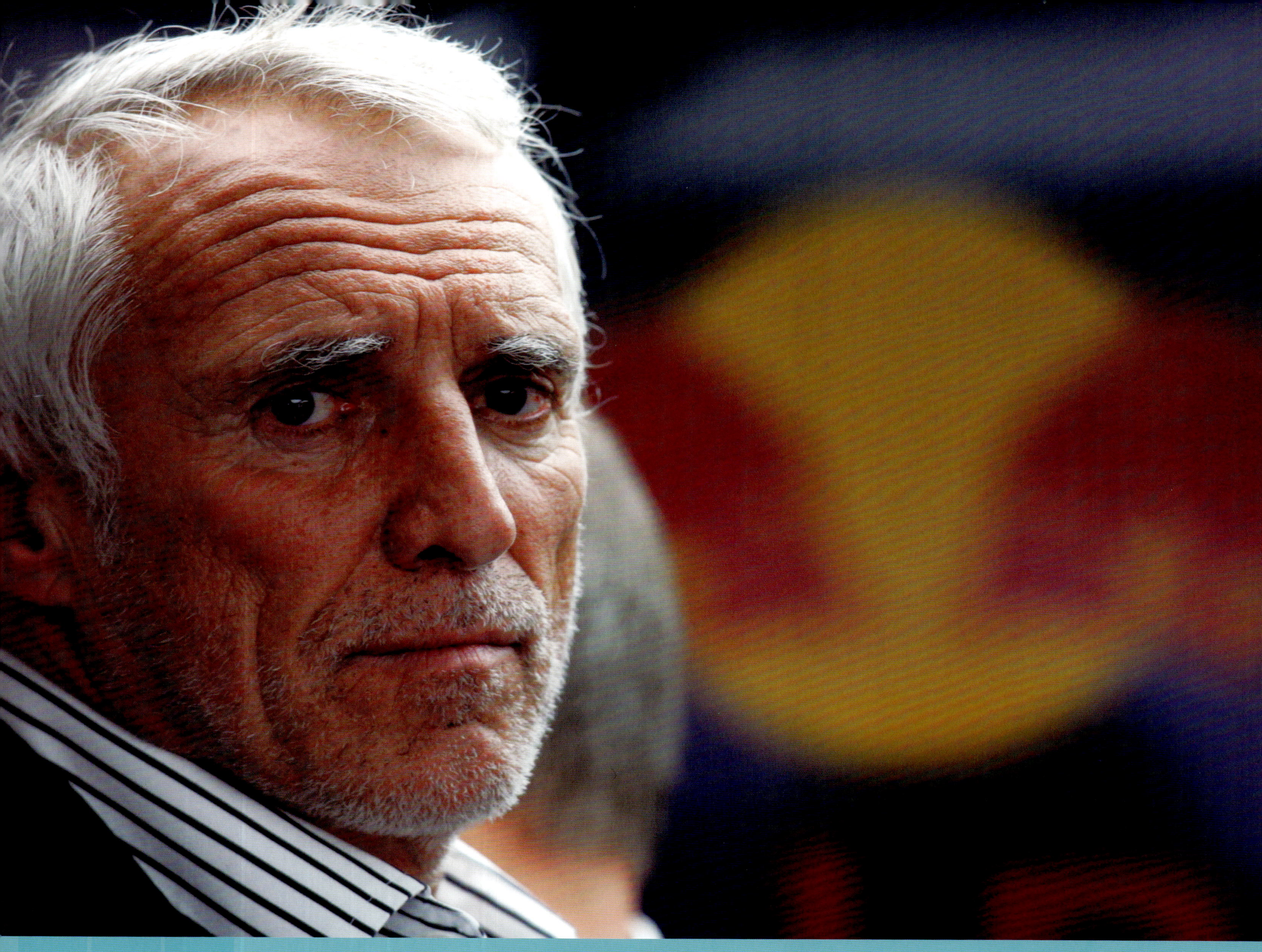

# DIETRICH MATESCHITZ

**IT IS NO SMALL IRONY THAT DIETRICH** Mateschitz, owner of Red Bull Racing – the brashest team ever to crash into Formula One – was a reclusive Austrian billionaire who preferred the mountain vistas of his homeland to the clamour and glitz of the racing paddock.

Mateschitz was a marketing savant who spotted the sales potential of a Thai energy drink, Krating Deang, during a business trip in the early 1980s and set about building the global phenomenon that would become ubiquitous as Red Bull. Armed with the 'Red Bull gives you wings' slogan, Mateschitz focused from the outset on the thrill and danger of extreme sport to promote his self-proclaimed health elixir. It was perhaps inevitable that his attention would turn to Formula One, which he regarded as 'the original extreme sport'.

His motivation was more than cold calculation: Mateschitz was a self-confessed F1 fan from a country with a proud tradition in Grand Prix racing. Long before Red Bull had become a household name, Mateschitz sponsored Austrian F1 driver Gerhard Berger in 1989, thus making Berger the first Red Bull athlete. Thousands would follow, in myriad sporting disciplines.

Little by little, Mateschitz crept from sponsorship to ownership, acquiring a majority stake in the Sauber team by the early noughties and buying outright the collapsed Jaguar Racing team at the end of 2004. Sales of his addictive, highly caffeinated product were already measured in the billions, with marketing teams driving sales, high-profile activations and athlete partnerships around the globe. Picking up an unloved F1 team for a bargain-basement price barely troubled Mateschitz's loose change.

The story of Red Bull Racing over the following two decades is one of vision, investment, transformation and a ruthless top-down commitment to victory, entirely at odds with early presentation as F1's barmy army. The packaging of a singular drive for success in a marketing artifice of fun, lifestyle and parties was the genius of Mateschitz's vision and within the team, indeed within the whole of the wider Red Bull organisation, no employee was ever in doubt that it was the Mateschitz way or the highway. As he once intoned to a gathering of Red Bull Media House staff: 'I welcome you to enjoy the Red Bull playground that I have created. But if you don't like the playground, you know where to find the exit.'

Nowhere was the fusion of business with brand more obvious – or successful – than in Formula One. Initially dismissed by F1's old guard as dilettantes with too much cash, Red Bull Racing gained instant respect by recording a double points finish on their debut at the 2005 Australian GP. After two races they had scored more points than Jaguar had managed in the entire previous season.

The cultivated 'good times' vibe remained much in evidence, thanks to innovations such as a paddock motorhome labelled 'The Energy Station' and a satirical magazine – *The Red Bulletin* – printed daily at every race, but this was a team on a mission. Mateschitz was far too astute a businessman simply to squander cash on a vanity project: he was funding this operation to win. The scale of his ambition became further apparent with the purchase of a second team, the perennial tail-enders, Minardi, at the end of 2005. Under Red Bull ownership, Minardi became Scuderia Toro Rosso, with a brief to finesse promising young drivers already contracted to Red Bull for promotion to the senior team.

Any remaining doubts as to Mateschitz's objectives were silenced when it was announced that Adrian Newey, Formula One's pre-eminent designer, would be joining Red Bull for 2006 to lead their technical department. The façade had dropped. Any team that hired Newey on a salary estimated at $10m per season was no bit-player.

A first Grand Prix victory came at the 2008 Italian GP, where the prodigy Sebastian Vettel, aged 21 years, two months and eleven days, became the youngest ever F1 winner, although – against script – driving for Toro Rosso rather than Red Bull Racing. That minor blip was rectified in 2009 when the first signature Newey Red Bull chassis, the RB5, rolled out of the team's Milton Keynes HQ. True to Mateschitz's ideals, the RB5 went its own way: it looked like no other car that year and was conceptually the most coherent machine, having pioneered a high-rake aerodynamic philosophy. Vettel and Mark Webber won six Grands Prix and only the rulebook-manipulating double-diffuser design of the Brawn team kept Red Bull Racing and Vettel from world titles.

Then came the flood: over the following four seasons, the Vettel–RBR juggernaut was unstoppable: four consecutive title doubles echoed the domination of Michael Schumacher and Ferrari a decade earlier. A reset of technical regulations for 2014, which introduced hybrid engines and emphasised powerplant efficiency over aerodynamic iteration, brought Red Bull Racing up short, as engine partner Renault had no answer for Mercedes' power unit supremacy. But by the end of the decade, with Honda power matching Mercedes' best, RBR once again held their rivals in a vice.

Having unearthed Max Verstappen, another megastar from their young driver programme, Red Bull toppled Mercedes as top constructor in 2022, repeating their success in '23. Indeed, the 2023 Championship set a new mark for success, with 21 victories from 22 Grands Prix – a 95.45 per cent success rate, F1's highest ever. Mateschitz didn't live to see his race team's finest hour – he died from pancreatic cancer in October 2022. He would surely have enjoyed the discomfiture of his more straitlaced rivals that this one-time party team had out-flown them all.

**ADRIAN NEWEY WAS SO COMMITTED TO** maximising the aerodynamic efficiency of his first Formula One car that he made its cockpit too tight. He conceived the March 881 to be shrink-wrapped around the frame of its compact lead driver, Ivan Capelli. Trouble was, when Capelli came to sit in the form-fitting monocoque, he found that with the fingers of his right hand wrapped around the gear stick, his knuckles hit the side of the carbon-fibre bodywork. The tight fit, along with other innovations such as a raised nose and a front wing without underside obstruction, would enhance the car's aerodynamic performance and fulfil an early Newey vision of 'less is more', except that this svelte, elegant creation was un-raceable.

Newey got to work, cutting a hole in the tub where Capelli's knuckles rubbed, then making a mould from wax and filler around which a carbon-fibre blister could be created. With the blister covering the hole, Capelli's hand had space to shift gears. All the graft was done by Newey himself, overnight before the car's first track test in February 1988, in a manner unthinkable for a modern-day F1 team. The mistake was a rare one, but the episode illustrated both the intense focus of which Newey's brilliant engineering mind was capable, as well as the hands-on ability to fix problems that a pure theoretician would have lacked.

Adrian had learned rudimentary engineering skills as a child, encouraged by his father's own enthusiasm for science, engineering and automobiles, and by the age of six had decided he wanted to work in motorsport. By age 12, designing racing cars was the goal. Newey didn't have long to wait. After an unhappy secondary education, he alighted at Southampton University to study aeronautics and astronautics, gaining a first-class degree then landing a job with the Fittipaldi Formula One team in 1980, soon after graduation. There, he worked under another fabled British Formula One engineer, Harvey Postlethwaite, and the whirlwind of ideas inside his head began to find practical expression.

For much of the following decade, Newey worked with March, initially as an aerodynamics specialist but soon overseeing the design of whole cars to race in US endurance categories and its premier single-seater series, CART. His designs were race and championship winners; their success led to Newey's appointment as chief designer for the March Formula One project from 1988 to '90, where he rose to become technical director. The thinly financed entry returned little in the way of championship results, though the occasionally exceptional performance of Newey's cars, as well as their obvious aerodynamic sophistication, drew attention from other teams.

Williams, rebuilding with new engine partner Renault, made Newey an offer for 1991 to become chief designer alongside technical director Patrick Head, and they set about creating Formula One history. Working for the first time at a front-running, fully resourced F1 team and with the engineering oversight of Head (once memorably dubbed 'the Isambard Kingdom Brunel of Formula One' by Damon Hill), Newey penned the FW14. It married Newey's trademark aerodynamic elegance with Williams' engineering rigour and a highly competitive Renault engine, to become a toe-to-toe match for the McLaren MP4-6 that won the '91 Constructors' Championship and the Drivers' Championship with Ayrton Senna.

A year later, Williams were in the ascendent. The Williams FW14B, equipped with electronically controlled active suspension, blitzed the Constructors' Championship, outscoring McLaren by 164 points to 99, as Nigel Mansell strolled to the drivers' title. The championship wins were the first for Newey in F1, but the dam had burst. Williams won every constructors' title through to 1997, with the exception of 1995, the success making Newey the most coveted engineer in Formula One.

Those years were also marked by the death of Ayrton Senna in the Williams FW16, whose design had been overseen by Newey and Head. The accident that killed Senna at the 1994 San Marino GP has never been definitively explained, though engineering defects were identified as possible causes. In his autobiography, *How to Build a Car* (2017), Newey writes: 'People ask me if I feel guilty about Ayrton. I do. I was one of the senior officers in a team that designed a car in which a great man was killed. What I feel the most guilt about though is not the possibility that steering column failure may have caused the accident, because I don't think it did. But the fact that I screwed up the aerodynamics of the car.'

Despite the tragedy, Newey's eminence continued to grow, as did his realisation of his worth to a team. He pushed for a share of equity in Williams; when that was denied, a cooling of relations, along with legal tribulations resulting from Senna's death, left Newey ripe for an approach by McLaren to join for 1997. By now Newey was the nearest thing to a silver bullet in F1. After a fallow period, McLaren won the last race of '97, teeing up Mika Häkkinen to win back-to-back drivers' titles in 1998–99, with McLaren taking the '98 constructors' title.

Newey's relationship with McLaren team boss Ron Dennis was never entirely harmonious, however, and in 2006 Newey joined the nascent Red Bull Racing team, lured by a $10m annual salary and the chance to build a technical structure entirely to his liking. There, with Sebastian Vettel from 2010 to 2013, Newey's cars achieved four consecutive title doubles; latterly, with Max Verstappen, new levels of domination have been achieved. The team's 21 wins from 22 races in 2023 established a record winning percentage of 95.45.

To this day, Newey sketches designs with a pencil on a technical drawing board, just as he'll wander along pre-race grids, A4 notebook in hand, studying rivals' work and harvesting ideas. Aged 65 on the eve of the 2024 F1 season, and with a total of 25 Drivers' and Constructors' World Championships won in cars he has designed, Newey is emphatically the most successful designer in F1 history. The man once described by Frank Williams as 'the most competitive person I know' shows no signs of laying down his pencil just yet.

## ADRIAN NEWEY

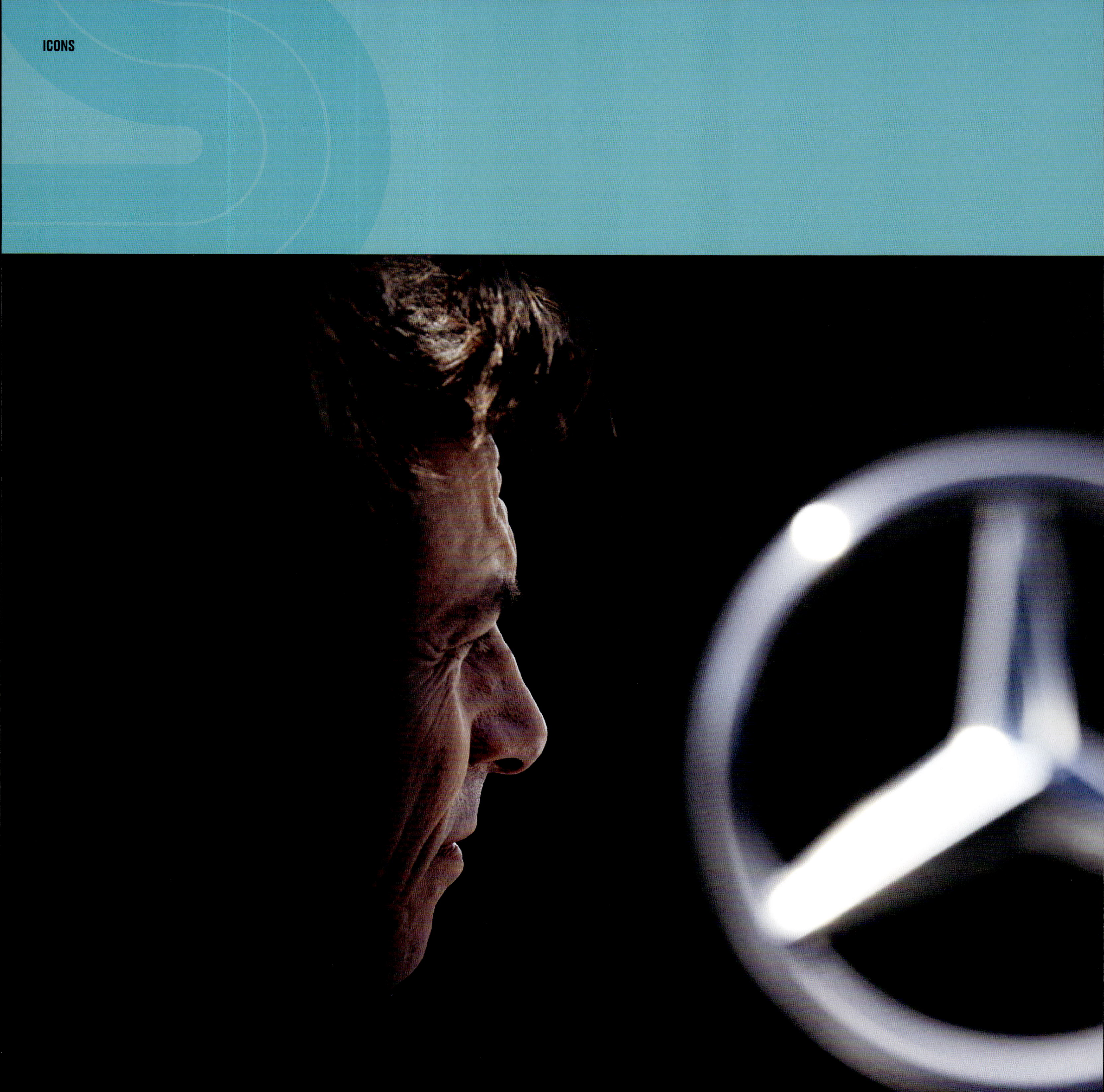

# TOTO WOLFF

**THE NAME TOTO WOLFF WAS LITTLE** known outside Austria when he bought a stake in the Williams Formula One team in 2009. A self-made Viennese businessman, who had become wealthy through investments in tech companies, he was regarded initially as little more than a background figure – a racing enthusiast and ex-competitor who relished the F1 environment and would back his passion with cash.

Few outside a close circle of Austrian friends and associates realised the scale of Wolff's ambition. His 16 per cent share – the first sold by Williams to an outside investor – bought him a seat on the board; within three years he was executive director and being spoken of as a future team principal. Those predictions were correct, though not entirely.

Early in 2013, Wolff resigned his role at Williams to become executive director of the Mercedes F1 team which, since 2010, had returned to the sport as a full, manufacturer-backed race team, having stepped up from their role as engine supplier. The approach from Mercedes left him 'gobsmacked', he said at the time, as their return to F1 had not yet brought the anticipated levels of success. Behind the scenes, Mercedes were investing heavily in the hybrid engine technology that was due for introduction in 2014. They wanted a team boss sufficiently committed to invest his own cash in the business, as well as lead commercial and political functions. Wolff chewed on the offer for several weeks, seeking counsel from wise heads, including Frank Williams, before accepting. 'I had his blessing, which was very important for me,' Wolff told *F1 Racing* magazine in 2013.

As history records, it was a smart move, for Mercedes were about to steal a huge march on their competitors. Neither of F1's two rival engine manufacturers, Ferrari and Renault, had matched Mercedes' technological investment and they would be blown away by a tsunami of Silver Arrows success that dwarfed anything previously achieved in F1. Wolff, having bought a 30 per cent stake in the team, would be at the helm for the ensuing run of seven consecutive world title doubles, from 2014 to 2020, with a further constructors' title in 2021.

While Mercedes F1 benefitted from unprecedented levels of investment, all of this was achieved on Wolff's watch, establishing him as a significant power broker in the sport. His rise from outsider to primus inter pares had been astonishingly rapid and achieved without the backing of family riches or a nurturing motorsport benefactor. Born to a Polish mother and a Romanian father, Torger Christian Wolff studied economics, honing the interest in finance that would fund both his amateur racing exploits and his Formula One odyssey. An imposing figure, almost two metres tall and weighing 100kg, Wolff's competitive urges briefly led him to play rugby for Austria's national team, though it was through motorsport that his drive found its true expression. 'Controlling the uncontrollable, riding the wild horse. That was the big appeal of motorsport to me,' Wolff told the BBC in 2023.

Outwardly approachable and personable, Wolff's charm disguises a sometimes volatile temper – a character trait he admits to – and the degree of ruthlessness essential in all F1 and business leaders. Some noses were pushed out of joint as he exerted greater influence and control at Williams, while at Mercedes he oversaw the departure in 2013 of the vastly experienced and widely respected Ross Brawn as team principal. Brawn later wrote that he felt unable to trust Wolff and fellow Mercedes director Niki Lauda, who had joined the team after Brawn.

A few years later, the high-profile departure of Mercedes' technical leader Paddy Lowe also raised eyebrows, but such was the team's domination (by the end of 2016 they had won three consecutive title doubles) any troubled waters were quickly smoothed over. The internal manoeuvrings had little detrimental effect on Mercedes' F1 operation; indeed one of the team's hallmarks while it set about crushing the opposition was its achievement of unruffled ultra-professionalism and a team bond that, to outsiders at least, appeared exceptionally strong. In a 2021 interview with *The Race*, Wolff spoke of how the death of his father, when Toto was only 15, had fostered a need in him to protect his 'tribe': 'It is my responsibility to look after everybody in this organisation, and my family,' he said. 'That's maybe also because I had to take responsibility at a very early age for my sister and I. What it triggers in me is an instinct of "this is my tribe, and I need to protect my tribe, no matter what". This is the most important part.'

Wolff's management style and the sustained success he had nurtured became the subject of academic research by Harvard Business School, where he appeared as a guest lecturer. At the end of 2021, however, Mercedes' stranglehold on F1 was finally loosened by Max Verstappen's first Drivers' Championship win, even as Mercedes won an eighth straight constructors' title. Over the following two seasons, Red Bull assumed their former position as F1's dominant team, sweeping aside Mercedes, whose interpretation of a new technical ruleset left them with a far slower car. It seems certain the assault on Wolff's tribe will be met with a fierce response.

# RIVALRIES

*Wheel to wheel, at the limit of competition, these are the rivalries that have compelled F1 fans through the decades.*

Juan Manuel Fangio vs Stirling Moss

Jackie Stewart vs Emerson Fittipaldi

James Hunt vs Niki Lauda

Gilles Villeneuve vs Didier Pironi

Nigel Mansell vs Nelson Piquet

Alain Prost vs Ayrton Senna

Damon Hill vs Michael Schumacher

Mika Häkkinen vs Michael Schumacher

Fernando Alonso vs Lewis Hamilton

Lewis Hamilton vs Nico Rosberg

Lewis Hamilton vs Max Verstappen

8
Vanwall

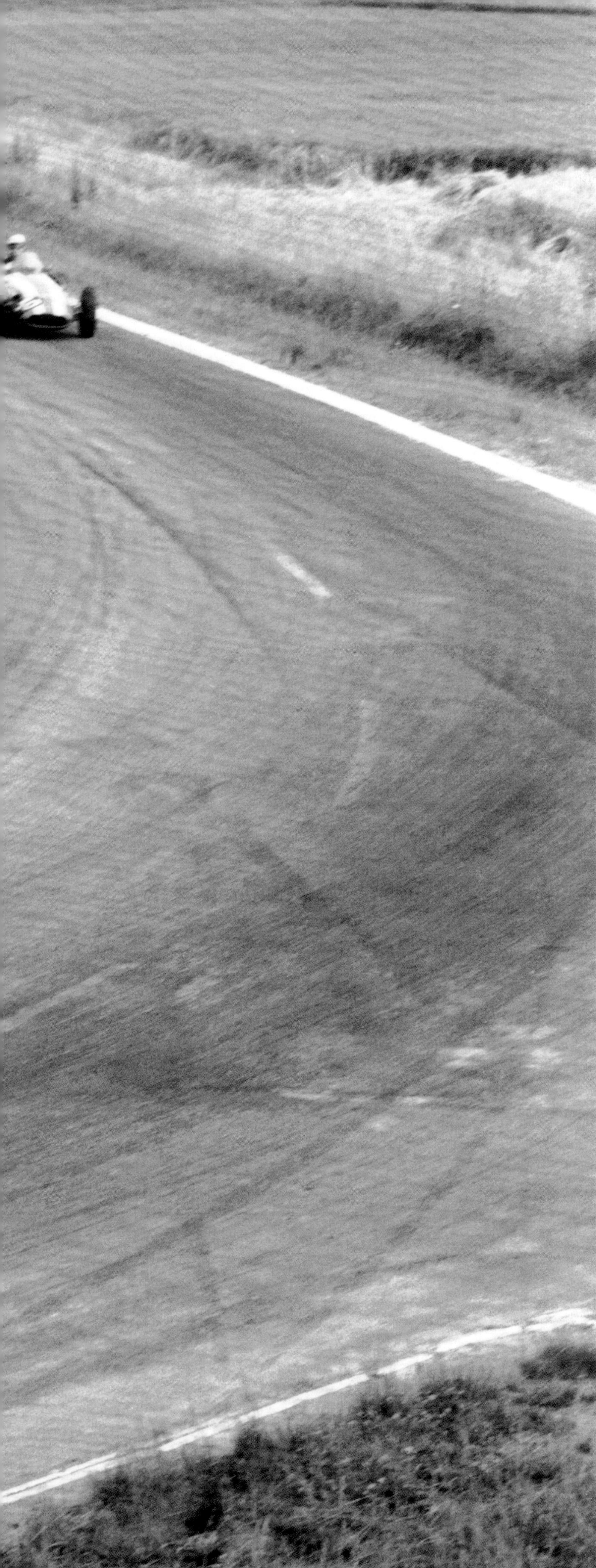



# JUAN MANUEL FANGIO vs STIRLING MOSS

**THE GRANDEE AND THE PRODIGY, JUAN** Manuel Fangio and Stirling Moss were the two greatest drivers of the 1950s, alongside Alberto Ascari. In age, they were a generation apart – Fangio was 18 years Moss's senior – and Fangio's five world titles far outshone Moss's statistical record: notoriously, Stirling never became a Formula One World Champion. But on track they were sometimes inseparable, never more so than in 1955 as teammates at Mercedes. Driving the dazzling W196 cars, they achieved seemingly effortless superiority, finishing one–two in the Drivers' Championship and amassing a points total that would have made Mercedes dominant Constructors' Champions, had the title existed.

Never, though, was there a hint of animosity between the two, as there would often be in later decades between other close-matched teammates in front-running cars. For all his own prodigious talent, Moss held Fangio in awe and was comfortable in accepting an understudy role, without explicit team orders. During a period when drivers routinely died during competition, risks were obvious enough; there was little appetite for off-track machinations to add to the drama. Moss was runner-up to Fangio in the Drivers' Championship over three consecutive years from 1955 to '57, yet never was there rancour between them. Theirs was a rivalry from a more noble age.

# JACKIE STEWART vs EMERSON FITTIPALDI

**FORMULA ONE IN THE EARLY 1970S WAS** dominated and defined by Jackie Stewart and Emerson Fittipaldi. Both were immaculate stylists at the wheel, both combined huge natural talent with intelligence. It was inevitable they would rise to pre-eminence among their peers.

Stewart's F1 career began in 1965, five years earlier than Fittipaldi's, whose own F1 record stretched to 1980. Briefly though, a commanding Stewart, who won world titles in 1969, '71 and '73, was the benchmark for Brazil's rising superstar, who would become champion in '72 and '74.

In 1972 and '73, their closely matched teams – Stewart with Tyrrell, Fittipaldi with Lotus – made them direct championship rivals. Writing in his autobiography *Winning Is Not Enough* (2009), Stewart observed that Fittipaldi 'had become a major force... one of the great trailblazers in the history of our sport'. During '72, Stewart developed a duodenal ulcer and was forced to miss the Belgian GP on medical advice. In the Lotus 72, Fittipaldi won five Grands Prix to Stewart's four, comfortably out-scoring him to take his first title and become the (then) youngest World Champion.

Stewart hit back in '73, fully recovered and having already resolved to retire at the end of the season. His five wins trumped Fittipaldi's three, though they had scrapped for supremacy throughout the first half of the year. Their time as rivals was brief: Stewart retired as World Champion with a career-record 27 wins, while Fittipaldi moved to McLaren, taking his second title in 1974. It took their successors generations to match their standards.

GOODYEAR
Ford
elf
1
Ford
Tyrrell

CHRONOGRAP
HEUER
parmalat
Marlbo

# JAMES HUNT vs NIKI LAUDA

**THE STORY OF THE 1976 FORMULA ONE** season is so implausibly dramatic it became a Hollywood movie: *Rush* (2013). McLaren's dashing, highly strung Brit, James Hunt, pitched against the rapid though canny Austrian Niki Lauda, reigning World Champion with Ferrari.

On paper there was balance between the rival camps: Lauda's pace and cool conviction were getting the most from Ferrari's 312T; Hunt brought a dash of inspiration to a McLaren whose M23 had the edge over a gaggle of competitive British teams powered by Cosworth engines. By mid-season, however, it seemed as if Lauda would waltz to a second title – he held a 31-point lead in the Drivers' Championship after nine races. Everything changed at the German GP, where Lauda crashed and suffered burns that came close to killing him, inhaling smoke that scarred his lungs for life.

Lauda missed three races, while Hunt scored heavily and continued to do so after Lauda's miraculous, blood-stained return at the Italian GP. They entered the season finale at Japan's Fuji circuit, with Lauda holding a three-point advantage. There, in a deluge, he quit on lap two; Hunt finished third to win the title by a point.

Through the most tumultuous season, one that almost cost Lauda his life, James and Niki remained close friends, as they had been throughout their junior racing careers and into Formula One. Rivals, yes, but comrades.

# GILLES VILLENEUVE vs DIDIER PIRONI

**THE SEASON OF 1982 WAS ONE OF GREAT** promise for Ferrari. Their 126C2 had a turbocharged engine at least the equal of its rivals, while a major chassis upgrade from the previous year gave grip levels to match leading competitors. As for drivers, in Gilles Villeneuve and Didier Pironi they had two incendiary talents – Villeneuve more flamboyant and instinctive, Pironi more calculated, but both brilliant and potential champions.

At round four, the San Marino GP, they ran one–two as the race progressed, Villeneuve ahead, no one near them. They swapped and re-swapped positions in the closing stages, leaving Villeneuve leading into the final lap. Approaching the Tosa hairpin for the last time, Pironi passed Villeneuve – contrary to team orders in Villeneuve's view – and charged to the chequered flag. Villeneuve believed he had been duped and later told *Autosport* magazine, 'I trust anyone until they break that trust and I will not speak to Pironi again – ever. From now on it's war. Absolute war'. Two weeks later, Villeneuve crashed fatally at the Belgian GP, he and Pironi still unreconciled.

SAN
CHAMPION
FILA
Marlboro
Candy
Candy Racing Team
HARIBO
CHAMPION
MOËT
GIACOBAZZI
brut N.H. gran premio

PHILIPS
Canon
ICI
Tactel
HONDA
Mobil
5
DENIM
GOODYEAR

# NIGEL MANSELL vs NELSON PIQUET

**SUCCESS HAD COME QUICKLY TO NELSON** Piquet in Formula One. He was a race winner in only his second full season and a World Champion in his third. A second title came two years later in 1983, and to many eyes he was the sport's best driver at that time; certainly its most glamorous.

He would not have expected, three years later, to be beaten up – almost literally, such was the venom of their intra-team rivalry – by a flat-capped Brit called Nigel Mansell, who just happened to be every bit as fast as Piquet. Mansell had served a far tougher apprenticeship to earn a ride in the rocketship that was the 1986 Williams FW11. No way was he going to let Piquet's reputation halt his progress.

By the end of the season, Mansell went into the finale, the Australian GP, leading Piquet and their only title rival, Alain Prost, with a plush points cushion. Tyre trouble blew his title hopes into strips of flailing black rubber, however, allowing Prost through to a second consecutive World Championship. A year later, Williams' advantage with the FW11B was once again huge and this time Piquet used all his guile (even goading Mansell's wife) to get under his teammate's skin and find a way to win his third world title. Mansell crashed out of contention during practice for the Japanese GP, pushing too hard to claw back Piquet's advantage. He had won six races to Piquet's three, but it wasn't enough.

# ALAIN PROST vs AYRTON SENNA

**FOR THREE UNFORGETTABLE SEASONS, AS** the 1980s tipped into the next decade, the two greatest drivers of their era staged a mesmerising fight that came to define their careers. It began in 1988, when Alain Prost, already a double World Champion, and Ayrton Senna, a multiple race winner of immense talent, were paired together at McLaren. Neither was accorded number-one status – the thought of either accepting a number-two position was inconceivable – allowing them the freedom to race each other as well as anyone else.

And race they did in the mighty McLaren-Honda MP4-4, a machine so dominant in '88 that it won 15 out of 16 races. They had only each other to beat: Prost as the serene incumbent, reaching for a third title; Senna, the new boy, still racing with the desperation of a man yet to win his first. Relations between these titans were respectful, even cordial at first, but as each strove harder for perfection, pressure increased.

A flashpoint was inevitable, and it came at the Portuguese GP, round 13. Prost needed to beat Senna, as his younger rival held a slight points advantage and had already won seven races to his four. On the main straight at the start of lap two, Senna led, but Prost began to tow past as they reached 190mph. Instinctively, with the edge of menace that would become his hallmark, Senna edged his car towards Prost's, squeezing him to within 18 inches of the pitwall. Prost stood firm and went on to take the win and championship lead, although Senna ended the year as champion.

Just over a year later, they arrived at the Japanese GP, still as teammates, locked in their own, private title battle. Their 1989 dominance was less, but by the penultimate race, Prost was 16 points clear at the top of the championship table, with Senna his only title rival. After 46 laps, Prost led, with Senna chasing hard and drawing alongside Prost to make a pass for the lead at the chicane. As they both turned right, Prost's McLaren nudged into Senna's, putting Prost out and damaging the nose of Senna's car. Senna pitted for repairs and recovered to cross the line first – only later to be disqualified for missing the chicane where he and Prost had clashed. Prost was champion, Senna was seething.

No longer could McLaren contain these feuding super-egos and Prost switched to Ferrari for 1990. Their battle raged on all year, peaking once again at Suzuka, the penultimate round. With cold-blooded resolve, Senna took Prost off at the first corner to secure the title. He admitted one year later, again at Suzuka having just won his third title, that his 1990 targetting of Prost was revenge for what he regarded as the injustice of '89.

They never fought again for a title, as the competitive trajectories of their teams fell out of alignment. Prost dominated 1993 with Williams and retired as champion; Senna took the drive Prost had vacated and crashed fatally at the 1994 San Marino GP.

Marlboro
EAGLE
GOODYEAR
GOODYEAR
GOODYEAR
Marlboro
Marlboro
HONDA
Marlboro
HONDA

Rothman

# DAMON HILL vs MICHAEL SCHUMACHER

**DAMON HILL WASN'T THE FIRST DRIVER** to feel the hard edge of Michael Schumacher's ruthless competitive instincts. Nor would he be the last. But when the two clashed on lap 35 of the 1994 Australian GP, pitching Schumacher's Benetton onto two wheels and Hill out of title contention, Damon instantly became the most infamous of Michael's 'victims'.

Their journey to a title shoot-out at the final race of the year had been turbulent and tragic. Williams lead driver, Ayrton Senna, had died in an accident at that year's San Marino GP, leaving Damon to assume team leadership. Schumacher's Benetton had in the meantime been docked points for alleged technical irregularities. They went to the Adelaide street track only a point apart (Schumacher's 92 to Hill's 91); they left the same way, title decided in Schumacher's favour by their clash.

They went at it again in 1995, once more taking each other out – this time at the British GP – but Schumacher's season was by far the more impressive: he was champion with a 33-point advantage and nine wins to Hill's four. Hill's redemption came a season later, still with Williams, but Schumacher having switched to a less competitive Ferrari. Damon was comfortably the 1996 Champion, able to breathe at last for the first time since his dramatic promotion two-and-a-half years earlier. Meanwhile, Schumacher raged on, hungry for new opponents...

# MIKA HÄKKINEN vs MICHAEL SCHUMACHER

**THE TWO FASTEST DRIVERS OF LATE-1990S** Formula One, Michael Schumacher and Mika Häkkinen both broke into the sport in 1991, yet not until 1998 did they go wheel to wheel in equally matched cars. By then, Schumacher was already a two-time World Champion, while Häkkinen had only just won his first Grand Prix. But, finally in a machine that could match Ferrari's best, Mika would show he was Michael's equal.

Armed with a McLaren penned by master designer Adrian Newey, Häkkinen flew to the 1998 and '99 world titles, but it was in 2000 that the Häkkinen–Schumacher rivalry reached its zenith. At the 2000 Belgian GP, both battling for the race win and the drivers' title, Häkkinen and Schumacher touched wheels at almost 200mph (as related by Häkkinen in Chapter 2). Häkkinen won the race, then took Schumacher to one side immediately afterwards to make his feelings clear about what he believed was overly aggressive driving. Schumacher eventually won the 2000 World Championship and Häkkinen quit Formula One a year later.

When Schumacher announced his own (first) retirement during 2006, he was asked who his greatest rival had been. 'Mika,' was his immediate, emphatic response.

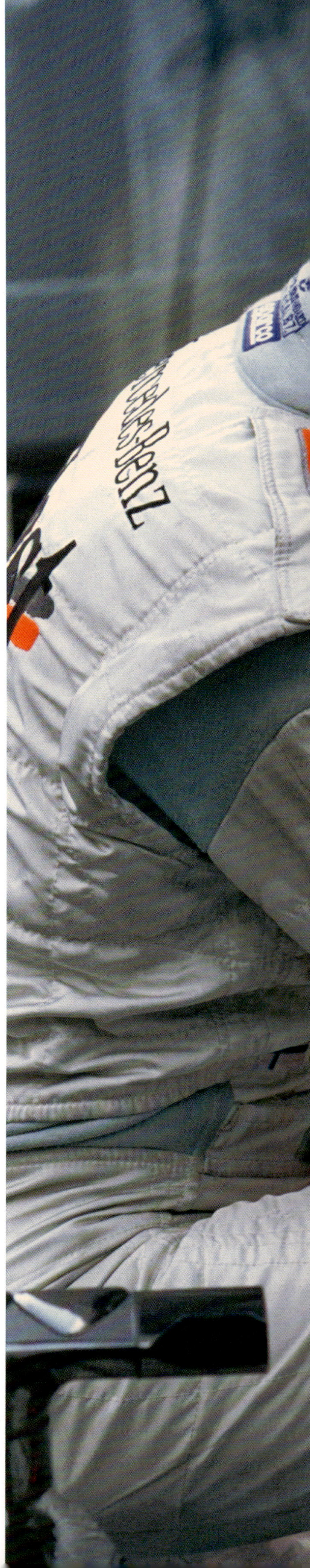

FedEx
Marlboro
Marlboro
BRIDGESTONE
Marlboro
OMP
M. Schumacher

FedEx
BOSS
HUGO BOSS
Mercedes

# FERNANDO ALONSO vs LEWIS HAMILTON

**IN 2007, RON DENNIS, HEAD OF THE** McLaren team, was driven to replicate the superteam he had formed two decades earlier by pairing Alain Prost and Ayrton Senna. To do so, he partnered Fernando Alonso, reigning double World Champion, poached from Renault, with the McLaren-groomed prodigy, Lewis Hamilton, making his F1 debut.

The talent quotient of the pairing was off the charts – but so was the potential for trouble. Alonso was a notoriously feisty character, not shy of manipulating in-team politics for his own advantage; Hamilton was regarded almost as The Second Coming, such was the reverence for his abilities within the team. After only six races, at the Canadian GP where Hamilton scored his first F1 victory, tensions began to surface. The win placed Hamilton at the top of the drivers' table, an astonishing achievement for an F1 rookie, and Alonso, who believed he had been assured of lead driver status at McLaren, was not happy. 'Right from the start I've never felt totally comfortable,' he said. 'I have a British teammate in a British team, and he's doing a great job and we know that all the support and help is going to him and I understood that from the beginning.'

One week on and Hamilton won again, this time at the US GP, which extended his championship lead to 10 points over Alonso. Lewis bit back: 'I don't know why he would say what he said but I guess because he is Spanish and I am English. So it's a very difficult situation.' At the Hungarian GP, round 11, both drivers tried to compromise each other's qualifying sessions. This was civil war.

Hamilton: 'Fernando doesn't seem to have been speaking to me since yesterday, so I don't know if he has a problem.'

Alonso: 'Right now Hamilton isn't talking to anyone in the team. I don't have any problems, it's the team who have the biggest one.'

Alonso's comment carried weight beyond the drivers' toxic rivalry. Away from the track, McLaren had become embroiled in the 'Spygate' affair, in which they were accused of obtaining Ferrari technical secrets via illicit means. Alonso himself was accused of sharing information that might harm McLaren.

On the two drivers feuded, coming close to taking each other out at the Italian GP, and ending the season tied on 107 points. Ferrari's Kimi Räikkönen pipped them both to the title by a single point and McLaren, Alonso and Hamilton were left to rue the loss of a championship that might easily have been theirs, had one driver been backed over the other.

As Dennis reflected, 'The easy option at the beginning of the season would have been to nominate a number-one and a number-two. The price that I pay for being able to say to Fernando and Lewis, "Race on the circuit and don't try to pressure me off the circuit" is certainly, for various reasons, much greater than in previous seasons.'

# LEWIS HAMILTON vs NICO ROSBERG

**WHEN FORMULA ONE'S TECHNICAL** regulations mandated all-new hybrid turbo engines for the 2014 season, no one was ready like Mercedes Benz. The F1 team owned by Germany's most fabled auto maker had invested hugely in its F1 engine tech, and the cars those power units drove largely dominated the following eight seasons: Mercedes won consecutive Constructors' Championships from 2014 to 2021.

For drivers Lewis Hamilton and Nico Rosberg, who were in at the start of Mercedes' hybrid odyssey, that meant pole positions, race wins and world titles were almost guaranteed. Hamilton, true to form and reputation, capitalised immediately and a world title double was his across 2014–15. Rosberg had taken a pounding, but he refused to lay down and, during 2016, took advantage of early-season unreliability for Hamilton to establish a point's lead he maintained for most of the year.

There was an edge of desperation to Nico's campaign, however. He knew that Hamilton was the faster driver and that fate had handed him a vanishing chance to out-sprint Lewis to the title. At the Spanish GP, the pressure told. Rosberg out-dragged Hamilton from the grid to lead through the first three corners, but on the approach to Turn 4, a power unit glitch slowed Rosberg's car and allowed Hamilton a split-second passing opportunity. Rosberg blocked, Hamilton kept coming and the two collided, putting both out of the race.

The clash had no effect on their championship standings (neither scored), but already tense internal relations were soured thereafter. By the season finale, Rosberg had given everything to stay ahead and the strain of competition prompted him to quit Formula One as World Champion within days of his title win.

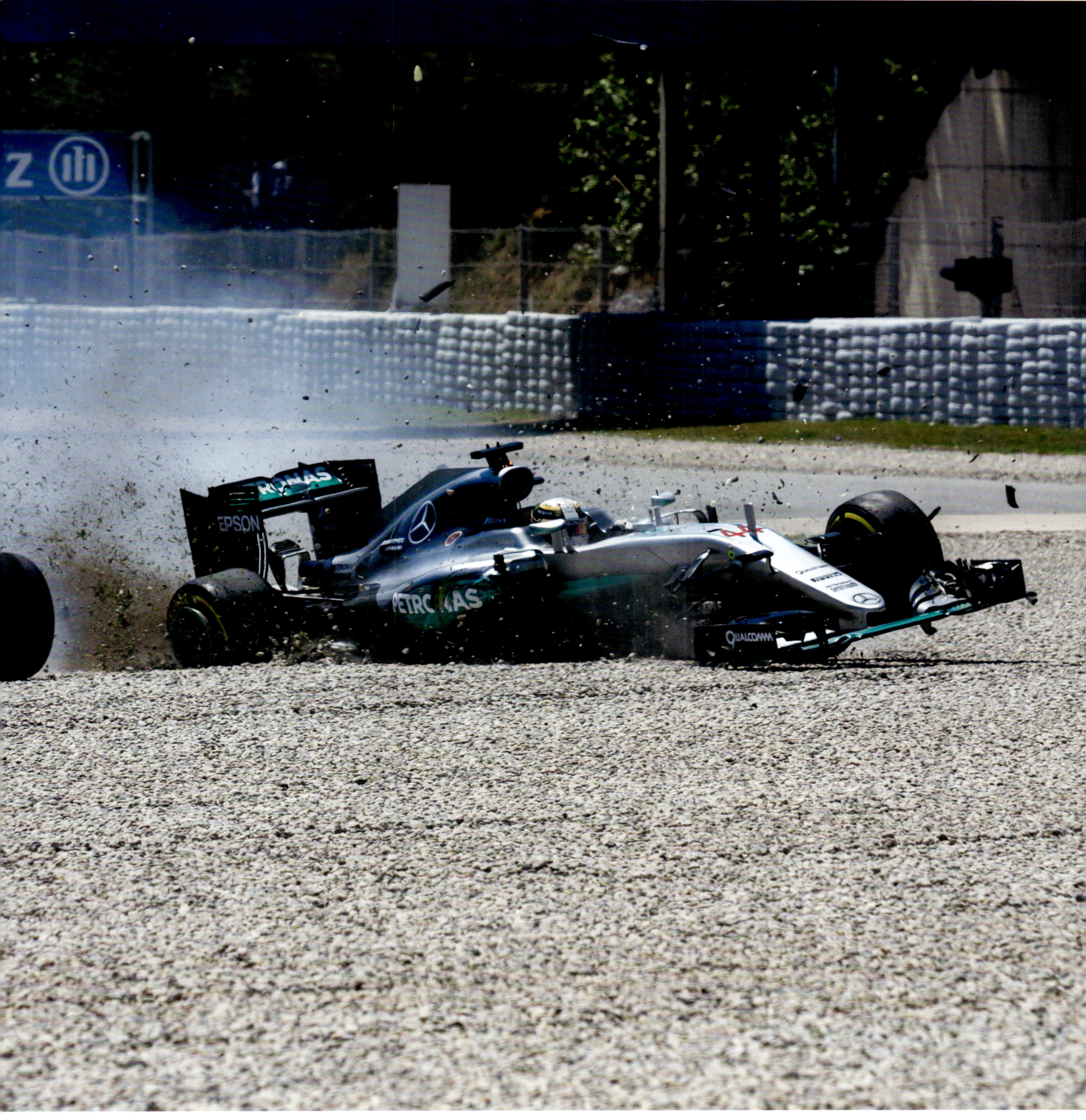
EPSON
QUALCOMM

HONDA
Claro
33
ESSO
HONDA

# LEWIS HAMILTON vs MAX VERSTAPPEN

**TO LOOSEN THE MANACLE-GRIP OF LEWIS** Hamilton and Mercedes on the Formula One World Championship that had endured from 2014 through to 2020, it was always going to take something very special. A commitment to excellence in all operations, backed by the financial heft that required, had been the hallmark of Mercedes' operations since the introduction of hybrid-engine technical regulations. Their reward? Seven consecutive title doubles.

By 2021, however, the beast that was Red Bull Racing had stirred. Once a team as dominant as Mercedes, RBR had suffered for lack of a front-running engine partner throughout the hybrid era. Finally, though, Honda had raised the standard of their power unit to match Mercedes', allowing the underlying excellence of the team to shine once more. In Max Verstappen, RBR had found Hamilton's heir apparent and in Adrian Newey they retained the most gifted F1 engineer of the past 30 years. It was game on.

A measure of how closely pegged these two superteams had become was evident from a glance at the drivers' points table ahead of the season finale in Abu Dhabi: both Hamilton and Verstappen had 369.5 points. Their rivalry during the season had teetered on the edge of gloves-off conflict. At the British Grand Prix, opening lap contact sent Verstappen hurtling into 51G impact with the barriers; at the Italian GP, both cars ended up in the gravel trap, Red Bull perched on top of Mercedes, after a clash at the first chicane. Multiple other incidents peppered their season, fuelling a growing hatred between fans of either team and driver, played out on social media.

The final drama concluded on the very last lap of the championship. Hamilton had looked secure in the lead and set to claim a record-breaking eighth world title. But a late safety car period, during which Verstappen had changed to fresh tyres, set the protagonists up for a last-gasp shoot-out. On older rubber, Hamilton could not defend against Verstappen, who took victory and his first world title. Multiple protests and a social media outcry followed the race, Mercedes insisting that regulations had not been followed during the race restart. It was to no avail. The result stood and Verstappen prevailed after one of the most intense title fights in the sport's history.

*The breathtaking technical masterworks that have challenged F1's greatest drivers to tame them.*

# THE GREAT CARS

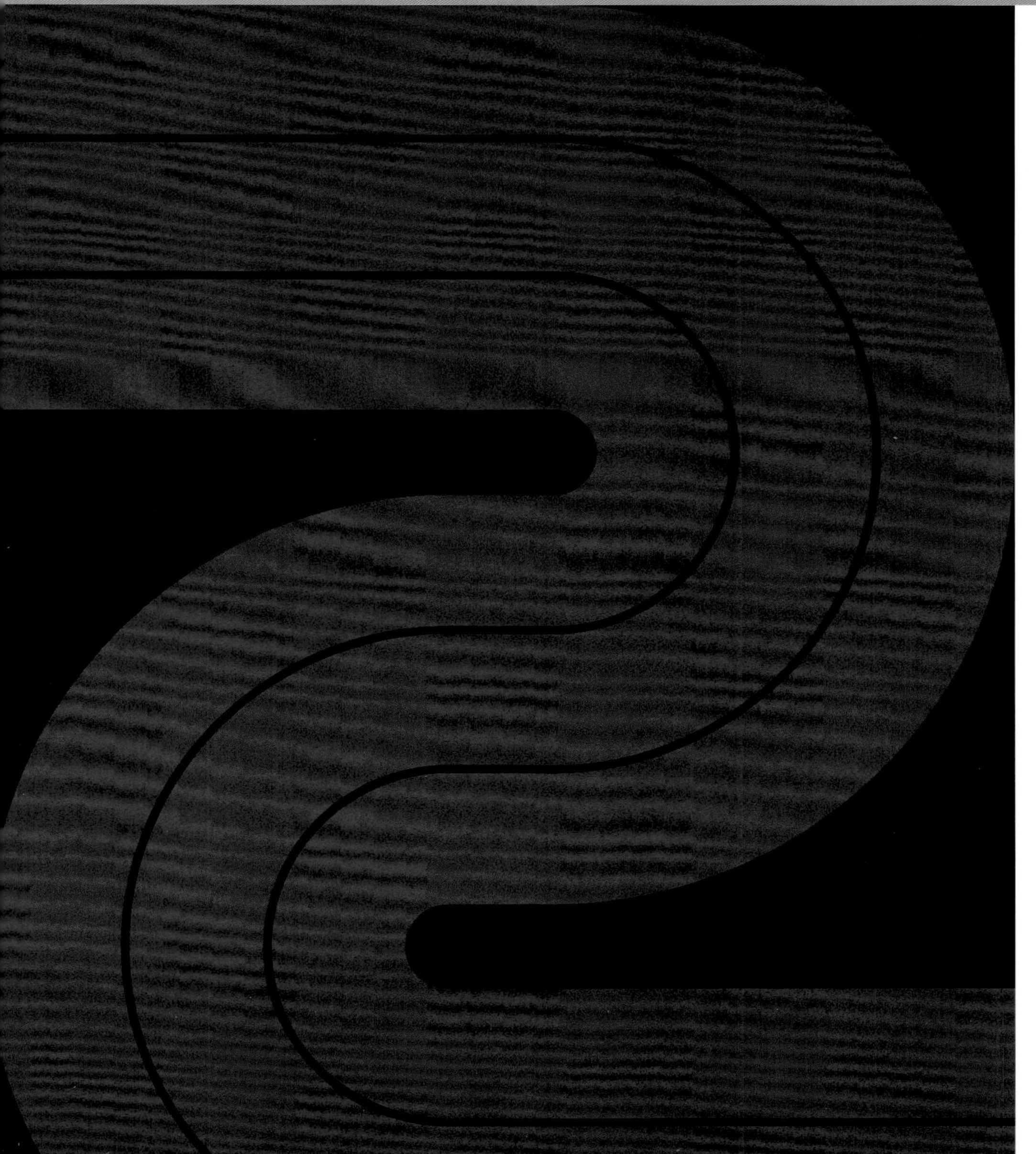

1950s: Mercedes W196

1960s: Lotus 49

1970s: Ferrari 312T

1980s: McLaren MP4-4

1990s: Williams FW15C

2000s: Ferrari F2004

2010s: Mercedes W09

2020s: Red Bull RB19

# 1950s: Mercedes Benz W196 (1954–55)

**IN THE SUMMER OF 1954, WHEN THE** Mercedes W196 'streamliner' cars were wheeled from their transporter into the paddock of the Reims circuit in northern France, the future touched down. The long, low Silver Arrows, wrapped in all-enveloping bodywork fashioned from magnesium alloy, looked like nothing else, their design the product of a rulebook loophole which permitted wheels to be enclosed.

Lined up alongside the Ferraris, Maseratis and Gordinis of the day, they looked like a vision not just of another age, but of another planet. They went like rocketships, too. Around high-speed Reims, the aerodynamic benefits of the curvaceous surface form were instantly apparent: nothing could touch the W196 in a straight line. Drivers Juan Manuel Fangio and Karl Kling took the chequer nose-to-tail in a staged finish, having lapped the field and put another 48 seconds on the third-placed Ferrari. The game had been changed. Grand Prix racing had experienced just this kind of silver sensation before the Second World War, when a previous generation of Mercedes racing cars and their Auto Union rivals rendered opposition futile.

The mid-1950s Mercedes assault picked up where their predecessors left off, employing the same team manager, Alfred Neubauer, to drill perfectionist rigour into team operations, alongside a winning mindset. Factory backing bankrolled engineering of the highest standard, overseen by the totemic chief designer Rudolf Uhlenhaut, who was also a top-calibre driver, quite capable of track-testing the technical developments he had conjured.

The swoopy form of the W196 concealed multiple fine touches, such as every tube of the space-frame chassis being individually stress-tested to optimise strength-to-weight ratio. Brakes were mounted inboard to reduce unsprung weight, while the straight-eight 2.5-litre engine was tilted at an angle 20 degrees from horizontal, permitting a lower bonnet line and thus enhancing aerodynamic efficiency. The use of an antiquated swing-axle arrangement for the rear suspension was anomalous, given the sophistication of the W196 in all other aspects, and bestowed less-than-fluid handling traits. This was one of the car's few weaknesses: while the W196 was a straight-line bullet, it was not capable of benign four-wheel cornering drifts in the manner of its direct contemporary, the Maserati 250F.

Another was a price exacted by the elegant bodywork beyond material cost: at tighter tracks, concealment of the front wheels prevented drivers from precise positioning at the apex of corners. A fortnight after the Mercedes' Reims debut, the cars contested the British Grand Prix at Silverstone, where the corners were marked out with oil drums. These proved invisible from the cockpit and during the race Fangio, despite starting from pole position, clipped several, besmirching the immaculate contours of his car, as he slid to fourth place.

It was a rare blip. The W196 used a more conventional open-wheel layout for most of its remaining races through 1954–55, and more often than not, it was the car to beat: nine wins from 12 starts – eight victories for Fangio, one for Moss at the '55 British GP. Fangio remembered it fondly: 'With Mercedes there was always peace of mind. Those cars were amazingly reliable and to win in 1954 and 1955 was easy, because they were undoubtedly superior to every other car. They were quicker, they lasted longer.'

**RACE RECORD**

**Championships: 2**
**(2x Drivers'; Constructors' not awarded until 1958 season)**
**Race wins: 9**
**Pole positions: 8**
**Fastest laps: 9**

*Juan Manuel Fangio leads Stirling Moss, Circuit de Monaco, 1955*

*(Above)*

## ALFA 158/9 (1950–51)

*Based on a successful pre-war design, the Alfa 158/9 was the pre-eminent machine at the birth of the F1 World Championship. Giuseppe Farina and Juan Manuel Fangio drove it to drivers' titles. (Guiseppe Farina, Silverstone, 1950)*

*(Right)*

## MASERATI 250F (1954–60)

*A drivers' favourite in its prime, this car was raced by Juan Manuel Fangio at the start of his 1954 title-winning season and throughout '57 for his fifth and final drivers' title. (Juan Manuel Fangio, Nürburgring, 1957)*

*(Above)*

**VANWALL (1958)**

*The British riposte to the might of Ferrari and Maserati, Vanwall was the first team to win the F1 constructors' title in 1958, with Tony Brooks and Stirling Moss as their race-winning superstars.(Tony Brooks, Spa-Francorchamps, 1958)*

*(Left)*

**COOPER T51 (1959)**

*The first rear-engine F1 car to win races and championships, the Cooper T51 tore up the design rule book and forced others to follow. (Jack Brabham, Sebring, 1959)*

*Jim Clark,*
*Nürburgring, 1967*

# 1960s: Lotus 49 (1967–70)

**FEW CARS HAVE HAD SO LASTING AN** influence on Formula One design as the Lotus 49. While not conceptually radical in the manner of, say, the Cooper T51, which introduced mid-engine layouts to F1 in 1959, or the Lotus 79, which was successful in harnessing ground-effect aerodynamics in 1978, the Lotus 49 set a template still employed today.

Its fundamentals were a monocoque 'tub' to house the driver and around which the car's front end would be built; to this was mounted the Cosworth DFV engine, deployed as a load-bearing component at the heart of the car's rear-end. Neither idea was new: Lotus had introduced monocoque construction with its 25 in 1962, and the Lancia D50 had a load-bearing engine in 1954. Their seamless integration was, however, novel and genre-defining.

The arrangement, overseen by Lotus chief designer Maurice Philippe and visionary team owner Colin Chapman, allied simplicity, lightness and strength – the holy trinity of Formula One architecture. Its efficacy relied on the excellence of the Cosworth DFV engine, for which the 49 had been tailor-made. Funded by Ford, the DFV was the first successful, bespoke engine drawn under the 3.0-litre engine regulations introduced for 1966. Much like the 49, the DFV had been conceived with efficiency and simplicity as its watchwords and it was supplied exclusively to Lotus in 1967. Thereafter it would be the vital building block for myriad small teams through the '70s and '80s. A lightweight, compact V8, the DFV – double four valve – packed a 430-horsepower punch, but its manners were rude. So much so, drivers Graham Hill and Jim Clark bemoaned the too-abrupt power delivery of early-spec units, while revelling, nonetheless, in their muscle.

The 49 might have been a handful, but on its debut at the 1967 Dutch GP, Hill took pole position by half a second, while Clark won with a 24-second advantage, Hill having retired from the lead. On pace alone, nothing could touch the 49. Either Clark or Hill took pole for every '67 race in the 49 and Clark won four Grands Prix in his – doubling the tally of Brabham twins Denny Hulme and Jack Brabham, who finished ahead of him in the championship.

Unreliability was a bugbear for both chassis and engine in the 49's first season, but there was no holding it back in 1968. Hill and Lotus swept to a title double, despite Clark's fatal accident in a Formula Two race held after the season-opening South African GP, which he had won.

By now in 'B' specification, the 49 benefitted from numerous suspension modifications designed to eliminate its tendency to nose-dive under braking and squat while accelerating. More obvious was the introduction of nose fins and upswept rear bodywork for the '68 Monaco GP. Their appearance marked the advent of performance-chasing aerodynamic development in F1 and by mid-season, the 49B was running with a wide, high-mounted rear aerofoil attached directly to the rear suspension via thin aluminium struts.

The 49 raced on through 1969, winning twice, and even took a final victory at the 1970 Monaco GP, driven by Jochen Rindt, before being superseded by the radical Lotus 72. Arguably the first 'modern' F1 car, the Lotus 49 passed on its DNA to every one of its successors.

**RACE RECORD**

**Championships: 2**
**(1x Drivers'; 1x Constructors')**
**Race wins: 12**
**Pole positions: 19**
**Fastest laps: 13**

(Below)

## LOTUS 25 (1962–67)

*A Colin Chapman classic, the 25 introduced monocoque construction to F1. A race winner from 1962 to '65, it dominated 1963 with Jim Clark. (Jim Clark, Circuit de Monaco, 1962)*

(Right)

## FERRARI 156 (1961)

*The first mid-engine F1 Ferrari and a double-title winner in 1961, with Phil Hill as champion. (Richie Ginther, Circuit de Monaco, 1961)*

*(Left)*

## EAGLE WESLAKE (1966–69)

*Often cited as F1's most beautiful car, the Eagle Mk 1 famously won the 1967 Belgian GP with V12 Weslake power, driven by Dan Gurney. (Dan Gurney, Circuit de Monaco, 1967)*

*(Below)*

## MATRA MS80 (1969)

*French-built and run by Tyrrell, the MS80 gave Jackie Stewart his first drivers' title in 1969. (Jackie Stewart, Clermont-Ferrand, 1969)*

# 1970s: Ferrari 312T (1975–80)

**THE SMALLEST CHANGE – FROM A 'B' TO A** 'T' – denoted a shift in technical philosophy that would establish Ferrari as the team to beat for the second half of the 1970s. It was made as the 312B of 1974 became the 312T of 1975, the 'T' referring to the orientation of the car's gearbox. 'T' stood for 'traversale' – transverse – meaning the box had been turned through 90 degrees from the conventional arrangement in line with the engine. By virtue of this single conceptual change, the engine and transmission components could be packaged more compactly behind the driver while the positioning of the gearbox in front of the rear axle line brought its mass towards the centre of the car. For the driver, this meant a more nervous machine, albeit more nimble and ultimately faster. For a driver called Niki Lauda, it meant a car good enough to fly to a first world title with five wins and nine pole positions, as Ferrari eased to the constructors' title.

The 312T was the masterwork of Ferrari's technical Svengali Mauro Forghieri, who also designed the powerful 3.0-litre flat-12 motor at its heart. With surface aerodynamics to match the elegant efficiency beneath the skin, the 312T was a classic example of holistic, integrated design, the fundamentals of which could be enhanced over subsequent seasons. Indeed, the 312T, in iterating specifications, was a race and championship winner through to the 1979 312T4, guided by a glittering roster of drivers: Clay Regazzoni, Carlos Reutemann, Gilles Villeneuve, Jody Scheckter, and of course Niki Lauda.

Their success charted a turnaround in Ferrari's fortunes after largely uncompetitive seasons in the early '70s, when upstart British rivals Lotus, Tyrrell and McLaren, and their superstars Jochen Rindt, Jackie Stewart and Emerson Fittipaldi, shared championship spoils between them. These were the *garagistas*, impudent start-up teams with modest facilities and low headcount, all relying on off-the-shelf Cosworth V8 engines for power. Their very existence, let alone their success, was an affront to the dignity of Maranello's maestros.

Ferrari's upswing had begun in 1974, as the pugnacious trio of Lauda, Forghieri and youthful team boss Luca di Montezemolo gelled to bring new cohesion and direction. They were additionally blessed with a private test track, Fiorano, located opposite the race HQ, which permitted unlimited time for development of chassis, tyres, aerodynamics, engine and transmission. Lauda relished 'test pilot' duties and Ferrari soon harvested the fruits of their labours. At the 312T's second race, the 1975 Spanish GP, Lauda and Regazzoni qualified 1–2 and a fortnight later in Monaco, Lauda won from pole. By mid-season, Lauda was deep into a groove, winning four races out of five and losing only to James Hunt, by a second, at the Dutch GP. The world titles were a formality.

Ferrari had hit upon their interpretation of a success template pioneered in F1 by Mercedes in the 1950s and subsequently replicated by all 'superteams': stable leadership, magic in the design office, a cockpit ace. The Montezemolo–Forghieri–Lauda axis delivered Ferrari the first constructors' title hat-trick and a drivers' treble would surely have been Lauda's, had it not been for his Nürburgring inferno in '76.

The car at the heart of that success wasn't a radical show-stopper in the manner of seventies peers such as the Lotus 72 or 79, the Tyrrell P34 six-wheeler, or the outrageous, fan-assisted Brabham BT46B. Instead, the 312T owed its success to sublime technical integration, excellence of manufacture and a commitment to continual improvement. As Forghieri fondly recalled to *F1 Racing* magazine in 2014, 'It was the first F1 car with aerodynamic bodywork and the engine and chassis worked well together. It was probably my favourite car.'

**RACE RECORD (1975–80)**

**Championships: 7**
**(3x Drivers', 4x Constructors')**
**Race wins: 27**
**Pole positions: 19**
**Fastest laps: 25**

*Niki Lauda,*
*Anderstorp, 1975*

*(Below)*

## McLAREN M23

*Another seventies classic, winning Grands Prix from 1973 to '76. Made champions of Emerson Fittipaldi and James Hunt, winning constructors' honours in '74. (James Hunt, Nürburgring, 1976)*

*(Right)*

## LOTUS 72

*The most successful F1 Lotus. A race winner from 1970 to '74 with three constructors' and two drivers' titles. (Ronnie Peterson, Österreichring, 1973)*

*(Left)*

**TYRRELL P34**

*Unique as a race-winning six-wheeled F1 car. (Patrick Depailler, Anderstorp, 1976)*

*(Below)*

**RENAULT RS01**

*Historically significant as the first turbocharged Formula One car. Sparked an arms race in F1 engine technology lasting from 1977 to '88. (Jean-Pierre Jabouille, Zandvoort, 1977)*

*(Left)*

**LOTUS 79**

*The first F1 car to fully harness ground-effect aerodynamics and the last championship-winning Lotus, both for the team and Mario Andretti. (Ronnie Peterson, Anderstorp, 1978)*

*Ayrton Senna,*
*Circuit Paul Ricard,*
*1988*

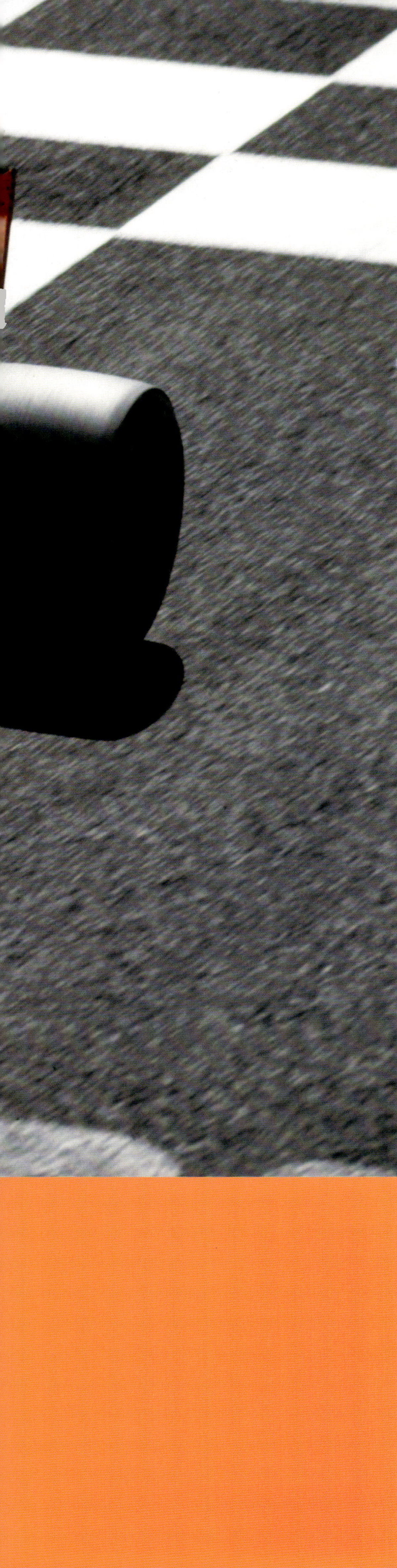

# 1980s: McLaren MP4-4 (1988)

**RACE RECORD**

**Championships: 2**
**(1x Drivers'; 1x Constructors')**
**Race wins: 15**
**Pole positions: 15**
**Fastest laps: 10**

**THE GREATNESS OF THE MCLAREN MP4-4** results not only from the elegant simplicity of its design and engineering, it was also the car that allowed the two best drivers of their age – Ayrton Senna and Alain Prost – to stage a mesmerising fight for the 1988 drivers' title on a plane completely separate from their rivals.

As teammates, they won 15 of the year's 16 Grands Prix, with 15 pole positions and ten 1–2 finishes, having led 1,003 laps of the 1,031 total. Only a fumble at the Italian GP, where Senna tripped over the hapless Jean-Louis Schlesser at the Rettifilo chicane, two laps from the chequered flag, sullied what would otherwise have been a clean sheet for McLaren – an astonishing achievement in an era when mechanical unreliability would regularly end a driver's race.

McLaren's stranglehold of the 1988 season was their peak during a decade they largely co-owned with Williams. McLaren had controlled the mid-'80s with the Porsche-powered MP4-2 series of cars before Williams hit back with their Honda-driven FW11s of 1986–87. The power and efficiency of the 1.5-litre Honda V6 turbo motor was a league apart from any rival offering (thanks in no small part to an estimated $50m annual budget) and McLaren boss Ron Dennis knew he simply had to have it. He snatched the prized engines from Williams during '87, then plundered Lotus for Senna – still yet to win a championship despite the brilliance he had shown since his F1 debut in 1984.

But what of the chassis? Dennis had lost his technical superstar, John Barnard, to Ferrari in 1986, and with him went a design lineage that stretched back to the early '80s. A reset was needed for '88 if McLaren were to capitalise on their advantage in all other departments. Dennis, in his pomp as a team principal, achieved another masterstroke by luring the free-spirited, free-thinking design maverick Gordon Murray from Brabham. As technical director of a team that included chief designer Steve Nichols, Murray contributed to a design that would prove devastatingly effective.

The hallmark of the MP4-4 was its low-line profile, a design concept sometimes attributed to Murray's pioneering 'skateboard' Brabham BT55 design of 1986. Others maintain the MP4-4 was evolutionary and that the car's stance resulted from a new Honda engine designed to be as compact as possible, plus fuel tank limits mandating a capacity of only 150 litres for turbo-engine cars. Clever transmission engineering allowed maximum benefit to be gained from the low-lying engine, but little else was radical. Clarity of concept and excellence of execution were the MP4-4's winning strengths.

In *Art of the Formula One Race Car* (2010), Murray explains: 'It was such a simple car, but we found a massive improvement in aerodynamics. And it handled very well. I've always liked very simple things. I wanted to bring the driver back down to Chapman levels. Over the years they'd been creeping back up again, the designers were looking to package more and more fuel behind the driver and the engines were getting bigger. There was no point in having the driver low – until we got to the turbo era.'

The results speak for themselves: the MP4-4's win rate was 93.75 per cent – a mark which stood until 2023, when Red Bull's RB19 pipped it with 21 wins from 22 races (95.45 per cent). And while its scorecard benefitted from the relative disarray of rival teams in '88, there is little argument that Senna, Prost, McLaren and Honda made the most of what they had. The MP4-4 remains a high-water mark for F1's turbo era: turbo-charged engines were banned at the end of the season.

*(Below)*

## BRABHAM BT52 (1983)

*Powered by BMW, the BT52 took Nelson Piquet to his second F1 title – the first for a driver in a turbocharged car. (Nelson Piquet, Circuit de Monaco, 1983)*

*(Right)*

## WILLIAMS FW07 (1979–82)

*The Williams FW07 series cars were archetypal ground-effect F1 machines. They won the 1980–81 constructors' titles, with Alan Jones as the 1980 World Champion. (Alan Jones, Circuito del Jarama, 1979)*

*(Left; far car)*

## WILLIAMS FW11 (1986–87)

*Honda-powered sledgehammers, the FW11 and FW11B cars made Williams dominant Constructors' Champions in 1986–87. Nelson Piquet won his third drivers' title in '87. (Nigel Mansell, Hungaroring, 1986)*

*(Left; near car)*

## LOTUS 98T (1986)

*Driven by Ayrton Senna, the Lotus 98T was one of the outright fastest turbo cars – and one of the most beautiful. (Ayrton Senna, Hungaroring, 1986)*

*(Above)*

## MCLAREN MP4-2 (1984–86)

*All-conquering in 1984, this was the car to beat in '85, and still a title winner for Alain Prost in '86. Another McLaren classic. (Alain Prost, Autodromo Nazionale Monza, 1985)*

**THIS WAS THE CAR FOR WHICH NIGEL** Mansell had waited his entire life. An elegant and technically advanced machine, it was swift and robust enough to answer his uncompromising demands and together they hurtled to the 1992 drivers' title.

Mansell won the year's first five races on the bounce and had won eight out of ten by the German Grand Prix in late July. Two weeks later, second place at the Hungarian GP was enough to confirm him as champion and by year-end he had accrued almost double the points of his teammate, Riccardo Patrese. The constructors' title was an inevitability for Williams; indeed the FW14B set up a run of championship wins for the team and for engine partner Renault that lasted through to 1997. Only in 1995 were they beaten, famously, by Benetton and Michael Schumacher, also using Renault power.

Like many great Formula One designs, the FW14B achieved a harmonious blend of tried-and-true with brave new world. One of its racing certainties was the 3.5-litre Renault V10 motor, which shoved out around 750bhp from a compact and relatively fuel-efficient package; it was the engine to beat for much of the 1990s. Also nailed on was the engineering authority of technical director Patrick Head and the mastery of packaging and aerodynamics brought by chief designer Adrian Newey. As a race team, Williams were battle-hardened veterans of multiple successful title campaigns during the 1980s, while Mansell's unrelenting speed galvanised the squad to reach for ever-higher standards.

So much for the bricks and mortar; the razzle-dazzle came in the form of electronically controlled hydro-pneumatic active suspension. Replacing conventional arrangements of springs and dampers, Williams' active system used pressurised hydraulics to control ride height and maintain a consistently stable platform for the surface aerodynamics and wings.

Active ride was by no means speculative radical engineering – that wasn't the Williams way. The Lotus 99T of 1987 used active suspension and was twice a Grand Prix winner with Ayrton Senna. That year Williams also won a Grand Prix with an active car, having developed the technology since the mid-80s. Their FW12 of 1988 ran with active ride for half a season.

By 1992, Head deemed the system fully race-ready, having overcome reservations from Mansell, who had experienced unsettling active ride failures while testing prototype installations as a Lotus driver in the early '80s. Mansell and Patrese reported receiving sometimes-disconcerting feedback from the 14B, compared with the feel of its conventionally sprung predecessor, the FW14. The engineering explanation for the drivers' experience was milliseconds of delay in the active system responding to driver inputs. Mansell learned to adapt once he became confident the car would obey his commands, but Patrese, who had been a close competitor to Mansell in 1991, never quite acclimatised.

There was no holding Mansell back as he charged to the world title his talent had long demanded. At the British GP, surfing a wave of fan fever, he took pole position with a two-second margin and led every lap to win by 40 seconds. The FW14B was in a class of its own in '92 and, with Mansell at the helm, became one half of an iconic F1 car–driver partnership.

# 1990s: Williams FW14B (1992)

**RACE RECORD**

**Championships: 2**
**(1x Drivers'; 1x Constructors')**
**Race wins: 10**
**Pole positions: 15**
**Fastest laps: 10**

*Nigel Mansell,
Adelaide, 1992*

*(Above)*

## FERRARI 641 (1990)

*Developed from the pioneering Ferrari 640 of 1989, the svelte 641 combined speed with reliability, although wasn't quite enough to allow Alain Prost to beat Ayrton Senna and McLaren to a 1990 title double. (Nigel Mansell, Circuit de Monaco, 1990)*

*(Right)*

## WILLIAMS FW15C (1993)

*Designed from scratch as an active-suspension car, the FW15C allowed Alain Prost a cruise to his fourth world title and Williams' sixth. (Alain Prost (right), Damon Hill (left), Circuit de Catalunya, 1993)*

*(Left)*

## JORDAN 191 (1991)

*One of the most elegant Formula One cars ever designed, the Jordan 191 was the team's first chassis. It has historical significance as the car in which Michael Schumacher made his F1 debut at the 1991 Belgian GP. (Michael Schumacher, Spa-Francorchamps, 1991)*

*(Below)*

## MCLAREN MP4-13 (1998)

*The first McLaren designed with Adrian Newey as technical director, the MP4-13 eclipsed all other interpretations of that season's narrow-track technical regulations. A championship winner for Mika Häkkinen and McLaren. (Mika Häkkinen (left), David Coulthard (right), Melbourne, 1998)*

*Michael Schumacher,*
*Nürburgring, 2004*

**FOR ALMOST TWO DECADES, SINCE** mopping up serial constructors' titles in the mid-to-late 1970s, Ferrari had been bit players in Formula One. Throughout the 1980s and '90s, with the exception of two turbo-powered constructors' titles in 1982 to '83, Ferrari were trounced by better-run, better-engineered teams operating out of the UK. Williams, McLaren and Benetton won every teams' title from 1980 to '98 ('82–83 aside), despite Ferrari having done their darnedest to buy in some of that Anglo-savvy by poaching revered master technician John Barnard from McLaren in 1986.

Barnard's arrival didn't bring the world titles Ferrari craved, but the tide began to turn with the appointment of the nuggety Jean Todt as Ferrari team boss in 1993. Todt's first bold stroke was to lure Michael Schumacher from his 1995 Championship-winning Benetton seat; others closely associated with that title success swiftly followed, technical director Ross Brawn and chief designer Rory Byrne the most prominent. Together, this core team began to remodel dysfunctional racing and design departments to match the existing excellence of Ferrari's in-house engine operation. Brawn had long regarded Ferrari as a slumbering giant and set about unlocking the unique potential of a team blessed not only with its own in-house chassis and engine departments, but with its own wind tunnel and private test track, too.

Schumacher was soon scoring improbable Grand Prix victories and through 1997 to '99, he was making life difficult for champions Jacques Villeneuve and Mika Häkkinen, despite the handicap of a car not quite the match of its best rivals. Ferrari took their first constructors' title for 16 years in 1999 and it seemed the dam must surely burst for Schumacher, such was the pressure he and Ferrari were exerting. And it certainly did. From 2000 to 2004, Ferrari and Schumacher won five consecutive title doubles, essaying Grand Prix domination, the like of which had never previously been witnessed.

The cars Schumacher drove to those titles, of which the F2004 was the ultimate expression, did not stand out as being dramatically better than their rivals in any single area. Their genius lay in maximising the potential of all constituent elements and blending them into a series of stunningly successful packages. The F2004's 920bhp 3.0-litre V10 was a match for any rival motor; its aerodynamic performance was class-leading; Ferrari's relationship with tyre supplier Bridgestone, which tailored its designs for the team's needs, set new standards. And, of course, in Michael Schumacher, Ferrari had a driver without peer for much of the early noughties. Add the leadership skills of Todt and Brawn to that mix, as well as both men's political acumen, and the result was a truly formidable racing team.

The F2004 won 15 out of 18 Grands Prix in its sole year of competition; its forebear, the F2002, achieved 14 out of 16. Neither quite matched the 15 out of 16 record set by McLaren's MP4-4 in 1988, but Ferrari's arguably greater achievement was to create a winning unit which, for five consecutive seasons, was almost invincible. Their legacy was the establishment of a mindset later described by Brawn, in his book of the same name, as 'total competition'. The Red Bull and Mercedes teams, which followed Ferrari with their own periods of dominance through the 2010s and '20s, learned those lessons well.

# 2000s: Ferrari F2004 (2004)

**RACE RECORD**

**Championships: 2**
**(1x Drivers', 1x Constructors')**
**Race wins: 15**
**Pole positions: 12**
**Fastest laps: 14**

*(Below)*

## MCLAREN MP4-20 (2005)

*The closest rival to Alonso and Renault during 2005. Often the faster car, but less reliable. (Juan Pablo Montoya, Circuit de Monaco, 2005)*

*(Right)*

## RENAULT R25 (2005)

*Driven by Fernando Alonso in 2005, this is the car that finally dethroned Ferrari and Michael Schumacher. (Fernando Alonso, Montreal, 2005)*

(Left)

### RED BULL RB5 (2009)

*Designed by Adrian Newey for a new set of technical regulations in 2009, this car became Red Bull's first winner, establishing design principles that brought title doubles for Red Bull and Sebastian Vettel from 2010 to 2013. (Sebastian Vettel, Circuit de Monaco, 2009)*

(Above)

### BRAWN BGP001 (2009)

*The fairy-tale championship winner that rose from the ashes of Honda's axed 2008 F1 project to win both 2009 titles. (Rubens Barrichello, Yas Marina Circuit, 2009)*

**THE 2010 RETURN OF MERCEDES BENZ TO** Formula One as a factory-backed team was never going to be a passing footnote. Its history with Grand Prix racing stretched back to the 1930s when its W154 cars, driven by Rudolf Caracciola and Richard Seaman, among others, were silver visions of an automotive future. In the 1950s, Mercedes once again set new standards with the W196, Juan Manuel Fangio and Stirling Moss. It is safe to say that expectations were high for the Silver Arrows' return, not least because Michael Schumacher came out of retirement to spearhead the driving strength.

Mercedes' first four seasons back in the top flight were only moderately successful, by their standards. Still building strength at the UK factory they had taken over from Brawn GP at the end of 2009, they scored four wins in a period reigned over by Red Bull Racing and Sebastian Vettel. This relatively thin return mattered little, as Mercedes always had eyes on the reset of the technical regulations that would be introduced for 2014. These altered engine regulations more extensively than at any time since 1989, when turbocharging was outlawed. For 2014, turbos were back – though not in the power-crazed fashion of the 1980s. Now they would be mounted to 1.6-litre V6 internal combustion engines and paired with two electric motors designed to recover energy lost under braking and whizz the turbo up to speed at low engine revs. These hybrid power units – PUs as they quickly became known – were more sophisticated, efficient and expensive than any motors ever previously used in F1. By some estimates, Mercedes were spending around €500m per season on their Formula One entry, at least half of which was channelled to their bespoke UK powertrains factory, led by Andy Cowell. The spend would be justified by increased sales of road cars, made more desirable by sporting success.

Mercedes' commitment to the new technical framework was at a level beyond anything its rivals had countenanced and, just as they had in the 1930s and 1950s, they changed the game. In 2014, with Rosberg and Lewis Hamilton on the driving strength, they came out of the blocks with a fully joined-up racing machine. The W05, perfectly attuned to the new rule-set, favoured excellence in engine development over cutting-edge aerodynamic efficiency for the first time in decades. The rival PUs from Renault and Ferrari were totally outclassed by Mercedes' PU106A and the team romped to the constructors' title with a margin of almost 300 points: 701 to Red Bull's 405. Hamilton was similarly dominant in the Drivers' Championship, taking 11 wins and seven pole positions to earn his second title. Only his teammate offered any kind of opposition.

For the next six seasons through to 2020, the story was similar; Mercedes won seven consecutive title doubles with comfortable, often crushing, margins. The season of greatest supremacy was 2016 – also notable for Rosberg's sole championship win in Hamilton's otherwise seamless sequence of world titles. The 765 points notched up by Nico and Lewis in that year's W07 set a new mark for points scored in a season, as they shared 19 wins out of 21 races. That vast total would likely have been even greater, had the pair not taken each other out on the first lap of the Spanish GP, allowing the precocious Max Verstappen through for his first victory.

Only by the turn of the decade was Mercedes' peerless domination of the hybrid F1 era being challenged. The team took another constructors' title in 2021 – their eighth on the bounce – though Hamilton was pipped to drivers' honours by Verstappen, his Red Bull finally enjoying a Honda PU that could match the Mercedes. Max's title marked a shift in F1's balance of power for the first time in nearly a decade. Mercedes' run of success had been unprecedented and the W07 shone brightest in a quiver of glittering Silver Arrows.

# 2010s: Mercedes W07 (2016)

**RACE RECORD**

**Championships: 2**
**(1x Drivers', 1x Constructors')**
**Race wins: 19**
**Pole positions: 20**
**Fastest laps: 9**

*Lewis Hamilton,*
*Suzuka, 2018*

*(Above)*

### RED BULL RB9 (2013)

*In the last year of technical regulations framed around 2.4-litre V8 engines, Red Bull and Sebastian Vettel were untouchable. Thirteen wins, a title double, game over. (Sebastian Vettel, Yas Marina Circuit, 2013)*

*(Right)*

### FERRARI SF-71H (2018)

*For the first half of 2018, Sebastian Vettel and Ferrari had the measure of Hamilton and Mercedes, until the defending champions tightened the noose. (Sebastian Vettel, Spa-Francorchamps, 2018)*

*(Left)*

**LOTUS E21 (2013)**

*The last car bearing the fabled Lotus name to win a Grand Prix, with Kimi Räikkönen's 2013 victory in Melbourne. (Kimi Räikkönen, Sakhir, 2013)*

*(Below)*

**MCLAREN MP4-25 (2010)**

*The most recent McLaren to fight for a world title, the MP4-25 pioneered the drag-reducing F-Duct system. (Lewis Hamilton, Suzuka, 2010)*

*Max Verstappen, Yas Marina Circuit, 2023*

**IT'S A STATISTICAL CURIOSITY THAT MORE** than 70 years passed before the Red Bull RB19 broke a record set by one of its ancestors in the early 1950s. That mark was for the number of consecutive Grand Prix victories, established by Italy's great double champion Alberto Ascari, driving the Ferrari Tipo 500 across 1952–53. Sebastian Vettel, also racing for Red Bull, won nine on the trot during his 2013 title streak, but not until 2023 did Max Verstappen and the Red Bull RB19 win 10 consecutive Grands Prix, from Miami to Monza. The passage of time and the advancement of technology render comparisons moot, yet an essential truth traverses the decades: a great driver, fully attuned to a car with a technical advantage, can destroy the opposition.

This has never been more obviously the case than during the 2023 F1 season, when Max Verstappen and his Red Bull RB19 set about tearing the record book into confetti. The car scored 860 points between Verstappen and teammate Sergio Perez; by way of comparison, the 1958 Vanwall VW5 amassed a more modest 48 points to win the Constructors' Cup in its first year of being awarded. While the points table alone is largely meaningless, given the growth of the championship since the fifties and the multiple changes to the scoring system, Red Bull's towering scoreline is a true barometer of the near perfection achieved by both man and machine.

The RB19 refined concepts already proven in its predecessor, the RB18, another championship-dominating design. Fundamental to both cars' success was the resolution of aerodynamic goals with precise suspension control. Both cars were recognised standard-setters in terms of aerodynamic efficiency – i.e. the amount of downforce they could generate with wings, body surface and under-car air channels for a given amount of drag. The most efficient cars, such as the RB19 – typical of almost all machines authored by Red Bull's chief technical officer Adrian Newey – exact less of a drag penalty for a given amount of downforce. In crude terms, this means the car can be fast in a straight line (thanks to low drag) while also being quick around the corners (thanks to high downforce). Less efficient designs make more of an either/or choice.

The subtle sophistication of the RB19's aero package was shrink-wrapped around a chassis concept that sweated the intricacies of suspension design and weight distribution. Further technical sublimation was achieved with the creation of Red Bull Powertrains ahead of the 2022 season. This new technical department brought engine development in-house, in collaboration with outgoing partner Honda, and elevated Red Bull Racing to the status of full 'works' entry, in the manner of a Ferrari or Mercedes: i.e., a maker of both chassis and engines.

In tandem with the relentless brilliance of Max Verstappen to lead the driving attack and a race team which ascribed to 'aggressive competitiveness' as its mantra, the RB19 proved irresistible throughout 2023, its rivals left wondering how to mount a challenge. The flaccid opposition offered by Ferrari and Mercedes (whose combined points total fell short of Red Bull's) flattered the performance of the RB19 and led some to question the car's eminence. The answer to those doubters might be found in a winning record – 21 wins from 22 starts – which renders the RB19 Formula One's greatest car yet.

# 2020s: RED BULL RB19 (2023)

**RACE RECORD**

**Championships: 2**
**(1x Drivers'; 1x Constructors')**
**Race wins: 21**
**Pole positions: 14**
**Fastest laps: 11**

*(Above)*

**RACING POINT RP20 (2020)**

*Sergio Perez's win at the 2020 Sakhir GP made Racing Point one of only a handful of teams to win a race outside the 'big three' of Mercedes, Ferrari and Red Bull Racing in F1's hybrid-engine era. (Sergio Perez, Yas Marina Circuit, 2020)*

*(Right)*

**ASTON MARTIN AMR23 (2023)**

*Driven by the evergreen Fernando Alonso, the AMR23 lifted hearts with front-running competitiveness in the first half of 2023. (Fernando Alonso, Circuit de Monaco, 2023)*

# MOMENTS

*Frozen in the blink of a shutter, a selection of defining moments from 75 years of Formula One.*

1950 British GP

1957 German GP

1964 Belgian GP

1969 Spanish GP

1970 Spanish GP

1971 Italian GP

1975 Austrian GP

1976 Japanese GP

1979 French GP

1979 Dutch GP

1986 Portuguese GP

1986 Australian GP

1987 Austrian GP

1990 Japanese GP

1991 British GP

1993 Canadian GP

1994 German GP

1997 Canadian GP

1997 European GP

1999 British GP

2001 German GP

2002 Australian GP

2007 Canadian GP

2012 Belgian GP

2016 Australian GP

2017 Singapore GP

2020 Bahrain GP

1 2 3 4 5 6
70

*Giuseppe Farina takes the winner's laurels after winning the inaugural Formula One World Championship Grand Prix – the 1950 British GP, held on Saturday 13 May.*

*Fangio's greatest day? This rare colour shot captures The Maestro winning the 1957 German GP at the Nürburgring, having passed the Ferraris of Mike Hawthorn and Peter Collins on the penultimate lap, after an epic comeback drive.*

ifen
Continental Reifen
Continental Reifen
Continental

*1964 Belgian Grand Prix, Spa-Francorchamps. Winner Jim Clark, sitting on the exhaust pipes of his Lotus 25, chats with his great rival Dan Gurney, who had led the race for 29 laps before running out of fuel. Graham Hill and Bruce McLaren also ran out of gas on the final lap, allowing Clark through to win.*

DUNLOP

*Graham Hill climbs from the wreckage of his Lotus 49B on lap nine of the 1969 Spanish GP. The strut-mounted rear wing has just collapsed, causing a high-speed crash. Eleven laps later, Hill's teammate Jochen Rindt crashed even more heavily, after a similar failure.*

*Driving a March, Jackie Stewart threads through fire, foam and track marshals at the 1970 Spanish GP. The burning wrecks are the BRM P153 of Jackie Oliver and the Ferrari 312B of Jacky Ickx.*

1

AUTOBIANCHI A112

*At the 1971 Italian GP, Peter Gethin (BRM) beat Ronnie Peterson (March) by 0.01 seconds. The top five – Gethin, Peterson, François Cevert, Mike Hailwood, Howden Ganley – were covered by 0.61s. All five are in shot.*

*Vittorio Brambilla celebrates his sole Grand Prix victory at the 1975 Austrian GP. The damaged nose of his March is the result of a spin immediately after crossing the finish line.*

Beta
Beta
GOODYEAR
9

*In near-monsoon conditions at the 1976 Japanese GP, James Hunt has finished third, after a late-race puncture. McLaren team boss Teddy Mayer holds up three fingers to confirm the position to a disbelieving Hunt. His four points are enough to make him World Champion.*

*On the final lap of the 1979 French GP at Dijon, René Arnoux (Renault) and Gilles Villeneuve (Ferrari) scrap over second place.*

MICHELIN
MICHELIN
12
12
Agip
SKF
arexons
MICHELIN

Agip
12
12
MICHELIN

*Gilles Villeneuve refuses to concede defeat after a rear-tyre blowout at the 1979 Dutch GP. He three-wheeled his Ferrari back to the pits, with a flailing wheel and suspension, to the delight of adoring fans.*

*Gang of four. Ayrton Senna (Lotus), Alain Prost (McLaren), Nigel Mansell (Williams) and Nelson Piquet (Williams) were all in contention for the 1986 drivers' title when this shot was taken at the Portuguese GP, with three rounds to go. Prost won the championship, his second of four drivers' titles; Piquet won his third in '87; Senna was champion in '88, '90 and '91; Mansell won the title in '92.*

Marlboro
McLAREN INTERNATIONAL
HONDA
DENIM
BOSS
Isle of Man Bank
Mobil
1
DENIM
PMG
HONDA
Mobil
1
DENIM
HONDA
ICI
DENIM
Nelson
Piquet

Canon
Mobil
HONDA
GOODYEAR

*The moment that cost Nigel Mansell the 1986 world title. The left-rear Goodyear of his Williams bursts on the main straight of the Adelaide circuit, allowing Alain Prost through to win the Australian GP and the World Championship.*

*During the 1980s, skid plates made from titanium were attached to the underside of F1 cars' chassis, to prevent them grounding on track surface bumps. The resulting sparks were spectacular, captured here as the Brabham of Andrea de Cesaris hurtles along the straight of the Österreichring during the 1987 Austrian GP, tailed by Stefan Johansson's McLaren.*

2

Marlboro
FIAT
Agip
BOSS
Marlboro
Marlboro
POWERED by HONDA
27

*Prost vs Senna, the sequel. This is the 1990 Japanese GP, seconds after the start. Prost beat Senna away from the grid, but Senna held an inside line into the high-speed Turn 1, refused to lift off and the pair collided. Both cars retired, deciding the World Championship in Senna's favour. A year earlier, when both were McLaren teammates, they collided at Suzuka. Prost won the '89 title.*

*A victorious Nigel Mansell salutes the crowd after winning the 1991 British GP. Ayrton Senna hitches a ride back to the pits having run out of fuel.*

HONDA
NACIONAL
Labatt's
RENAULT
Bull

Dirt Devil
TAG HEUER
olivetti
TAG HEUER

*A study in concentration. Ayrton Senna watches a timing screen in his McLaren garage during the 1993 Canadian GP weekend.*

*Benetton mechanic Paul Seaby is engulfed in flames as spilled fuel ignites into a fireball during a pitstop for Jos Verstappen at the 1994 German Grand Prix. Verstappen and his mechanics all escaped without permanent injury.*

*Ralf Schumacher's Jordan slams into the barriers approaching Turn 1 of Montreal's Circuit Gilles Villeneuve, on lap 15 of the 1997 Canadian GP.*

*The decisive moment of the 1997 world title fight between Jacques Villeneuve and Michael Schumacher. As Villeneuve attempts to pass for the lead on lap 47 of the European GP at the Jerez circuit, Schumacher drives his Ferrari into Villeneuve's Williams. Schumacher retired and was stripped of his '97 points. Villeneuve finished third and won the title.*

Rothmans
Castrol
Rothmans
3

tic
tac

*At the 1999 British GP, Michael Schumacher suffered the most serious accident of his Formula One career. Lap one brake failure left him unable to slow his Ferrari, which ploughed into the tyre barriers at Stowe corner. A double fracture of his right lower leg caused Schumacher to miss six races and ruled him out of world title contention.*

*Luciano Burti flips his Prost at the start of the 2001 German GP at Hockenheim, after crashing into the back of Michael Schumacher's slow-starting Ferrari.*

Mobil 1
BENSON & HEDGES

vodafone

*Ralf Schumacher gets airborne at the start of the 2002 Australian GP. His Williams was launched after clipping the rear of Rubens Barrichello's Ferrari. A total of eight cars were eliminated in the scramble that followed this initial contact.*

*Robert Kubica in the eye of the storm at the 2007 Canadian GP. This enormous lap 26 accident destroyed his BMW, though Kubica suffered only concussion and a sprained ankle.*

intel

Trinasolar
ZERO
PIRELLI
TW STEEL
Business Exchange
Santander
œrlikon
CHELSEA
Mobil 1
vodafone
TELMEX
NEC
CERTINA
Emil Frey
Claro
15

*This crash at the first corner of the 2012 Belgian GP earned Lotus' Romain Grosjean (mid-air) a one-race ban. When he torpedoed Red Bull's Mark Webber on lap one of the Japanese GP later the same year, he became stuck with Webber's dismissive 'first-lap nutcase' tag.*

*Fernando Alonso's McLaren is rolled to destruction at the 2016 Australian GP, after contact with the Haas of Esteban Gutierrez on lap 17.*

KPMG

Red Bull
Santander
HUBLOT
Santander
7
5
MAHLE
MAHLE

*Under the lights of the Marina Bay Circuit, Ferrari's Kimi Räikkönen harpoons teammate Sebastian Vettel approaching the first corner of the 2017 Singapore GP. Räikkönen and Red Bull's Max Verstappen had touched wheels a split-second earlier, causing a ricochet which put all three cars out of the race.*

*The miracle escape for Romain Grosjean at the 2020 Bahrain GP. His Haas speared into the barriers at Turn 3 after first-lap contact with another car and split in two, rupturing the fuel cell. Grosjean's hands were burned but he suffered no other serious injuries. An accident like this would undoubtedly have been fatal in an earlier Formula One era.*

FIA
OMP
OMP
MEDICAL
DELEGATE
ACTION

# INDEX

# INDEX



## CIRCUITS

## CHASSIS & ENGINE

# PICTURE CREDITS

Front cover: Zak Mauger
Back cover: Sam Bloxham
Frontispiece: Rainer Schlegelmilch

Andre, Jerry 204–05
Bloxham, Sam 234
Bumstead, Gareth 230
Coates, Charles 165, 176, 179, 230–31, 235, 238, 280–83
Colombo, Ercole 22, 70, 77, 82, 89, 98, 158, 190–91, 258–59
Dunbar, Glenn 5, 139, 235, 239
Dunbar, John 73, 152–53, 169, 219, 222, 260–61
Easton, Ron 29, 30, 69
Elford, Martyn 106, 136–37, 227, 270–71, 284–85
Etherington, Steve 180, 231
Ferraro, Andrew 234, 286–87
Galloway, Simon 148–49
Hone, Andy 125, 236–37, 292–95
Hutson, David 85, 90
Kalisz, Daniel 290–91
LAT Images 26, 146–47, 210
Mauger, Zak 133, 202–03
Morton, Laurie 66, 188–89, 212–13, 215, 218–19, 252–55
Ng, Lionel 154–55
Phipps Photographic (David Phipps, Nigel Snowdon, David Winter, Pam Rowe, Duncan Cubitt) 57, 81, 145, 173, 186–87, 214–15, 219, 248–49
Rose, Clive 113
Rowe, Maurice 41, 138
Schlegelmilch, Rainer 17, 45, 52–4, 58, 61–2, 65, 74, 78, 86, 93–4, 97, 105, 117, 121, 140–41, 162, 166–67, 174, 192–93, 196–97, 216–18, 220–22, 226, 228–29, 250–51, 266–67
Smythe, Tony 210, 244–45
Sutton Images 102, 122, 129, 268–69, 276–77
Sutton, Keith 18, 264–65
Sutton, Mark 21
Tee, Michael 14, 33–4, 37–8, 42, 46, 49, 51, 142–44, 161, 184–85, 208–09, 211, 242–43, 246–47
Tee, Steven 13, 101, 109–10, 114, 118, 126, 130, 150–51, 170, 194–95, 198–201, 223–27, 232–33, 262–63, 272–75, 278–79, 288–89



ISBN: 978-178884-268-6



A CIP catalogue record for this book is available from the British Library.

The author and publisher gratefully acknowledge the permission granted to reproduce the copyright material in this book. Every effort has been made to trace copyright holders and to obtain their permission for the use of copyright material. The publisher apologises for any errors or omissions in the text and would be grateful if notified of any corrections that should be incorporated in future reprints or editions of this book.

Senior Editor: Alice Bowden
Designer: Peter Allen
Colour Separation: Corban Wilkin

Printed in China
for ACC Art Books Ltd., Woodbridge, Suffolk, UK

*www.accartbooks.com*